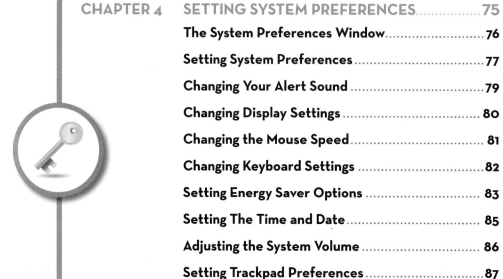
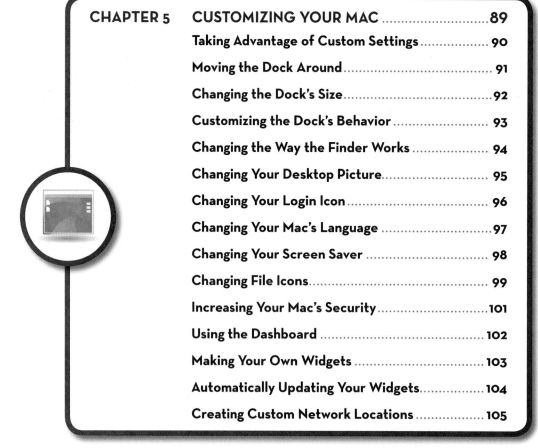

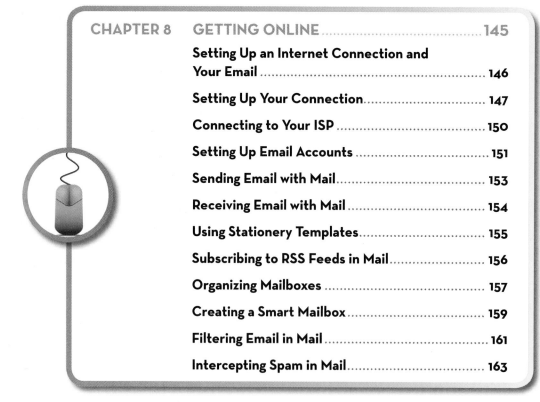

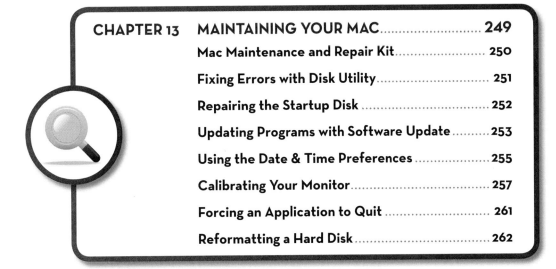

EASY MAC® OS X SNOW LEOPARD™

ISBN-13: 978-0-7897-4044-1

ISBN-10: 0-7897-4044-3

U.K. ISBN-13: 978-0-7897-3979-7

U.K. ISBN-10: 0-7897-3979-8

Library of Congress Cataloging-in-Publication data is on file.

Printed in the United States on America

First Printing: September 2009

TRADEMARKS

WARNING AND DISCLAIMER

BULK SALES

Que Publishing offers excellent discounts on this book when ordered in quantity for bulk purchases or special sales. For more information, please contact

U.S. Corporate and Government Sales
1-800-382-3419
corpsales@pearsontechgroup.com

For sales outside of the U.S., please contact

International Sales
international@pearsoned.com

Associate Publisher
Greg Wiegand

Acquisitions and Development Editor
Laura Norman

Managing Editor
Patrick Kanouse

Project Editor
Seth Kerney

Indexer
Cheryl Lenser

Technical Editor
Paul Sihvonen-Binder

Publishing Coordinator
Cindy Teeters

Interior and Cover Designer
Anne Jones

Composition
Bronkella Publishing, Inc.

ABOUT THE AUTHOR

Kate Binder is a longtime Mac lover and graphics expert who works from her home in New Hampshire. She has written articles on graphics, publishing, and photography for magazines including *Publish*, *PEI*, and *Desktop Publishers Journal*. Kate is also the author of several books, including *The Complete Idiot's Guide to Mac OS X*, and coauthor of books including *Sams Teach Yourself Adobe Photoshop CS3 in 24 Hours*, *Microsoft Office: Mac v.X Inside Out*, *SVG for Designers*, and *Get Creative: The Digital Photo Idea Book*. To those interested in a successful career as a computer book writer, Kate recommends acquiring several retired racing greyhounds (find out more at www.adopt-a-greyhound.org)—she finds her four greyhounds extraordinarily inspirational.

DEDICATION

This book is for my daughter Pinkie Rose, a Mac-lover-in-training.

ACKNOWLEDGMENTS

Profuse thanks are due to Laura Norman for shepherding me through yet another one. Thanks, too, to the awesome editorial, design, and production people at Que—and especially my new favorite tech editor, Paul Sihvonen-Binder—for making it happen once again.

WE WANT TO HEAR FROM YOU!

As the reader of this book, you are our most important critic and commentator. We value your opinion and want to know what we're doing right, what we could do better, what areas you'd like to see us publish in, and any other words of wisdom you're willing to pass our way.

As an associate publisher for Que Publishing, I welcome your comments. You can email or write me directly to let me know what you did or didn't like about this book—as well as what we can do to make our books better.

Please note that I cannot help you with technical problems related to the topic of this book. We do have a User Services group, however, where I will forward specific technical questions related to the book.

When you write, please be sure to include this book's title and author as well as your name, email address, and phone number. I will carefully review your comments and share them with the author and editors who worked on the book.

Email: feedback@quepublishing.com

Mail: Greg Wiegand
Associate Publisher
Que Publishing
800 East 96th Street
Indianapolis, IN 46240 USA

READER SERVICES

Visit our website and register this book at www.quepublishing.com/register for convenient access to any updates, downloads, or errata that might be available for this book.

IT'S AS EASY AS 1-2-3

Each part of this book is made up of a series of short, instructional lessons, designed to help you understand basic information.

1 Each step is fully illustrated to show you how it looks onscreen

2 Each task includes a series of quick, easy steps designed to guide you through the procedure.

3 Items that you select or click in menus, dialog boxes, tabs, and windows are shown in **bold**.

Tips, notes, and cautions give you a heads-up for any extra information you may need while working through the task.

How to Drag: Point to the starting place or object. Hold down the mouse button (right or left per instructions), move the mouse to the new location, then release the button.

Click: Click the left mouse button once.

Click & Type: Click once where indicated and begin typing to enter your text or data.

Selection: Highlights the area onscreen discussed in the step or task.

Double-click: Click the left mouse button twice in rapid succession.

Right-click: Click the right mouse button once.

Pointer Arrow: Highlights an item on the screen you need to point to or focus on in the step or task.

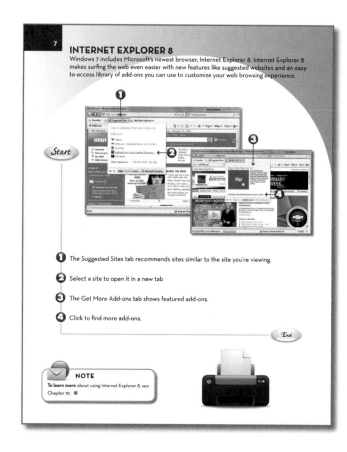

7

INTERNET EXPLORER 8

Windows 7 includes Microsoft's newest browser, Internet Explorer 8. Internet Explorer 8 makes surfing the web even easier with new features like suggested websites and an easy-to-access library of add-ons you can use to customize your web browsing experience.

1 The Suggested Sites tab recommends sites similar to the site you're viewing.

2 Select a site to open it in a new tab

3 The Get More Add-ons tab shows featured add-ons.

4 Click to find more add-ons.

NOTE
To learn more about using Internet Explorer 8, see Chapter 10. ■

INTRODUCTION TO EASY MAC OS X SNOW LEOPARD

Mac OS X is like no operating system, Macintosh or otherwise, that came before it. It's incredibly stable and powerful, and it looks amazingly sleek. But underneath the glitz and sparkle, it has the same old friendly nature that Mac users have enjoyed since 1984.

With *Easy Mac OS X Snow Leopard*, you'll learn how to take advantage of powerful and useful Mac OS X features such as the built-in instant messaging program iChat, controlling other Macs over a network, and the ability run Windows right on your Mac (if you really feel you must). Along the way, you'll get used to being able to run a dozen programs at one time on a stable system that doesn't crash. This book's step-by-step approach tells you just what you need to know to accomplish the task at hand, quickly and efficiently. All the skills you need to get the most out of Mac OS X, both online and on the desktop, are covered here.

If you want, you can work through the tasks in *Easy Mac OS X Snow Leopard* in order, building your skills steadily. Or, if you prefer, use this book as a reference to look up just what you need to know *right now*. Either way, *Easy Mac OS X Snow Leopard* lets you see it done, and then do it yourself.

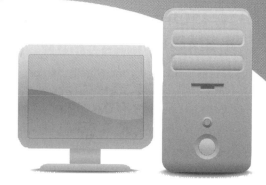

GETTING STARTED

Mac OS X 10.6 Snow Leopard is the latest big cat in a line that started with version 10.0 (Cheetah) and also included 10.1 (Puma), 10.2 (Jaguar), 10.3 (Panther), 10.4 (Tiger), and 10.5 (Leopard). So has the leopard changed its spots?

Yes and no. Mac OS X 10.6 is still many times more powerful than older systems, completely modern, capable of handling the latest innovations in hardware, and as easy to use as any Mac system that has gone before. But there are a few tweaks in Snow Leopard that you'll want to know about.

The starting point for any exploration of Mac OS X is the desktop: what you see when your Mac has finished starting up. The desktop is operated by a program called the Finder, and it's a central location where you'll gain access to your disks and their contents, move files around, and keep track of what your computer's up to—sort of like a hotel or office building lobby. This section covers the basics of working with the Finder, as well as other functions that work the same no matter what program you're using.

MAC OS X'S DESKTOP

Minimize window into the Dock, 7

Control your Mac with the Apple menu's commands, 4

Close window, 6

Maximize window, 7

Drag the title bar to move a window, 6

Set System Preferences, 13

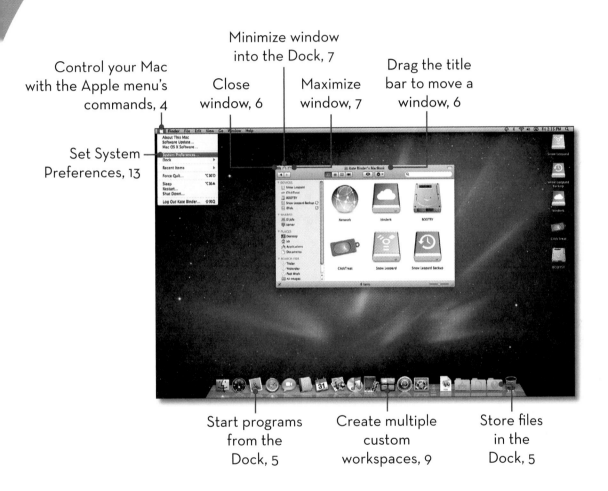

Start programs from the Dock, 5

Create multiple custom workspaces, 9

Store files in the Dock, 5

TOURING THE DESKTOP

If you've used an older version of Mac OS before, Snow Leopard's desktop won't look completely new to you—just a bit unfamiliar. On the other hand, if you're new to computers, concepts like *windows, icons,* and *menus* need a little explanation. Either way, this tour of the Mac OS X desktop should set you on your way.

Start

1 Double-click to view a window showing the contents of a drive or folder.

2 Click and drag to move icons on the desktop.

3 Click objects in the Dock to activate them.

4 Click a menu name, drag the mouse down, and release the mouse button when the menu item you want to use is highlighted.

Continued

NOTE

It's Okay to Explore If you're not sure what something on the desktop does, try clicking or double-clicking it—it's safe to explore and experiment. If something *does* go wrong, you can usually undo the last thing you did by pressing ⌘+Z or choosing **Edit > Undo**. ∎

NOTE

Making the Desktop Your Own Turn to the task called "Changing Your Desktop Picture" in Chapter 5, "Customizing the Mac," to learn how to change the desktop picture so you'll truly feel at home when you sit down in front of your Mac. ∎

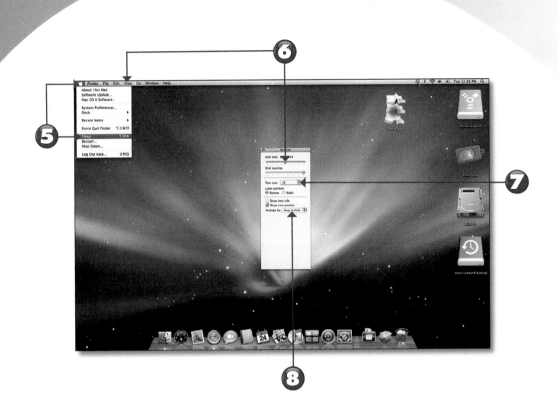

5 Click the **Apple** icon in the upper-left corner of the screen to access the Apple menu, where you can perform tasks that affect your whole computer.

6 Choose **View**, **Show View Options** to open the View Options dialog box. Drag the **Icon size** slider to change the size of desktop icons.

7 Change the **Text size** and **Label position** settings to change the appearance of icon labels.

8 Check any of the other options or choose an option from the **Arrange By** pop-up menu to set other options for files, folders, and drives on the desktop.

End

TIP

Cleaning Up the Place When your desktop gets cluttered with files and folders so that it's impossible for you to find anything, choose **View**, **Clean Up** to line up all the icons on the desktop in neat rows, so you can see what you've got.

NOTE

Where's the Trash? If you've used pre-OS X Macs, you're probably looking for the Trash, which used to live on the desktop. It's in the Dock now, but you can put it back on the desktop if you like by using a little program called Bin-it (www.fastforwardsw.com).

USING THE DOCK

The *Dock* serves more than one function. First, it's where you can see which programs are running and switch among them. The Dock contains an icon for each active program at any given time. Second, it's a good place to store things you use often, whether they're programs, folders, or documents. And finally, it's where you'll find the Trash. The Dock has a dashed vertical line dividing its two sides. Program icons are stored on the left side, whether the programs are running or not, and folders and documents you add to the Dock yourself are stored on the right side.

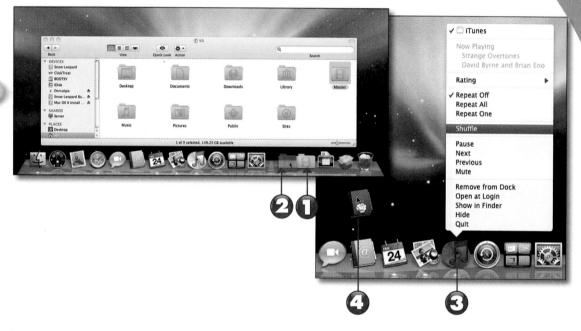

1 Click a program icon in the Dock to switch to that program (if it's running) or to start it up (if it's not running). Running programs are indicated by glowing dots under their icons.

2 Drag programs from the desktop into the Dock's left side and documents or folders from the desktop into the Dock's right side to store them for easy access.

3 Click and hold an icon in the Dock to see a menu of actions you can perform on that object or a list of folder contents. If you don't like waiting, you can Ctrl-click or right-click.

4 Drag icons of files, folders, and inactive programs off the edge to remove them from the Dock in a puff of virtual smoke.

End

NOTE

Disappearing Act When you drag programs or documents off the Dock, they disappear in a puff of smoke. But don't worry about the original files—they're still on your hard drive. Dock icons are just pointers to the files, not the files themselves. ■

TIP

Moving Day If you don't like the order of the icons in the Dock, you can drag and drop them into an order that suits you better. ■

MOVING AND RESIZING WINDOWS

Mac OS X is full of windows: document windows, folder windows, more windows than you can count. The Finder shows you the contents of each folder or disk in a window. Each of your open documents—a picture, a text file, a web page, and so on—appears in a window, too. All these windows, whether they belong to the Finder or to the program in which you're viewing or editing a document, have certain features in common. Knowing how to get windows to go where you want them is an important skill you'll use every hour of your Mac's life.

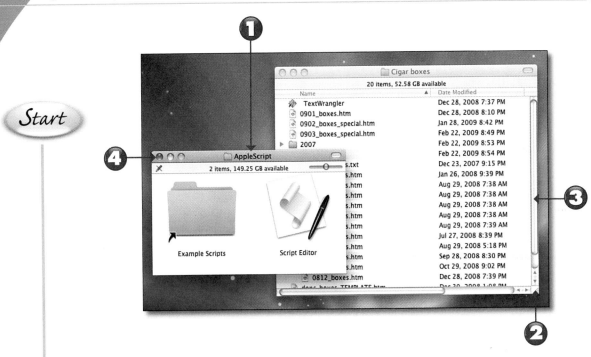

Start

1. To move a window so you can see what's underneath it, click its title bar and drag the window to a new position.

2. Click and drag the lower-right corner of a window to change the window's size.

3. View the remaining contents of a window by clicking and dragging the scrollbars.

4. To close a window, click the red button at the left end of the window's title bar.

End

NOTE

More to Windows Than Meets the Eye Keep reading for more about wrangling windows. The next task shows how to minimize and maximize your windows, and the results might not be quite what you're expecting. ■

MINIMIZING AND MAXIMIZING WINDOWS

Although windows are a great way to look inside folders, they never seem to open at just the right size for what you're trying to see. Getting the most from your windows requires learning to maximize their size when you need them and minimize them out of sight when you don't.

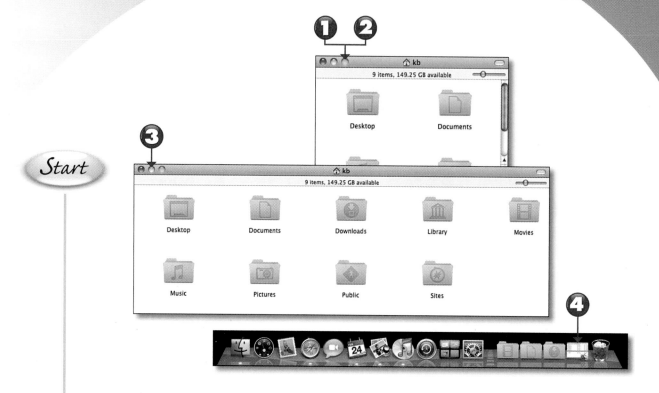

Start

① Click the **green button** at the left end of a window's title bar to size the window so that it shows its entire contents—or as much as will fit on the screen.

② Click the **green button** again to return the window to its previous size.

③ Click the **yellow button** at the left end of a window's title bar to shrink the window downward into the right side of the Dock.

④ Click the window's thumbnail image in the Dock to put it back onto the desktop.

End

NOTE

Window Identification Each minimized window in the right side of the Dock has a small icon attached to its lower-right corner that identifies the program to which the window belongs. Folder and disk windows belong to the Finder, so they have a Finder logo. ■

NOTE

The Wonders of Windows The Dock continuously updates the appearance of minimized document windows. For example, if you minimize a movie window while the movie's playing, you can monitor the movie's progress while its window is in the Dock. ■

MANAGING MULTIPLE WINDOWS

Exposé is a handy way to cut through window clutter instantly, no matter what program you're using. And if you tend to use a lot of programs at the same time, you'll definitely find Exposé's three little magic tricks very useful. They use the function keys, the row of "F" keys at the top of your keyboard.

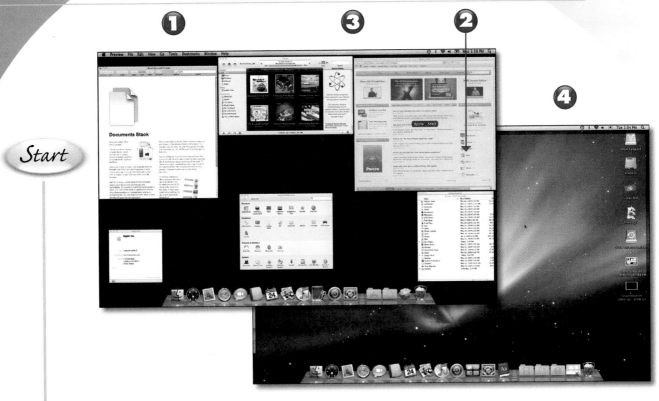

Start

End

① Press **F9** to scale down and tile all open windows.

② Click to select the window you're looking for and return all the windows to their normal size.

③ Press **F11** to hide all windows so you can see the desktop.

④ Press **F10** to tile all the windows in the current program and shade other windows.

TIP

For Those Who Prefer the Mouse Choose Apple menu, System Preferences, and click Exposé & Spaces to assign the Exposé functions to the screen's corners. Then perform any of these magical actions by simply positioning your mouse in the appropriate corner. ■

TIP

One Window at a Time Any time you've used Exposé to tile windows, either by pressing F9 or F10, you can highlight each window in turn by pressing ⌘-` repeatedly. When you reach the window you want, press Return or click to activate it. ■

USING CUSTOM SPACES

Time to quit work and take a Solitaire break! But wait—if you close all your Finder and document windows, you'll have to open them all back up again when you return to work. There's a better way—change Spaces. You can set up custom configurations of programs and documents that appear when you switch to the appropriate Space and slide neatly off the side of the screen when you switch to another Space. Switch back to the first Space, and there are all your windows, just waiting for you.

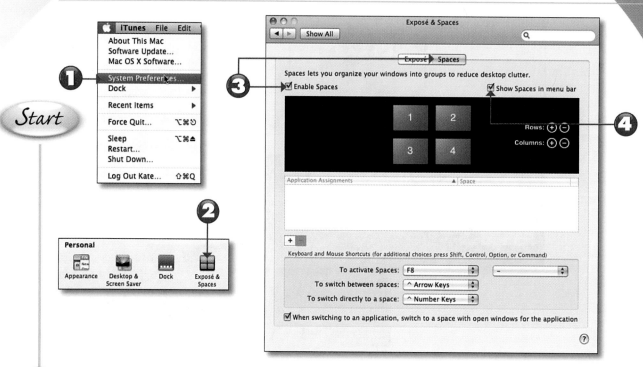

Start

1. Choose **Apple menu, System Preferences**.

2. Click **Exposé & Spaces** to display the Exposé & Spaces preferences.

3. Click the **Spaces** tab, and then click the check box labeled **Enable Spaces** to turn Spaces on.

4. Click the check box labeled **Show spaces in menu bar** to add a Spaces menu to your menu bar.

Continued

TIP

Making More Spaces To add more Spaces, go to the Spaces preferences in System Preferences and click the Rows and Columns icons in the display window. You can create up to 16 Spaces, in four columns and four rows. For efficiency's sake, don't set up more spaces than you're actually going to use, however. ■

TIP

A Spacey Shortcut Flip back and forth among your different Spaces by holding down Control and pressing the arrow keys. ■

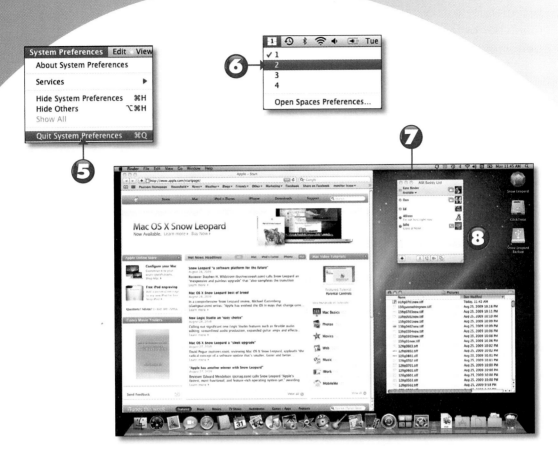

Choose **System Preferences**, **Quit System Preferences** to apply your changes.

Choose a Space from the menu bar by clicking its number in the Spaces menu.

Open programs and documents and arrange windows to set up your custom workspace.

Switch out of this Space and into another by choosing a different number from the menu bar or by pressing **Control** and a different Space's number.

End

TIP
Check 'Em Out To see pictures of all your Spaces, click the Spaces icon in the Dock or press F8. Click the Space to which you want to switch. (You can change this keyboard shortcut to a different key if you prefer.) ■

NOTE
Blast Off with Spaces How about a space for work, with project folders open and Mail running? Or one for web surfing, with your browser and iChat open? Or even a minimalist Space with nothing at all open? ■

USING CONTEXTUAL MENUS

The more you use your Mac, the more you'll appreciate time-saving techniques. Contextual menus pop up right where you're working, instead of requiring you to mouse up to the menu bar or take your hands off the mouse to use the keyboard. Their contents vary depending on what you're doing at the time.

Start

1 Press **Control** and click any object on the desktop.

2 Click the contextual menu command you want to perform.

End

TIP
Remember the Context Contextual menus contain different options depending on what you click to see them. Try Control-clicking the desktop itself, and don't forget to Control-click objects in document windows, such as pictures or misspelled words. ▪

NOTE
The Easy Way If you have a multibutton mouse, you can use the software that came with it to program one of the buttons to perform a Control-click. Most people use the right mouse button. ▪

RESTARTING OR SHUTTING DOWN THE MAC

Because they're commands that affect the entire system, Restart and Shut Down are located in the Apple menu, so you can access them from any program rather than having to switch to the Finder, as in pre-OS X versions of the Mac OS. You'll use Restart most often after installing new software, and you'll use Shut Down when you want to turn off your computer.

 Start

 End

1 To restart the Mac, choose **Apple menu**, **Restart**.

2 In the dialog box, click **Restart**. Click **Cancel** to exit the dialog box without restarting.

3 To shut down the Mac, choose **Apple menu**, **Shut Down**.

4 In the dialog box, click **Shut Down**. Click **Cancel** to exit the dialog box without shutting down.

TIP

No Fresh Start Needed You don't have to restart the Mac if you only want to switch users. Choose Apple menu, Log Out instead; this command quits all running programs and presents you with the login screen, but it doesn't require the computer to completely reboot. ∎

TIP

As Easy as Pressing a Button On a Mac laptop, press the Power key briefly to bring up a dialog asking you whether you want to restart, shut down, or sleep your Mac. ∎

SETTING BASIC SYSTEM PREFERENCES

You can't customize everything about your Mac, but you can get darn close (for more customization techniques, turn to Chapter 5). Here's a look at the most basic preferences you'll want to set on a new Mac.

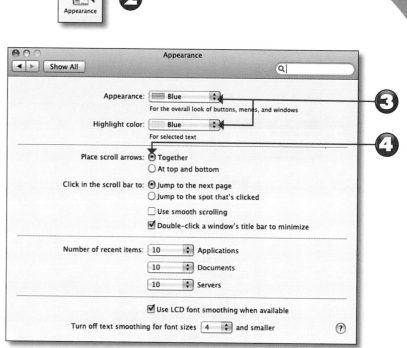

Start

① Choose **Apple menu**, **System Preferences**.

② Click **Appearance** to display the Appearance preferences.

③ Choose colors from the **Appearance** pop-up menu (for scrollbars, buttons, and menus) and the **Highlight Color** pop-up menu (for selected text and objects in list view).

④ Click a radio button to put scrollbar arrows together or at the top and bottom of each window.

Continued

NOTE

Blue Versus Graphite Your Appearance color preference starts out set to Blue. If you switch it to Graphite, all your dialog box buttons, menu highlights, and window components turn graphite gray. The only problem you might encounter with that setting is that the Close, Minimize, and Maximize buttons—normally red, yellow, and green, respectively—also turn gray. You can still tell them apart by placing the cursor over them; an X appears in the Close button, a minus sign in the Minimize button, and a plus sign in the Maximize button. ■

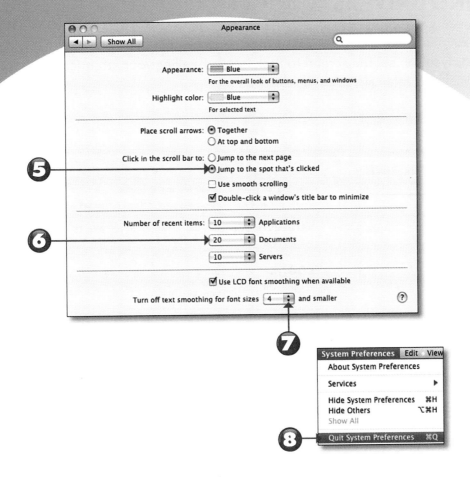

5 Click a radio button to choose how far clicking in the scrollbar scrolls the window.

6 Choose the number of recently used applications and documents that will appear in the Apple menu.

7 Choose a font smoothing size from the pop-up menus.

8 Choose **System Preferences**, **Quit System Preferences** to apply your changes.

End

TIP

Scroll, Scroll, Scroll Your Window Here's how the scrollbar settings work: Jump to the next page moves the view up or down one screen when you click in the scrollbar. With long documents, you might prefer Jump to the spot that's clicked, which moves the view to the location within the document that approximates the location of your click. In other words, click halfway down the scrollbar to see the document's midpoint. These settings apply within both application windows and folder windows in the Finder. ∎

USING UNIVERSAL ACCESS

Universal Access provides alternative ways of viewing the Mac's screen, hearing the sounds it makes, using the keyboard, and using the mouse. For example, if you can't hear alert sounds, you can set the screen to flash instead, calling your attention to what's happening just as clearly as an alert sound would.

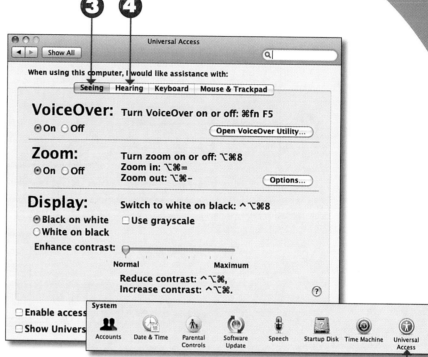

Start

1 Choose **Apple menu**, **System Preferences**.

2 Click **Universal Access**.

3 Click the **Seeing** tab and click the buttons to turn on the Zoom feature or switch to white text on a black background.

4 Click the **Hearing** tab and click the check box to flash the screen when an alert sound is played.

Continued

TIP

Shortcuts to Access No matter which Universal Access settings you want to use, you should click Allow Universal Access Shortcuts. This option activates the keyboard shortcuts shown on each tab of the Universal Access preferences pane. ■

NOTE

Yakkety Yak VoiceOver is the first setting in the Seeing section of the Universal Access preferences. This feature enables you to control your Mac with voice commands. Turn to the next task to learn more. ■

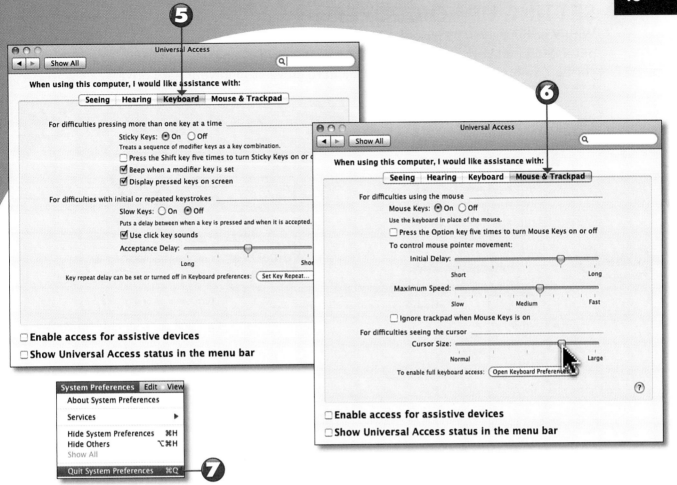

5 Click the **Keyboard** tab and choose from the various keyboard options.

6 Click the **Mouse & Trackpad** tab and choose from the various mouse options.

7 Choose **System Preferences, Quit System Preferences** to apply your changes.

End

NOTE

Special Assistance The **Enable access for assistive devices** setting at the bottom of the Universal Access preferences pane enables you to use special equipment to control your Mac, such as head tracking devices with which you can move the cursor by moving your head. ■

SETTING UP VOICEOVER

With VoiceOver, you can use the keyboard and Mac speech features to control your computer. Standard keyboard commands are augmented by special commands to enable you to start up, switch, and control programs, and to move around your hard drive.

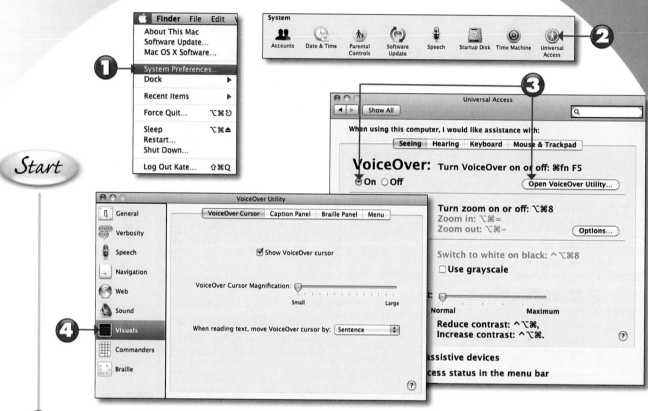

Choose **Apple menu**, **System Preferences**.

Click **Universal Access**.

Click **On** to enable VoiceOver, and then click **Open VoiceOver Utility** to configure VoiceOver settings.

In VoiceOver Utility, click **Visuals** to control when and how the VoiceOver feature is invoked.

Continued

NOTE

More or Less The Display settings determine how evident VoiceOver is as you use your Mac. For example, you can turn on the VoiceOver cursor to hear spoken descriptions of the objects and dialog boxes under your cursor, or you can turn off the cursor to hide this feature. ∎

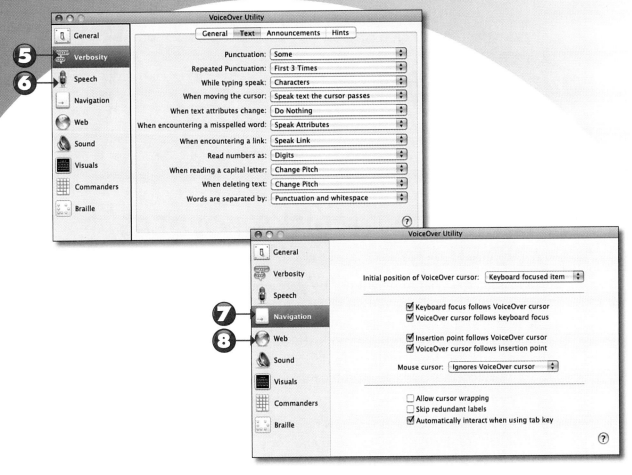

 Click **Verbosity** to control how much VoiceOver talks.

Click **Speech** to change the voice VoiceOver uses.

Click **Navigation** to control how VoiceOver moves around your screen.

Click **Web** to set how VoiceOver interprets web pages for you.

End

TIP

PatienceOver The level of your Verbosity settings should be proportional to your patience. If you want to get moving without listening for very long, lower the **Item Description** and **Punctuation** settings. ■

WORKING WITH DISKS, FOLDERS, AND FILES

The tasks in this chapter might not be glamorous or exciting, but they're the foundation of everything you do on your Mac. It's all about files, folders, and the disks that hold them. Every time you create a new document or receive an email attachment, that information is stored in a file on your hard drive, and the file is in turn stored within a folder. Mac OS X provides many ways for you to view and modify folder contents and file attributes, so you're in complete control of your Mac.

The tasks in this part teach you how to create new folders and view their contents in different ways, how to move and copy files, how to organize your hard drive and keep it uncluttered, and how to use Apple's MobileMe online service to perform regular backups of your important files and synchronize your vital information across multiple computers.

You might notice that windows on your Mac OS X desktop have two distinct guises—a "plain" dress that looks like any document window and a "fancy" version that includes racks of buttons down the side and across the top. These are, respectively, multi-window mode and single-window mode. Don't be deceived, though—you can have windows of both types open at the same time. This important aspect of Mac OS X is covered in the first task in this part.

Use single-window
mode, 21

Use multi-window
mode, 22

Find files, 43

Change folder
views, 25

Access favorite
folders, 49

See documents
in Cover Flow
view, 27

Get information
about files and
folders, 35

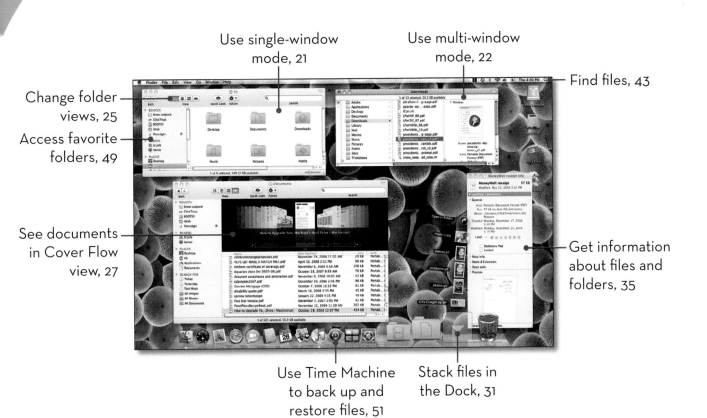

Use Time Machine
to back up and
restore files, 51

Stack files in
the Dock, 31

USING SINGLE-WINDOW MODE

Traditionally, the Mac spawned a new window for each folder or disk you opened. Mac OS X introduced single-window mode, in which the contents of each folder or disk appear in the same window, like each successive page in a web browser displays in the same window. It took a little getting used to, but it's a better way of working.

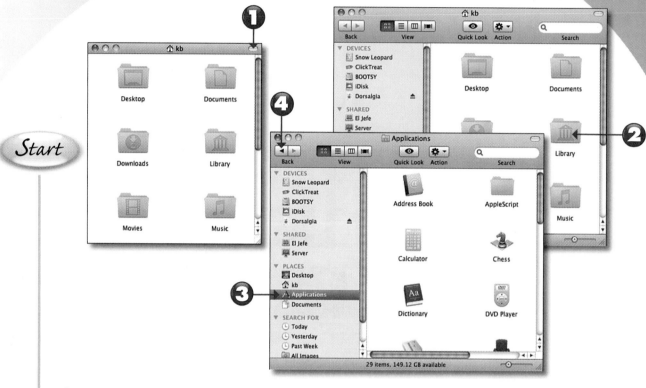

Start

1 If you're using multi-window mode, click the transparent button in the upper-right corner of the window to switch to single-window mode and display the toolbar and sidebar.

2 Double-click folders in the main window to see their contents.

3 Click a folder or disk in the **Places** sidebar to see its contents.

4 Click the **left** and **right arrows** to go back and forward in the series of windows you've viewed (similar to the Back and Forward buttons in a web browser window).

End

TIP

Single Versus Multi Single-window mode is at its most useful when you need to see the contents of only one window. If you're copying or moving files from one folder to another, you'll probably find multi-window mode a better bet. Don't forget that you can switch window views in single-window mode by clicking the Icon, List, Column, and Cover Flow view buttons at the top of the window. A special button with a picture of a gear next to these four summons up a contextual menu for any selected file in the window. ■

USING MULTI-WINDOW MODE

Sometimes you need to see the contents of two windows at once, and it's easier to focus on what you need to look at without the sidebar and toolbar in single-window mode. Multi-window mode makes copying or moving files from one folder or disk to another easier.

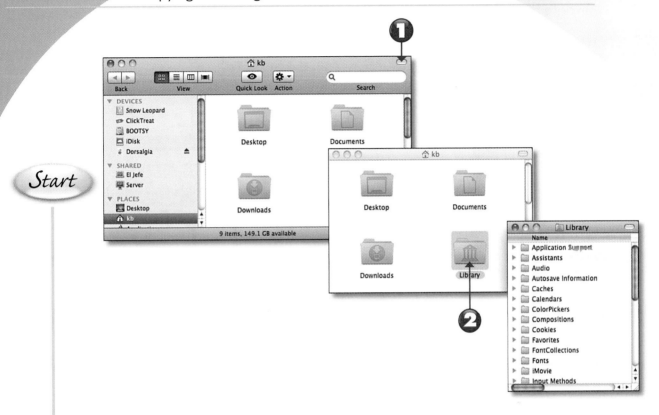

Start

1 If you're using single-window mode, click the transparent button in the upper-right corner of the window to switch to multi-window mode.

2 Double-click a folder in the window to open a new window showing its contents.

End

TIP

Quick Switch Even without the single-window mode toolbar, you can switch quickly from one window view to another. Click in a window and press ⌘-1 for icon view, ⌘-2 for list view, ⌘-3 for column view, and ⌘-4 for cover flow view. ■

USING THE TOOLBAR

In single-window mode, each window contains a toolbar that provides shortcuts to common tasks in the Finder, such as switching folder views and searching for files. After you get to know the toolbar, it quickly becomes your best friend. You can even customize it with your favorite buttons, too—see the next task.

Start

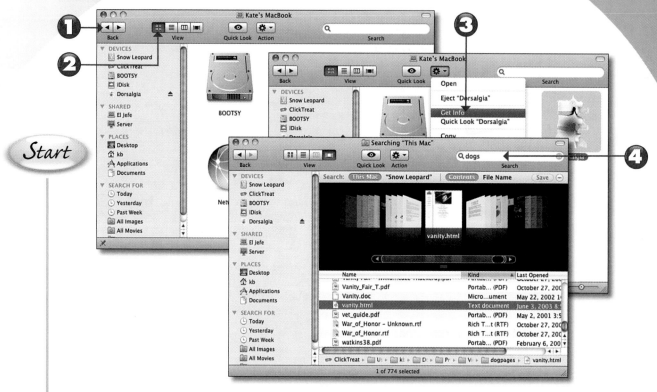

1 Click the **Back** and **Forward** buttons to see the contents of folders you've looked at before in this window.

2 Click the **Icon View**, **List View**, **Column View**, or **Cover Flow** button to change your folder view.

3 Choose an option from the **Action** menu to perform one of several common tasks.

4 Type in the **Search** field to search for files and folders by name.

End

NOTE

Where to Look The toolbar's Search field automatically starts out by searching your entire system. But as soon as the search begins, a toolbar pops up giving you a choice of other locations. If you can narrow down the search location, the search will go faster. ∎

TIP

Action Figures The commands available in the Action menu vary depending on what's selected. For example, if you click a disk icon, the Action menu adds an Eject command. Be sure to explore your Action menu options. ∎

CUSTOMIZING THE TOOLBAR

The row of buttons across the top of a window when you're in single-window mode is called the toolbar. These buttons offer you quick access to the most common functions in the Finder, such as changing window views and creating new folders. You can choose the buttons you want to display in the toolbar.

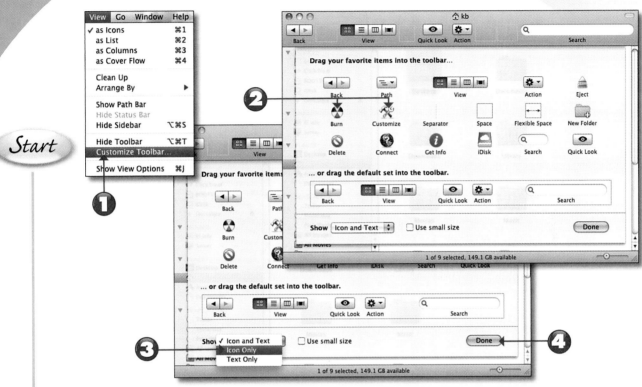

Start

1 Choose **View**, **Customize Toolbar**.

2 Drag buttons onto the toolbar to add them.

3 Choose an option from the **Show** pop-up menu.

4 Click **Done**.

End

TIP

Back Where You Started When you're customizing your toolbar, you can restore the default set of buttons by dragging the whole set from the bottom of the Customize dialog box up to the toolbar. ■

TIP

Cutting Back To remove buttons from the toolbar, choose View, Customize Toolbar and drag the buttons you don't want off the toolbar. ■

USING DIFFERENT FOLDER VIEWS

You can view Finder windows in four ways. Icon view is convenient when a folder contains just a few files and you want to be able to tell them apart quickly. List view enables you to sort the contents of a window, and column view provides a quick way of burrowing down into a series of nested folders. The glamorous Cover Flow view has the next task all to itself.

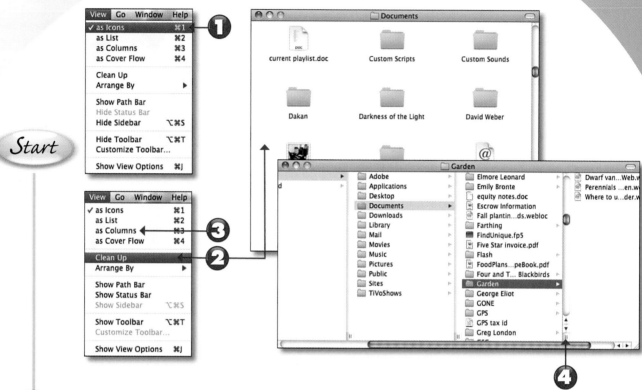

Start

1 To switch to icon view, choose **View**, **as Icons**.

2 If the icons are stacked on top of each other, choose **View**, **Clean Up** to space them out so you can see them all.

3 To switch to column view, choose **View**, **as Columns**.

4 Drag the bar between two columns to adjust the columns' width.

Continued

TIP

Wide Angle View To adjust column widths in column view, drag the small double line at the bottom of the column divider. It's only visible if the column contains a list of files and folders; you can't adjust empty columns. ∎

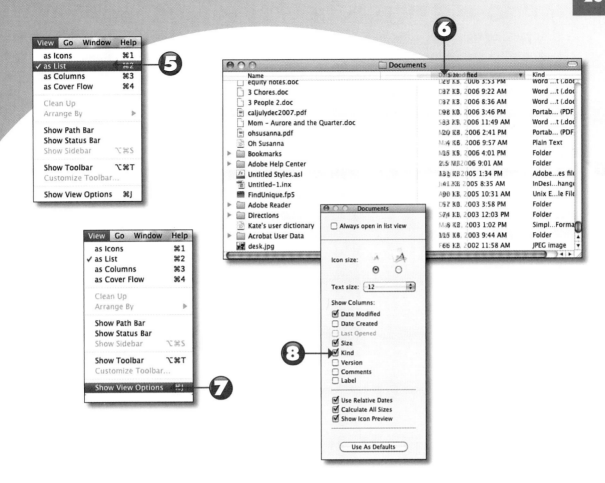

5 To switch to list view, choose **View, as List**.

6 Drag the right edge of a list column header to change that column's width, or drag a column header to a different position to change the order of the columns.

7 Choose **View, Show View Options** to select which list columns are visible.

8 Check boxes to choose which columns are visible in the active window.

End

TIP

Getting There via Buttons In single-window mode, you can click the buttons in the upper-left corner of the window to switch window views. Turn to the task "Using Single-Window Mode," earlier in this part, to learn more about using single-window mode. ■

TIP

Switch Hitting Lists can be sorted in ascending or descending order. Click the active column header to switch from ascending to descending order or vice versa. An arrow in the list column header indicates which way the list is sorted. ■

CHOOSING FILES IN COVER FLOW VIEW

Leopard brings you a new way of flipping through folder contents in the Finder, courtesy of iTunes. In Cover Flow view, your files are lined up like discs in a jukebox, so that you can see a large preview of each one. You can scan through them slowly with a slider, or you can skip from one to another as you please.

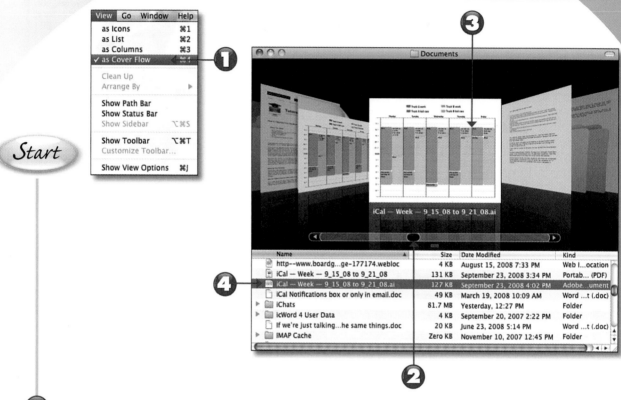

Start

1 To switch to Cover Flow view, choose **View**, **as Cover Flow**.

2 Drag the slider to move back and forth through the "covers."

3 Click a "cover" in the window or an item in the list to select that file.

4 Double-click a "cover" or a list item to open the file.

End

NOTE

All the Same to Me Cover Flow is another way to look at the files in a folder. Drag files from a Cover Flow view window onto the Dock, into the sidebar, or into other folders, just like files in any other view. ■

NOTE

Play Me If the file you're looking at in Cover Flow is a movie or music file, you can click it to bring up a Play button. Click that button, and the file will play. You can also play the file full-screen in Quick Look view. ■

USING THE GO MENU

To make getting around your system easier, the Go menu contains commands that instantly take you to specific locations, including any of the special folders Mac OS X creates for your programs and documents. The Go menu also keeps track of the last several folders you've opened so you can return to any of them with a single click.

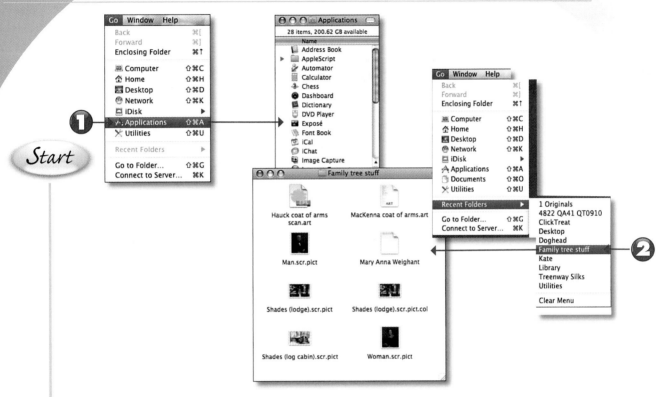

 Start

End

1 To go to one of Mac OS X's special folders, click **Go** and choose **Computer**, **Home**, **Applications**, or **Utilities**.

2 To go to one of the folders you've opened recently, choose **Go**, **Recent Folders** and choose a folder.

TIP

Using the Keyboard You can also go to the special folders with keyboard commands. Press ⌘-Shift-C to see the Computer window; press ⌘-Shift-H to open your home folder; press ⌘-Shift-A to open the Applications folder; and press ⌘-Shift-U to open the Utilities folder. ■

SELECTING FILES

It might seem obvious, but before you can do anything with a file, folder, or disk in the Finder, you must select it so that the Finder knows which object(s) you want it to act on. A couple of selection methods enable you to select more than one item at a time while leaving out those you don't want to use at the moment.

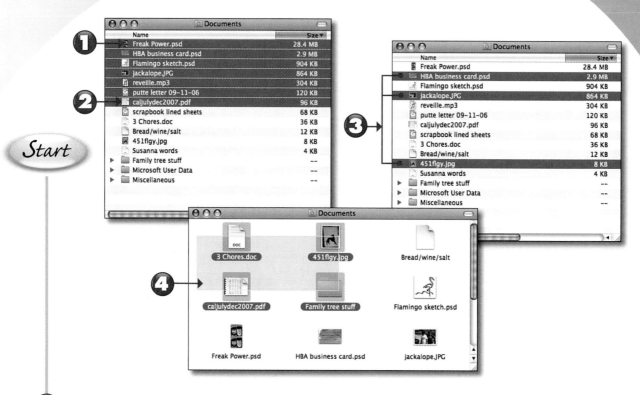

Start

End

① In any folder view, click a file or folder to select it.

② **Shift-click** another file or folder to select it along with all the items between it and the first object you selected.

③ ⌘-**click** to select noncontiguous items.

④ In icon view, click and drag to select a group of icons.

TIP

Selecting Everything at One Time To select all the items in a folder (or on the desktop), click the folder's title bar to make sure it is the active folder; then either press ⌘-A or choose Edit, Select All. ∎

MOVING AND COPYING FILES AND FOLDERS

Keeping your computer tidy is mostly a matter of putting things where they belong. That means moving and copying files and folders to different locations. You have to be authorized to open folders to which you're copying items, which means you can't put files in other users' folders, for the most part.

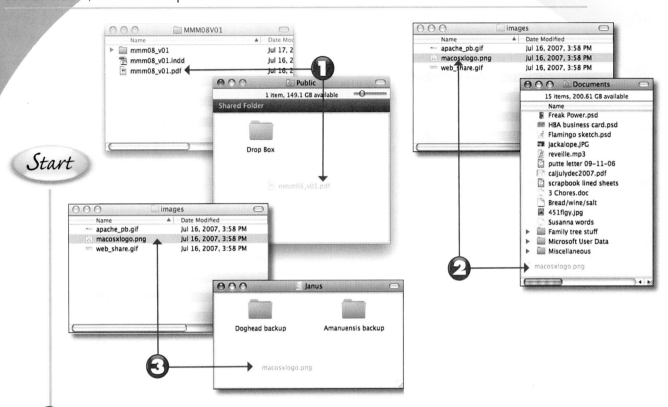

1 To move an item to another folder on the same disk, drag and drop it into the folder's window.

2 To copy an item to a location on a different disk, drag and drop it into the folder's window.

3 To copy an item to a different location on the same disk, press **Option** while you drag and drop it into the folder's window.

End

TIP

Another Way to Copy To make a copy of an item in the same place, press Option and drag the icon a little away from its current location or choose File, Duplicate. ■

TIP

Using Copy and Paste to Copy Files Control-click the file you want to copy and choose Copy from the menu. Control-click in an open area of the folder's window where you want to put the copy and choose Paste Item. ■

31

MAKING A STACK

Folders are great but the more organized you are, the more folders you use and the more time you spend digging through them. With Leopard, Mac OS X has a new way to show you the contents of a folder: stacks. Stacking files in your Dock is like stacking them up on top of your desk, only better, because you can see them all with just a click.

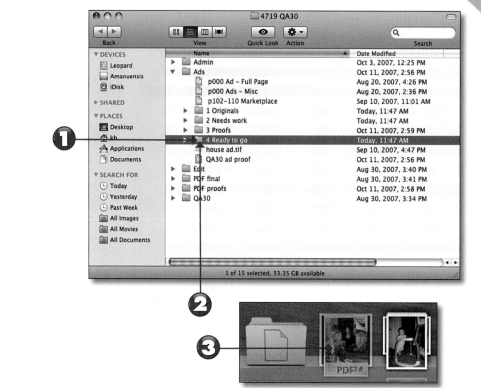

Start

1 In the Finder, select the folder you want to make into a stack.

2 Drag the folder to the right side of the Dock.

3 To add an object to the stack, drag it onto the stack icon in the Dock.

End

 TIP

What's Your Name? Each stack is named after the folder it's made from. To rename a stack something more useful, Control-click its icon on the Dock and choose Rename Stack. ■

 TIP

Begone! When you no longer need quick access to the files in a stack, it's time to get rid of it and make more room in your Dock for stuff you do need. Deleting a stack is as simple as dragging it off the Dock. ■

VIEWING STACKED FILES

So now that you have your files neatly organized into stacks on the Dock, what can you do with them? First, take a minute to savor the satisfaction of being so organized. Then, start working! Stacks are that simple; there's no learning curve.

Start

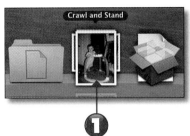

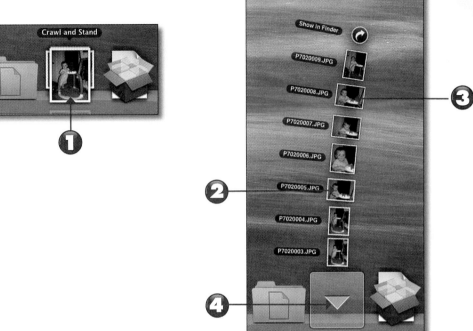

To see the files in the stack, click the stack icon.

To open a stacked file, click its icon in the stack.

To delete an object from the stack, drag it to the Desktop or a different folder.

To restack the files without opening one, click the arrow in the Dock.

End

NOTE

Arc or No Arc? If a stack contains more items than will fit in a neat arc above the Dock, clicking the stack icon reveals the files in a grid rather than an arc. ∎

NOTE

A Folder Within a Folder What happens if you've got a folder in your stack? That depends on how many other things are in the stack. If it's still arcing, as shown here, clicking a folder opens it in the Finder. If the stack is displayed as a grid, however, clicking a folder brings up a new grid showing the contents of that folder. ∎

MAKING A NEW FOLDER

This is one task that often trips up Mac users, who used to press ⌘-**N** to create a new folder. That keyboard shortcut brings up a new Finder window instead of creating a new folder. You'll get used to the change, and you'll find that being able to create new Finder windows this way is pretty useful, too.

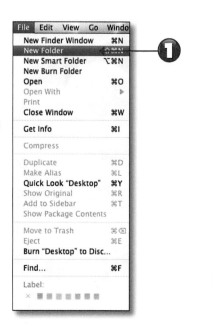

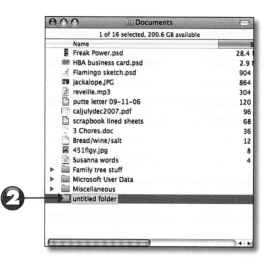

Start

To create a new folder, choose **File**, **New Folder** (or press ⌘-**Shift-N**).

Type a name for the untitled folder; to change the name, see the next task.

End

TIP

You Don't Have to Start from Scratch If you need several folders with the same name and, perhaps, a different number tacked onto the end of each, create the first one and create copies of it as described earlier in the task "Moving and Copying Files and Folders." Then replace "copy" in the folder name with the numbers or text you want. ∎

RENAMING FOLDERS AND FILES

Some people like to include dates and similar information in filenames so anyone can tell what's inside; others don't care if anyone else can make sense of their filenames. Whichever camp you fall into, you'll need to know how to change the names of files and folders.

Start

1 Click to select the item whose name you want to change.

2 Keep the mouse cursor positioned over the name.

3 When the item's name becomes highlighted, type to replace the old name with the new one. Press **Enter** when you're done.

End

CAUTION

Adding Extensions Hate documents with blank, white icons? You can't open them by double-clicking because your Mac doesn't know which program to use. If you know which kind of document it is, add the correct filename extension. ■

TIP

Extended Filenames Each filename has two components: the name and the extension, such as .pdf or .doc. Mac OS X uses extensions to determine which program can open which files, so don't change an extension unless you know what you're doing. ■

VIEWING FILE INFORMATION

Each file or folder on your computer has a lot of information associated with it—not just the data it contains, such as recipes or pictures or programming code, but data about the file, such as when it was created, the last time it was modified, and which program made it.

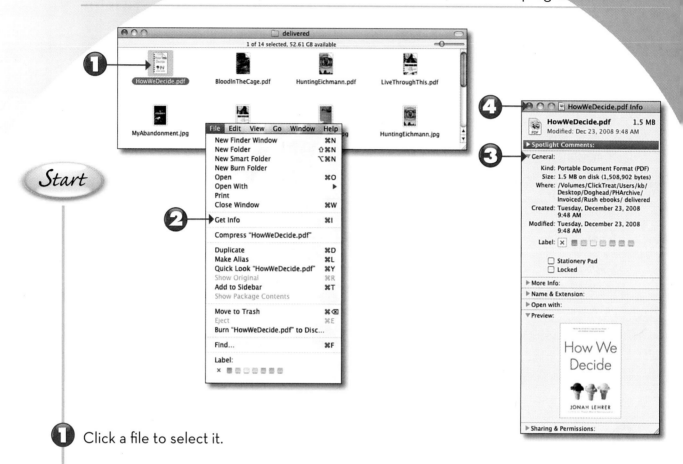

Start

1. Click a file to select it.

2. Choose **File**, **Get Info**.

3. The Info window opens to the General pane; to see the contents of another pane, click the gray triangle next to its name.

4. Click the red **Close** button to close the Info window when you're done.

End

TIP
Avoiding a Trip to the Menu Bar You can also press ⌘-I or use a contextual menu to get information about an item. ■

NOTE
Getting Info Some file information can be changed in the Info window, if you're the owner of a file. You can change the name and extension, the program that opens a document, and the file's ownership (if you're an admin user), and you can add comments. ■

PREVIEWING A FILE

If you're looking through a lot of files at one time, the filenames and preview icons may not be enough to help you figure out exactly what's in each document. Say hello to Quick Look, a Mac OS X feature that enables you to see the contents of a file without having to open it. You can flip through each page, and you can even switch to full-screen mode to get a really good look.

Start

End

1. Click a file to select it.

2. Choose **File**, **Quick Look** "filename".

3. To view the document in full-screen mode, click the double arrows at the bottom of the window.

4. To close the Quick Look window, click the **X** button.

TIP

Quick Navigation To enlarge the preview image, drag the corner of the window to make it bigger—the image will expand to fill the window. Use the scroll bar on the window's right side to move through the document's pages. ■

TIP

Give Me My Space A quick way to take a Quick Look at one or more selected files in the Finder is to press the spacebar. Press the spacebar again to close the Quick Look window. ■

OPENING A FILE

When you're looking at a file's icon in the Finder, you can open that file in the correct program without having to first start up the program. Conversely, if you're already using that program, you can open more files without having to return to the Finder to locate them.

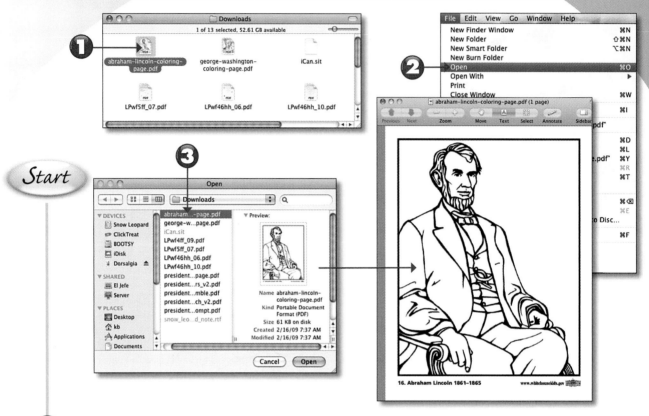

1. In the Finder, double-click the file's icon. The file opens in the program that created it.

2. Or, to open a file from within a running program, choose **File**, **Open**.

3. Navigate to the file in the pick list and double-click it or click the **Open** button. The file opens in the program.

End

TIP

Programs Some programs are picky about which types of files they'll open, so your file might be unavailable in an Open dialog box. If a pop-up menu below the pick list has an option such as Show All Files, choose this option to make your file available. ▪

NOTE

It's a Drag A third method of opening a file is to drag it on top of a program icon, either in the Finder or in the Dock. The program starts up, if it wasn't already running, and opens the file if it can. If it can't, its icon won't darken. ▪

CHOOSING A PROGRAM TO OPEN A FILE

Sometimes you disagree with your Mac about which program it should use to open a file. For example, perhaps you want to open PDF files in Adobe Reader instead of Preview, or RTF word processor files in Microsoft Word instead of TextEdit. You have the power to make the change; just follow these steps.

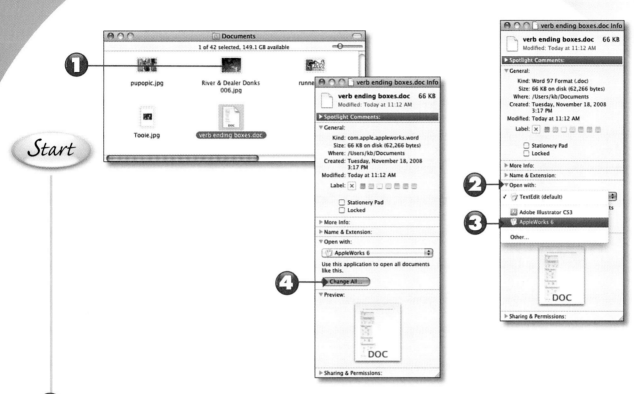

Start

1 Click to select the file and press ⌘-**I** to see its Info window.

2 Click the gray triangle next to **Open with** in the Info window.

3 Choose an application from the pop-up menu, or choose **Other** to navigate to the program you want if it's not listed.

4 Click **Change All** if you want to make the same change for all documents with the same extension. If you see a confirmation dialog box, click **Continue**.

End

TIP

There's More than One Way The directions here enable you to open a file in the right program by double-clicking its Finder icon. But if you're in a hurry, you can just start the program and choose File, Open as described earlier in the task "Opening a File." ■

HANDLING FILES WITH AUTOMATOR

Remember how computers were supposed to make our lives simpler? Well, Automator really does that. With Automator, you can set up a series of steps once, save them as a workflow, and then set that task in motion any time with a mere double-click or drag and drop. Here's how to create a workflow that backs up selected files.

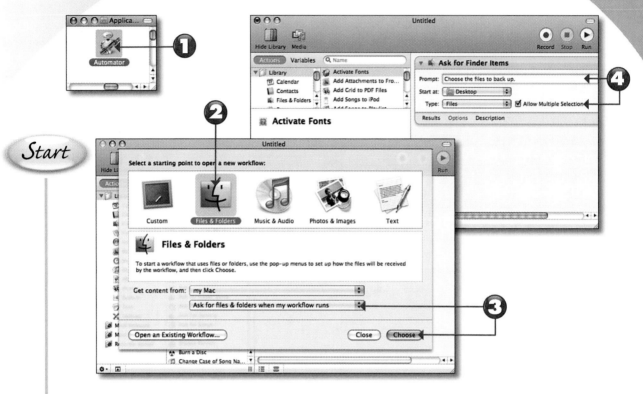

Double-click to start Automator (located in the Applications folder).

Click **Files & Folders** to start creating your workflow.

Choose **Ask for files & folders when my workflow runs** from the pop-up menu, and click **Choose**.

In the **Prompt** field, type **Choose the files to back up** and check the box marked **Allow Multiple Selection**.

Continued

TIP

Running Workflows Saving a workflow as an application enables you to run it without starting Automator. While it's running, you see a message to that effect in the menu bar; click the red stop sign button to cancel the series of actions. ∎

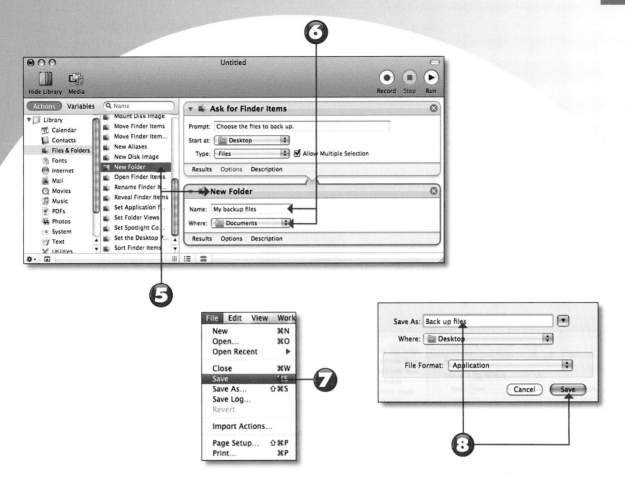

Drag the New Folder action into the work area from the Files & Folders section of the Library.

In the **Name** field, type **My backup files**, and then choose the location where you want the backup folder to be created.

Choose **File**, **Save**.

Choose a name and location for your workflow, choose **Application** from the File Format pop-up menu, and click **Save**.

End

TIP

The Endless Possibilities You can add other steps to make this workflow more useful. For example, you might add an Archive action to compress the backup folder after the files are copied into it. Another possibility is a Copy action to back up the files to another disk or server. ■

TIP

Making It Happen To run this workflow, just double-click its icon—you can put it in the Dock for quick access if you like—then select the files you want to back up in the dialog box. ■

RECORDING TASKS

Automator is easy to use, but it still takes a little more technical thought than you may have available before you've had your coffee. If you want to create workflows in the most intuitive way possible, set Automator to record your actions and then go to town! When you're done, you'll be able to repeat your actions any time by running the workflow you've just created.

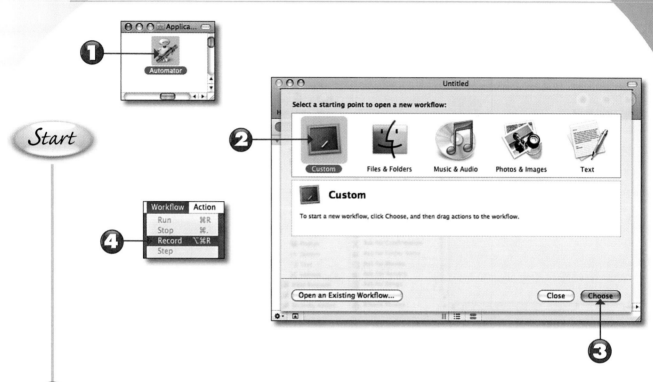

Start

 Double-click to start Automator (located in the Applications folder).

2 Click **Custom** to create an empty workflow with no steps automatically inserted.

3 Click **Choose** to start creating your workflow.

4 Choose **Workflow**, **Record** to begin recording.

Continued

CAUTION

What Will You Automate? There are two main categories of tasks to consider automating: repetitive tasks—ones that you do exactly the same way repeatedly—and ones that you want to happen without your intervention. For example, if you're spending hours each week converting PDF files to TIFFs, create a drag-and-drop workflow to do the job for you. Or if you want your Mac's volume muted every night at 7 p.m., that's another great candidate for a workflow. Record it, save it, and link it to an iCal appointment set for 7 p.m. each evening. ■

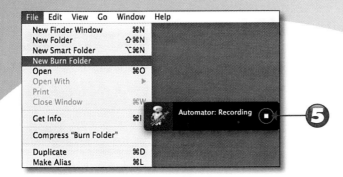

5 Perform the actions you want to record, then click **Stop**.

6 Make any adjustments to the steps recorded, such as deleting extraneous steps.

7 Choose **File, Save**.

8 Set the workflow's name and location, then click **Save**.

End

NOTE

Be Warned Automator's recording feature is very, very literal-minded. For example, if you record yourself clicking the Safari icon in the Dock to start up your web browser, Automator won't just record "Start Safari"—it will record "Click the Safari icon in the Dock." Then, if you go on a decluttering binge and remove the Safari icon from your Dock at some point in the future, that workflow will no longer execute. ■

FINDING FILES WITH SPOTLIGHT

Spotlight is a powerful and speedy search utility. Built into the Finder, it's always waiting for you in the upper-right corner of the screen. After it finds what you're looking for, Spotlight doesn't stop there; it organizes its results into categories and sorts them any way you like.

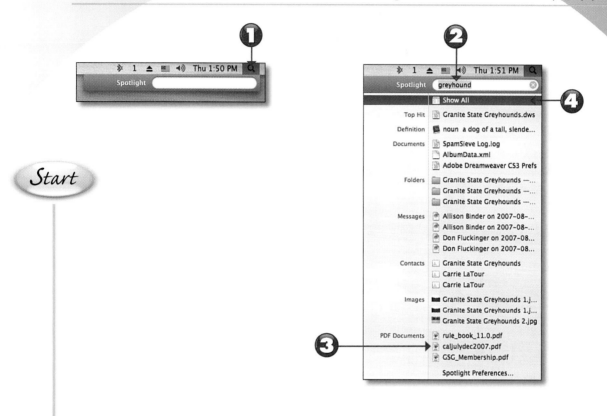

Start

① Click the **Spotlight** menu to display the search field.

② Enter search terms in the field.

③ Click a document in the results to open.

④ Click **Show All** to see more results.

Continued

TIP

Talking Your Language Spotlight is even smarter than it looks. Try adding natural-language search terms, such as "yesterday" (for files modified yesterday) or "image" (for image files), to narrow your searches. ■

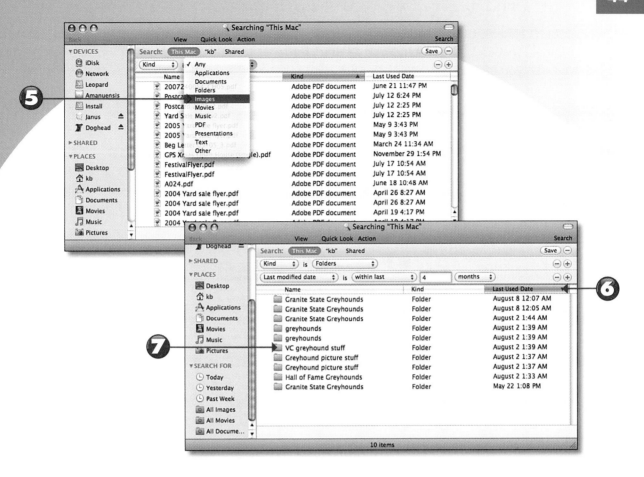

 Use the menus at the top of the window to filter the search results by time, location, or other criteria.

 Click a column head to sort the results differently.

7 Double-click an item in the list to open the file.

End

TIP

What's It Look Like? Spotlight search results always start out in List view, but you can use any of the other three view modes to sort through your results; Cover Flow and icon view work particularly well when you're searching for an image. ■

TIP

It's a Long Way to the Menu Bar If you don't want to make the trip all the way up to the right-hand end of the menu bar with your mouse, you can also perform a Spotlight search in any Finder window that's in single-window mode. ■

CREATING A SMART FOLDER

A smart folder collects related files into a single folder without moving the files from their original locations. One way to use a smart folder is to collect all the text modified in the last week so you can keep track of the files you're currently working on.

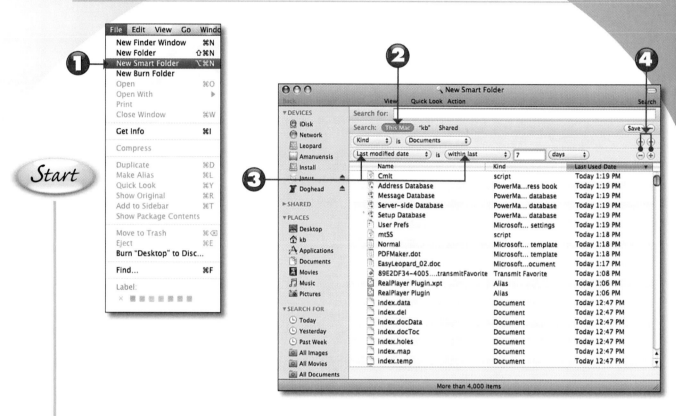

 Start

1 Choose **File, New Smart Folder**.

2 Click to specify a location for the files you want to track in this folder.

3 Select a search criteria category and make a setting within that category.

4 Click **Add** to add another search criterion, or click **Remove** to remove one.

Continued

TIP

On-the-Fly Smarts The system adds files to the smart folder as soon as you start setting search criteria. Don't worry about ending up with the wrong files in your smart folder, though; as you change the criteria, the folder's contents are updated to reflect the new criteria. ■

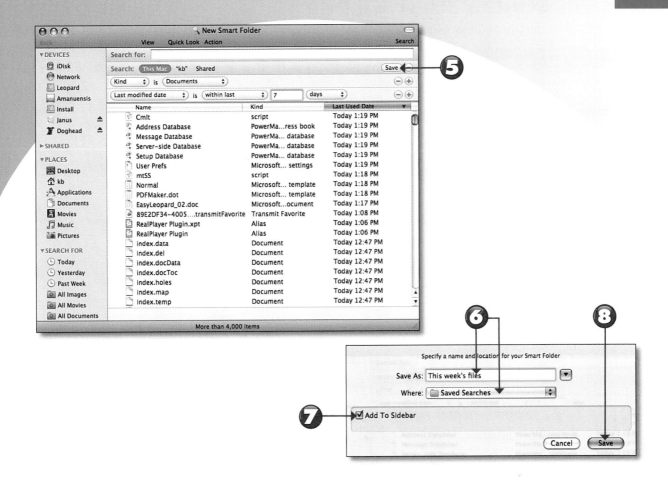

5 Click **Save**.

6 Enter a name and select a location for the folder.

7 Check **Add To Sidebar** if you want the folder to appear in the sidebar when you're using single-window mode.

8 Click **Save**.

End

TIP
Narrowing It Down In addition to a file's attributes, you can filter files for a smart folder based on text search terms. For example, to include files that contain the word Apple in the folder, enter that text in the search field at the top of the folder's window. ■

TIP
For Geeks Only (Not!) To get really specific about the kinds of files in your smart folder, select Other from any search attribute pop-up menu. In the dialog box, choose attributes. To add the selected attribute to the pop-up menu, check Add to Favorites. ■

CREATING A BURN FOLDER

Burn folders provide a way to collect files for burning later without having to actually move them. Dragging files into a burn folder earmarks them for burning later. When you're ready to burn, click and go! Meanwhile, the files stay in their original folders so you don't have to put them away after burning the disc.

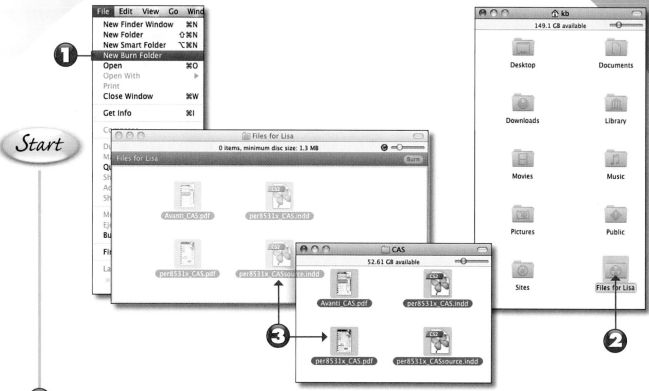

1 Choose **File, New Burn Folder**.

2 Type a new name for the folder; this name is also given to the disc you burn from this folder.

3 Drag files and folders into the burn folder's window to add them to the disc.

Continued

NOTE

But What's It For? Burn folders are useful for keeping track of files you regularly transfer to another person or location. Because the file you see in the burnable folder is really just a marker for the real file, you can edit the file in its original location and the changed version is burned to the disc. The burn folder sticks around after you burn the disc, so you can use it to create regular backups of the same set of files. ■

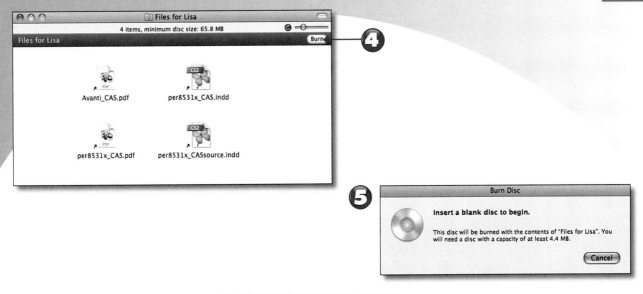

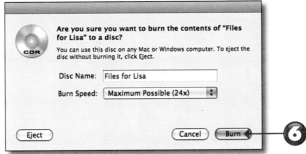

4 Click **Burn**.

5 Insert a blank CD.

6 Click **Burn**.

End

TIP

Better Backups You can use a smart folder in combination with a burnable folder to make weekly backups. First, create a smart folder with the parameters Last Modified and This Week. Then create a burnable folder and drag the smart folder into it. Every Friday afternoon, open the burnable folder, click Burn, and insert a CD—and presto! Your week's work is backed up to a disc that you can store offsite for true peace of mind. ■

49

ACCESSING YOUR FAVORITE FILES AND PLACES

Mac OS X offers a way to store and access your favorites. They're visible in a column called the Places sidebar at the left side of every window when you're using single-window mode. The top section of the Places list contains disks attached to your Mac, and the lower section contains anything you want.

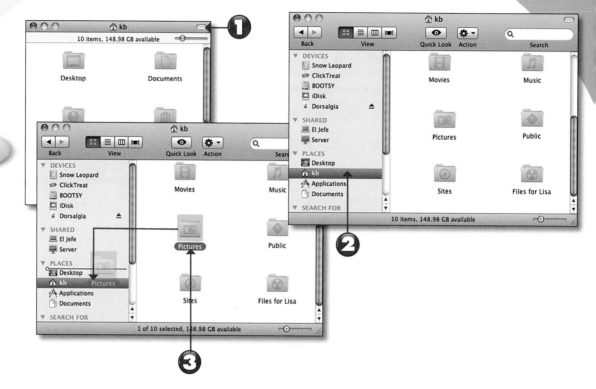

 Start

1 If you don't see the Places sidebar, click the transparent button at the upper-right corner of the window to enter single-window mode.

2 Click a disk or folder to view its contents in the window.

3 Drag files or folders into or out of the lower section of the Places sidebar to customize it.

End

NOTE

Quick Copy, Quick Move You can move or copy files to disks or folders in the Places sidebar by dragging them from the main section of the window over a disk or folder icon in the sidebar. ■

TIP

Customizing the Custom List To change the order of items in the bottom half of the Places sidebar, just drag and drop them into the order you prefer. Drag folders out of the lower section of the Places sidebar to remove them from the list. ■

DELETING A FILE

Mac OS X stores files you don't want any more in a trash can. You can rummage through the Trash to retrieve files you didn't mean to discard, just as you can in the real world. But—again, just like the real world—the Trash doesn't empty itself; you have to remember to empty it to truly delete the discarded files.

Start

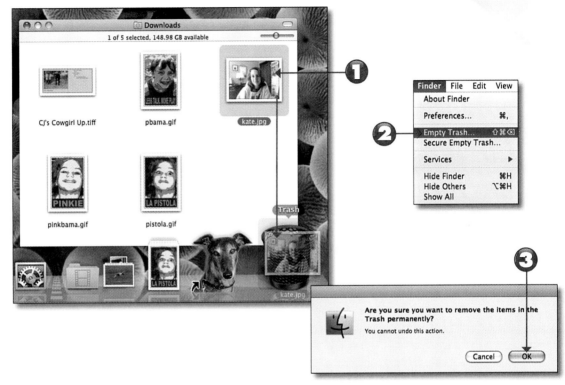

1 Drag the file to the **Trash** icon on the Dock and drop it when the Trash icon is highlighted.

2 To delete all the objects in the Trash, choose **Finder**, **Empty Trash**.

3 Click **OK** in the confirmation dialog box or **Cancel** to keep the items in the Trash.

End

NOTE

Here a File, There a File Applications leave files all over the place, so if you want to uninstall a program, you may need to do more than just drag the program's icon to the Trash. Consider using a clean-up utility such as AppCleaner—(www.freemacsoft.net/AppCleaner/). ■

TIP

Deleting Files Securely To make sure your files are removed from your hard drive, choose File, Secure Empty Trash. Secure Empty Trash writes gibberish data over the files so they can never be found, even by "computer detectives." ■

SETTING UP A BACKUP DRIVE

If you were to learn only one thing from this book, that thing should be how to back up your files. Fortunately, Mac OS X's new Time Machine utility makes it utterly simple to back up and retrieve files on your Mac. It keeps copies of all the versions of each file, so you can see exactly how your Mac looked in the past and retrieve files from that date.

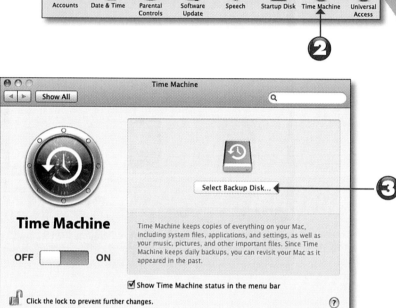

Start

1 Choose **Apple menu**, **System Preferences**.

2 Click the **Time Machine** button to see your backup settings.

3 Click **Select Backup Disk** to choose a hard drive where Time Machine can store backed-up files.

Continued

TIP
Better Safe Than Sorry If at all possible, use a drive for Time Machine that doesn't have any files stored on it. For one thing, you want the maximum amount of room available for backup files. For another, it's a remote possibility that Time Machine might overwrite your files. ■

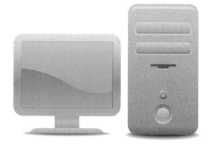

4 Choose a disk in the list.

5 Click **Use for Backup**.

6 Click **Options** to exclude disks from the backup.

7 Click the plus and minus buttons to add or delete disks; then click **Done**.

End

TIP

Skipping Along Check Skip system files in the Time Machine preferences if you haven't customized your Mac OS X system with a lot of add-ons. That will save a lot of space on your backup drive. ■

TIP

I Said No Another way to save space on your backup drive is to add disks or folders to the Do not back up list in the Time Machine preferences. These items will be ignored when Time Machine backs up the rest of your files. ■

RESTORING BACKED-UP FILES

You know right where the file was. You're sure of it. You even know when and why you deleted it—but now you need it back. Fortunately for you, Leopard brings a Time Machine to your Mac. All you have to do is take a look at past versions of your hard drive and choose the files you want to resurrect.

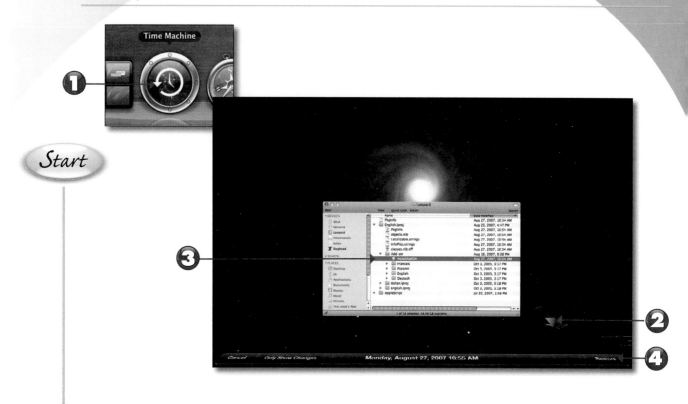

Start

① Open the folder where the file you want was previously located, then click **Time Machine**.

② Click back and forth through the previous versions of that folder to find a backup in which the file still exists.

③ Click to select the file you want.

④ Click **Restore** to return the file to your present-day Mac.

End

TIP

Take Me There If you know exactly what date you're looking for in Time Machine, click the bars on the right side of the screen to choose a specific backup date. You'll zoom right to the state of your Mac on that date. ∎

USING YOUR IDISK

Apple's special online services for Mac users, referred to collectively as MobileMe, include the use of an **iDisk**—an online storage area. You can mount your iDisk right on your desktop, where it appears along with your hard drive and any removable disks you insert (thumb drives, DVDs, or CDs).

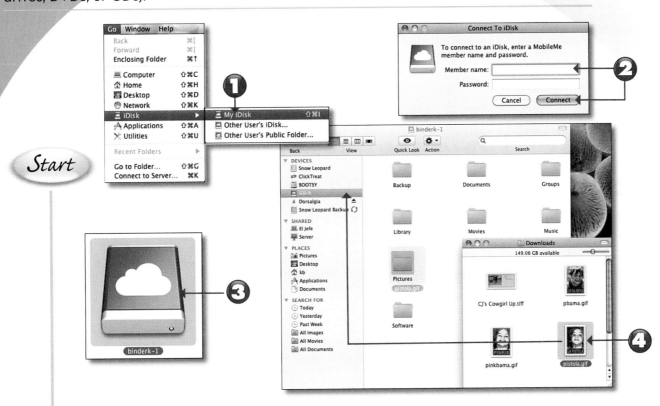

Start

1. In the Finder, either choose **Go**, **iDisk**, **My iDisk**, or press ⌘-**Shift-I**.

2. If you haven't entered your username and password in System Preferences, type that information into the dialog box that appears and click **Connect**.

3. Double-click the **iDisk** icon to view its contents.

4. Drag files into the **iDisk** folders to copy them to the iDisk.

End

TIP

Keeping Your iDisk at Home For easy access to your iDisk, go to the MobileMe pane in System Preferences. Click iDisk and click the Create a local copy of your iDisk check box. The iDisk copy appears on your desktop all the time; changes you make to it are automatically made to the real iDisk. ∎

INSTALLING AND USING APPLICATIONS

It's the programs that make using your Mac worthwhile, whether they're the applications that come with Mac OS X (such as Preview, TextEdit, and Safari) or the ones you buy and install yourself (such as Microsoft Word, Adobe Photoshop, or your favorite games). Apple even sells two collections of programs designed just for home and business users, called iLife (with iMovie, GarageBand, and the like) and iWork (featuring Pages, for page layout, Numbers for spreadsheets, and so on).

Some programs come with a special installer program that puts all their pieces in the right places. Other programs are so simple that you can just drag and drop them into your Applications or Utilities folder. You can store programs in other folders, too, but it's easier to find everything if you stick to the designated folders.

Some applications are, of course, commercially produced, with thick manuals and lots of shrinkwrap. But you may find your favorites turn out to be freeware or shareware—programs you download, try out, and then pay for if you keep using them. Be sure to pay your shareware fees, and check out www.versiontracker.com for the most comprehensive listing of downloadable software anywhere on the web.

MAC OS X'S PROGRAMS

Create text documents
with TextEdit, 61

Apply text
formatting with the
Font Panel, 63

Locate and start
up programs, 59

Switch programs
with the Dock, 71

INSTALLING PROGRAMS

Some Mac programs are small enough that you can drag them off their disks right into the Applications folder, but others require an installer program to make sure all their pieces get to the right places. When you run Installer, you have to enter an admin password to authorize the installation.

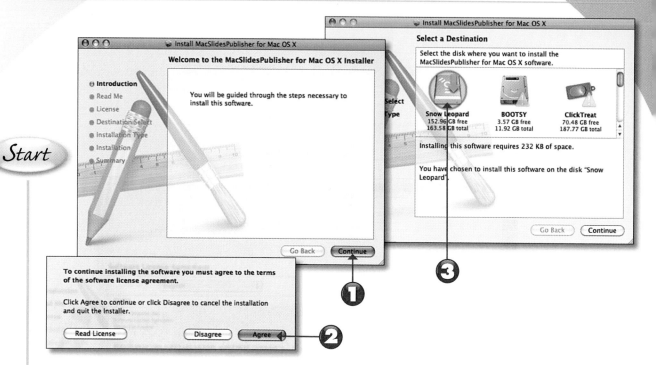

Start

1 After you read each screen of the installer, click the **Continue** button at the bottom of the window to move to the next screen.

2 Read the program information and the license agreement; then click **Agree** to agree to the license terms (or **Disagree** if you don't want to install the program after all).

3 If you have more than one hard drive, choose the drive where you want to install the software.

Continued

 NOTE

Applications in the Applications Folder You can install programs anywhere you want, but it's best to put them in the Applications folder on your startup drive. That way all users of your Mac can run the programs. ■

NOTE

Just Checking Many installers start out by asking your permission to run a program to see whether the program can be installed on your Mac. Just click OK. ■

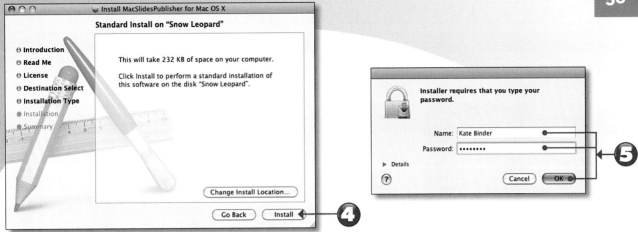

4 Click **Install** to begin the installation process.

5 Enter an admin username and password to authorize the installation and click **OK**.

6 When the installation is complete, click **Close** to quit Installer.

7 The application's icon now appears in the Applications folder (or whatever folder you chose).

End

NOTE

Installation Options Many installer scripts ask you to choose whether to install optional software such as sample files, fonts, or bonus features. The Easy Install or Full Install option usually installs everything that's available. ■

NOTE

Easy Uninstalling Some installer programs have an Uninstall option in case you decide you no longer want the software installed on your Mac. Using an installer to uninstall programs ensures that all the extra pieces scattered through your system are uninstalled. ■

FINDING AND STARTING UP PROGRAMS

Mac OS X is a very structured operating system, with a place for everything and everything in its place. Applications are no exception to this rule; all your programs live in the Applications folder where you and other users of your Mac can find them easily.

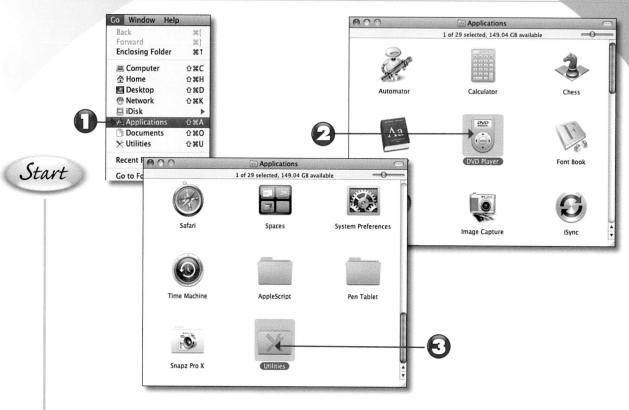

1 In the Finder, either press ⌘-**Shift-A** or choose **Go**, **Applications** to open the Applications folder.

2 Locate the program you want to use and double-click its icon to start it up.

3 If you can't find a program, look in the Utilities folder within the Applications folder.

TIP

Control Your Programs If the wrong program starts up when you double-click a document in the Finder, you need to specify a different program to open that type of document. Press ⌘-**I** to see the document's information and select an application in the Open with section of the Info window. Click **Change All** if you want the new program to open all documents of this type. ∎

SAVING FILES

Every program is different, of course, but some operations work almost the same no matter which program you're using. One of those is saving a file. Each program saves files in different formats, depending on which type of data that program works with, but the general process is the same no matter what. Here's how it goes.

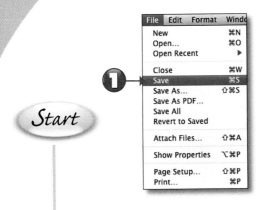

Start

1 In the application in which you're working, either choose **File**, **Save** or press ⌘-**S**.

2 Give the file a name and choose a location in the pick list. If you don't see the pick list, click the blue arrow button the right of the **Save As** field.

3 Choose file options such as format and compression (the available options vary depending on the program).

4 Click **Save**.

End

TIP

Pay Attention! Save dialog boxes usually open to the last place you saved a file in that program, which is unlikely to be the same place you want now. To save to the desktop, press ⌘-D—you'll have to put the file away later, but you'll be able to find it for the moment. ■

NOTE

Save Early, Save Often Don't wait until you're done working on a file to save it—start early and keep using the Save command as you continue to work. That way the file will be stored on your hard drive in case of a drive crash or power outage. ■

WRITING WITH TEXTEDIT

Mac OS X's TextEdit program can do a lot more than either of its ancestors. It's really a very compact, fast word processor with a lot of formatting options and tools as well as the capability to read and write Microsoft Word documents.

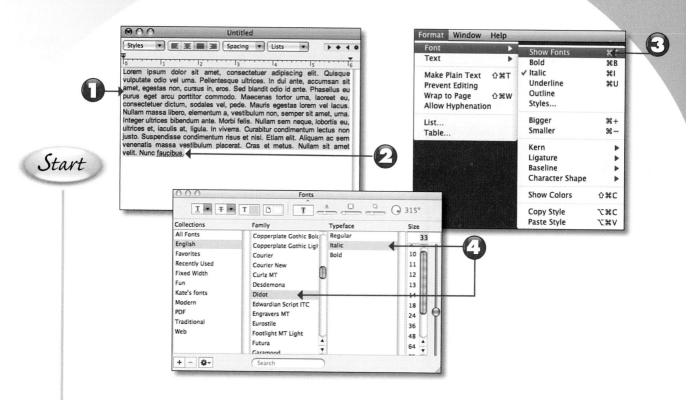

Start

1. Start TextEdit (located in the Applications folder) and begin typing in the new document window.

2. To copy text to another location, click and drag to select the text and press ⌘-**C**; place the cursor where you want the text to appear and press ⌘-**V** to paste it.

3. To change the font, select the text and choose **Format**, **Font**, **Show Fonts**.

4. Choose a new typeface and size in the Fonts panel. The change is applied immediately.

Continued

TIP

Learning How to Spell TextEdit gives questionable words a red underline; Control-click each and choose an option from the contextual menu. The Learn Spelling command adds the word to a system-wide dictionary. ■

NOTE

What's Not in There TextEdit is capable, especially with new features such as automatic bulleted lists, but it's not a full-featured word processor. If you need to use outlining or HTML conversion, you should use a program such as Microsoft Word. ■

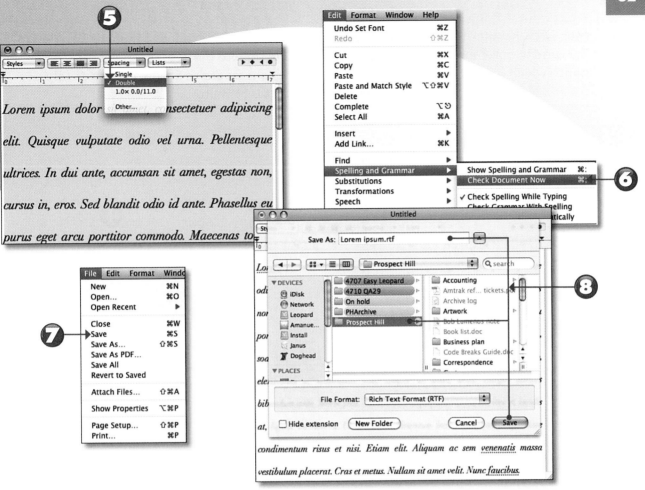

5 To change the text alignment or spacing, click and drag to select the text and choose an option from the controls at the top of the document window.

6 To run a spell check, choose **Edit, Spelling and Grammar, Check Document Now**.

7 Choose **File, Save** to save the file.

8 Give the file a name, choose a location for it, and click **Save**.

End

NOTE

Getting What You Pay For TextEdit's capability to open and save files in Microsoft Word format could keep you from having to invest in Word. Some complex features such as tables and hyperlinks can be lost when you edit a Word file in TextEdit, though. ■

NOTE

Word Compatibility When you're saving your document in step 8, you can choose RTF (Rich Text Format) or Word format. Either way, your document can be opened in Microsoft Word and retains all its formatting. ■

USING THE FONT PANEL

Mac OS X handles fonts very well. Apple's engineers have put a lot of thought into designing ways to make excellent typography more accessible to the average Mac user. The Fonts panel, which is the same in all the built-in applications, contains a wide variety of settings, from basic to advanced, for modifying the way text is formatted.

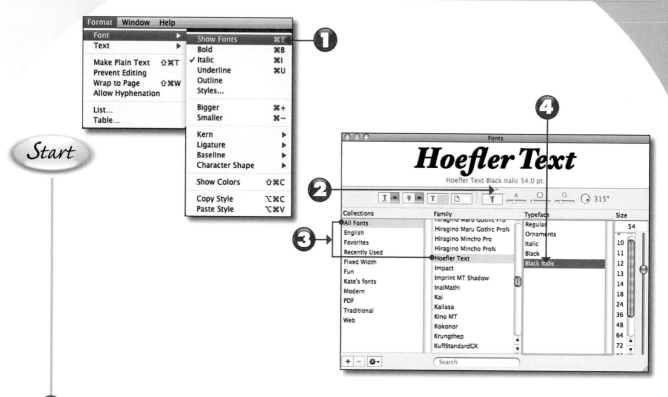

1 In TextEdit, choose **Format**, **Font**, **Show Fonts** to display the Fonts panel.

2 Click the dot below the window's title bar and drag downward to reveal the preview area.

3 Click **All Fonts** in the Collections column and choose a font family from the Family column.

4 Choose a style from the Typeface column.

Continued

TIP

Favorite Type Styles If you create a combination of type settings you plan to use again, click the Action menu at the bottom of the Fonts panel and choose Add to Favorites. Then you can apply this style to other text selections by choosing Font, Styles from the menu bar. ■

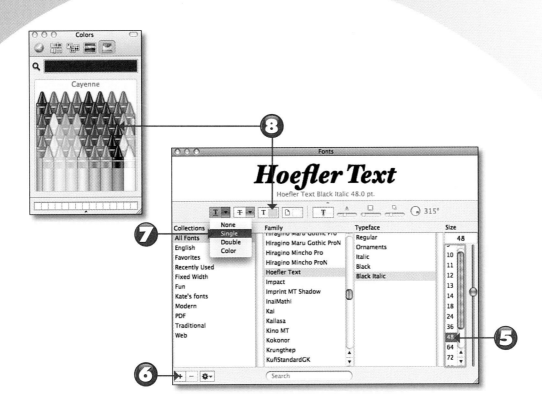

5 Choose a size from the Size column, or enter a value above the column.

6 Click the **Add** button to create a new font collection.

7 Click the **Strikethrough** or **Underline** button and choose an option to add strikethrough or underline style to the selected text.

8 Click the **Text Color** and **Paper Color** buttons to open the Colors panel; then choose a color for the text or the background.

End

NOTE

Beyond the Font Basics If you're interested in working more specifically with type, check out the Font Book program (located in the Utilities folder within Applications). This utility helps you install and manage fonts. ■

NOTE

Collectible Fonts Collections of your corporate fonts or the fonts for a particular project enable you to access those fonts without digging through a long list of fonts. To add a font to a collection, just drag its name from the Family column on top of the collection name. ■

WATCHING DVDS

Who needs a TV to watch DVDs? Not you! If you're looking for some entertainment while you work in the office, or if you just don't feel like getting up and moving to the living room, you can play DVDs right on your Mac. Mac OS X includes a full-featured DVD Player program that can do at least as much as your living room DVD player.

Start

1 Insert a DVD disc; DVD Player automatically starts up.

2 Click the navigation buttons on the remote control to make choices in the DVD's menus.

3 Click **Pause** on the remote control to stop playing the DVD.

4 Click **Eject** on the remote control to eject the disk.

Continued

TIP
Size Matters Use the Video menu to control the size of the virtual TV screen. Select Half Size, Normal Size, Maximum Size, or Enter Full Screen (to get rid of the window and hide the desktop entirely). ■

TIP
Zoom, Zoom, Zoom Choose Window, Video Zoom to zoom in on an area of the screen as the video plays or while it's paused. Click Auto Zoom to resize the window to hold the video image at the current zoom level. ■

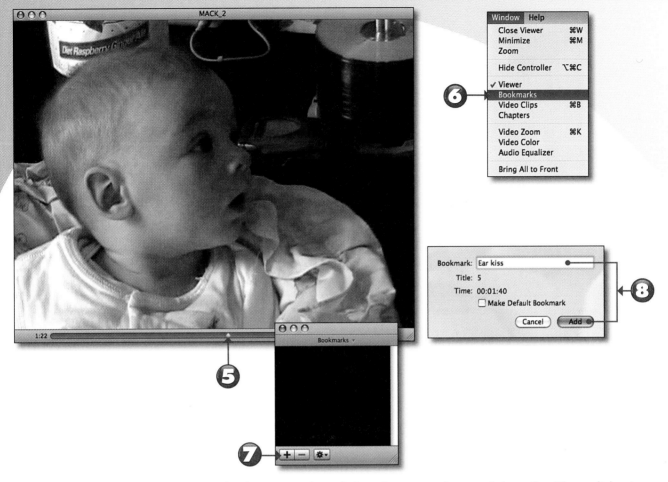

Place the cursor over the bottom edge of the player window and drag the **Time** slider to skip to any part of the video.

To add a bookmark so you can skip right to a particular moment in the video any time you play it, choose **Window, Bookmarks**.

Click the **Add Bookmark** button.

Enter a name for the bookmark and click **Add**.

End

TIP

Clip Me, Baby In addition to bookmarks, you can save video clips so that you can play just the highlights from any DVD. While the video is playing, choose Window, Video Clips. Click the Add Video Clip button and use the controls in the New Video Clip window to set the start and end points of your clip. ■

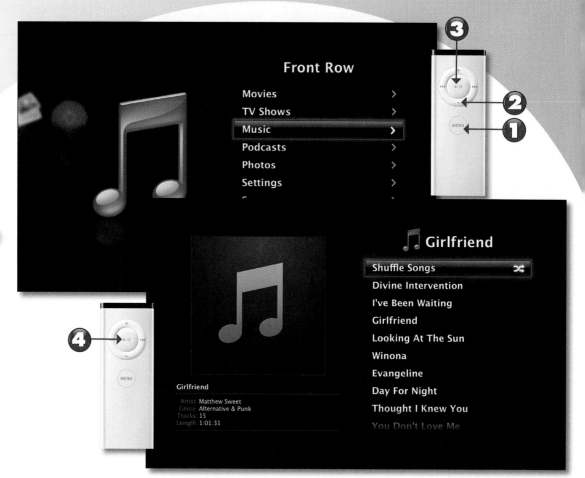

1 Press the Apple Remote's **Menu** button to bring up Front Row.

2 Use the up and down buttons to scroll through the media types: Movies, TV Shows, Music, Podcasts, and Photos.

3 Click the **Play** button on the remote to choose the media type you want to play.

4 On each menu screen, use the arrows to scroll through the options, and then press the **Play** button to select the option you want.

Continued

NOTE

I've Seen This Before If Front Row looks familiar, there may be a very good reason for that: It's based on the software that runs Apple TVs. These handy boxes hook up to your TV and stereo so that you can pipe all your audio and video right to the big screen. ■

TIP

We Want the Airwaves Add your favorite Internet radio stations to Front Row easily. Locate a station in iTunes and drag it into your Library. Create a smart playlist of files whose kind is "'MPEG audio stream." Now just pull up that playlist in Front Row. ■

5 When a song or video is playing, press the **Play** button on the remote to pause.

6 Press the **Menu** button on the remote to back up one screen.

7 On the main Front Row screen, press the **Menu** button on the remote to exit Front Row.

End

TIP
Lost in a Remote Location If you've lost or broken your Apple Remote, you can also access Front Row by pressing ⌘+Esc or F1 (depending on the computer). ■

USING THE APPLE REMOTE

As you saw in the previous task, "Playing Music and Video with Front Row," the Apple Remote is how you make Front Row work for you. But you can do much more with the Apple Remote. It comes with iPods, Apple TV, iMacs, the Mac Mini, and MacBooks, so if you've bought any of those items since October 2005, you should be good to go.

Start

1 Press the up and down arrows to control your Mac's volume.

2 Press the **Play** button and hold it down until you see a snoring remote on your screen to put your Mac to sleep.

3 Press any button on the remote to wake up your Mac when it's sleeping.

4 In iPhoto, press **Play** to begin a slide show of the images in the currently selected album.

Continued

TIP

When a Pair Beats Three of a Kind If you have more than one device that responds to an Apple Remote, or more than one remote, you can pair a particular remote with a particular device. Point the remote at your Mac or other device, then hold down both the Menu and Next buttons for five seconds. If you're working with a Mac, you'll see a screen showing a remote and linked chain, indicating that the remote is now linked only to this Mac. The same technique works with Apple's Universal Dock for iPods and with the iPod Hi-Fi. ■

In iTunes, press **Play** to begin playing the currently selected song or video.

In iTunes, press the **Next** and **Previous** buttons to move among songs or videos.

In Keynote, press the **Next** and **Previous** buttons to move among slides in a presentation.

End

NOTE

So Remote It Be Naturally, you can also use your Apple Remote to control your iPod, but you'll need either a Universal Dock (not the dock that came with your iPod) or an iPod Hi-Fi—Apple's combination of a Universal Dock and powered speakers. ■

TIP

For the Older Crowd If you want to use an Apple remote with older Macs that don't have built-in infrared receivers, you can buy a third-party IR receiver such as the Manta TR1 USB Infrared Transceiver (www.twistedmelon.com). ■

SWITCHING PROGRAMS WITH THE DOCK

The Dock acts as central storage for running programs and frequently used programs, but it has other functions, too. One of those is as an application switcher—a method of bringing different programs to the foreground so you can use them in turn. The Dock's location at the bottom or side of the screen makes it the most convenient way to switch applications.

Start

1 Move your cursor to the bottom of the screen and click a program icon on the Dock.

2 To hide windows belonging to the current program when you switch to the new program, press **Option** as you click.

3 To quit a program you're not using, click and hold its **Dock** icon (or **Control-click**) and choose **Quit** from the contextual menu.

End

TIP
Don't Touch That Mouse! If you prefer to use the keyboard to switch programs, press ⌘-Tab to see a list of the currently running programs in the center of the screen. Press ⌘-Tab as many times as needed to cycle through the list to the program you want. ■

HIDING PROGRAMS

Mac OS X enables you to run many programs at the same time because it hands over memory to each program as it's needed. But if you do like to run multiple programs, your screen can get pretty cluttered. Hiding program windows and palettes is a lifesaver for people who never quit programs until they shut down their Macs.

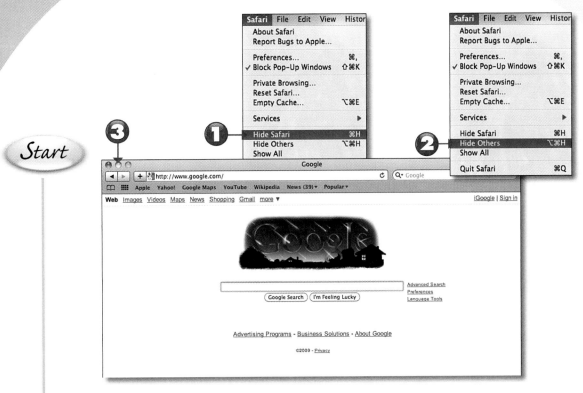

1. In the Application menu, choose **Hide** (or press ⌘-**H**) to hide the program you're currently using.

2. In the Application menu, choose **Hide Others** (or press ⌘-**Option-H**) to hide all other programs that are currently running.

3. To get one window out of the way instead of hiding the program, double-click its title bar or click the yellow **Minimize** button to send it to the Dock.

End

TIP

Another Way to Hide Another way to hide programs is to Option-click the desktop or a window from another program to simultaneously switch to the Finder or the other program, respectively, and hide the previous program. ■

NOTE

A Window Exposé Yet another way to maneuver among running programs and open windows is to use Exposé. Turn to "Managing Multiple Windows" in Chapter 1, "Getting Started." ■

RUNNING WINDOWS ON YOUR MAC

If you're reading this book, you probably love your Mac a lot. But sometimes you might need to use Windows—maybe your employer requires it, or perhaps you have a piece of hardware that doesn't have any Mac drivers. With Apple's current generation of Macs, you can have the best of both worlds by running both Mac OS X and Windows on your Mac using a little program called Boot Camp.

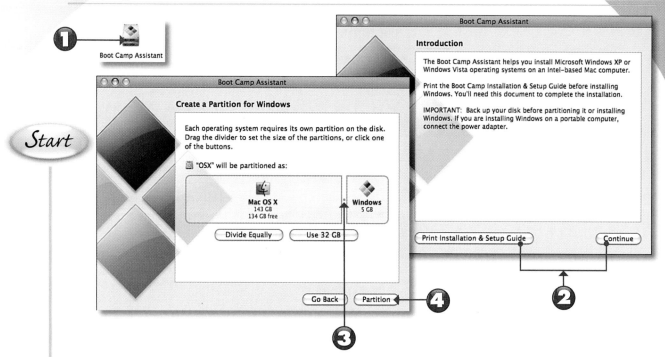

Start

1 Start up Boot Camp Assistant (located in the Utilities folder within your Applications folder).

2 Click **Print Installation & Setup Guide** to print out a copy of the important information you'll need to run Boot Camp; then click **Continue**.

3 Drag the divider between the partitions to determine the size of your Windows partition.

4 Click **Partition**.

Continued

TIP
Intel Inside Only Apple's current generation of Intel Macs can run Windows, because they have the same kind of processor that PCs have. To see whether your Mac is one of these, choose Apple menu, About This Mac. ■

TIP
Power Up If your Mac is a MacBook or MacBook Pro, be sure to connect the power adapter before you begin setting up your Windows installation. If the battery power runs out while the installation is taking place, you could lose data. ■

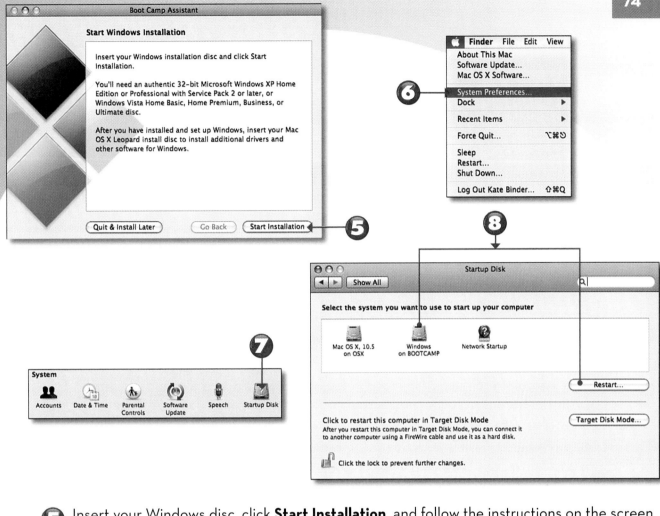

5 Insert your Windows disc, click **Start Installation,** and follow the instructions on the screen to install your Windows system.

6 To restart your Mac using your new Windows system, choose **Apple menu, System Preferences.**

7 Click the **Startup Disk** button to display startup disk preferences.

8 Click to choose your Windows partition, and then click **Restart.**

End

NOTE

Standard Precautions Before starting your Boot Camp installation, be sure you have a Windows XP or Vista system disc ready, and make sure you note the size of your Boot Camp partition so you will recognize it when you're installing Windows. ■

TIP

The Choice Is Yours If your computer is turned off, you can choose to start it up in either Windows or Mac OS X by holding down the Option key as you press the power button. Don't release the Option key until you see the Open Firmware screen. ■

Chapter 4

SETTING SYSTEM PREFERENCES

Preferences make the world go round—or, at least, they make your Mac more *your* Mac. You can control so many aspects of your everyday computing experience that it's worth a trip to the System Preferences window every once in a while just to remind yourself what's there. Be sure to explore all the tabs of each preference pane, too, to make sure you know what all your options are.

The System Preferences command in the Apple menu opens a command center for preferences. It contains buttons for each preference pane, organized into categories.

In this chapter you'll learn how to set preferences for everything from how your mouse or trackpad works to what size objects are displayed on your monitor. A couple of tasks—"Setting Trackpad Preferences" and "Monitoring Battery Use"—deal with preferences for laptop users only; if your Mac isn't an iBook or a MacBook, you won't even see these settings, so don't worry about them.

THE SYSTEM PREFERENCES WINDOW

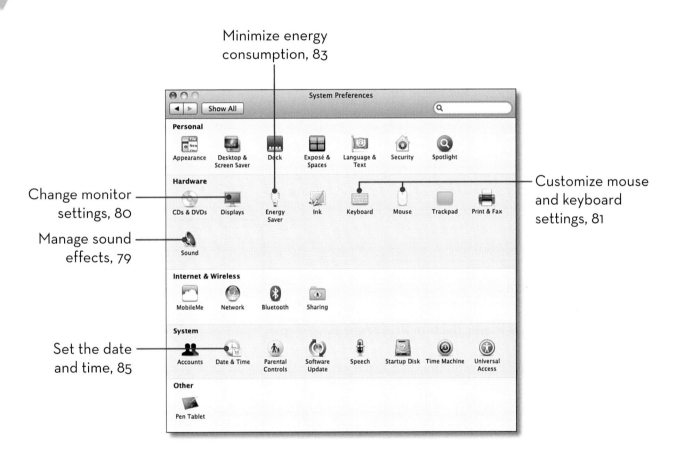

Minimize energy consumption, 83

Customize mouse and keyboard settings, 81

Change monitor settings, 80

Manage sound effects, 79

Set the date and time, 85

SETTING SYSTEM PREFERENCES

In a flashback to the days of the Mac's System 6, Mac OS X stores all its preferences in a central window called System Preferences. It's accessible via the Apple menu, so you can reach it from any program. Preference panes for non-Apple programs and utilities can also be found in System Preferences, in the Other section at the bottom of the window.

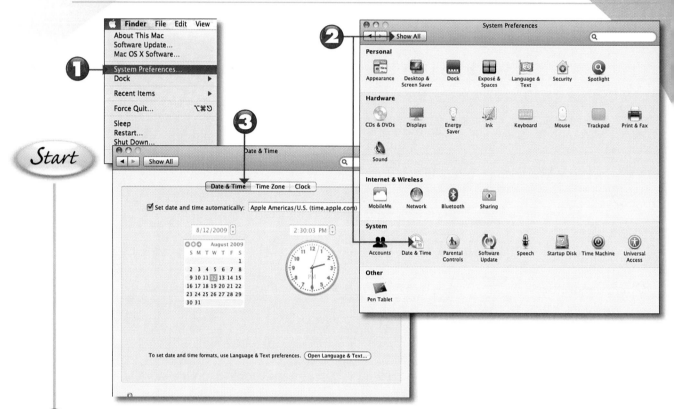

1 Choose **Apple menu**, **System Preferences** to display the System Preferences window.

2 Click **Show All** to see all the buttons; then click the button for the preferences you want to change.

3 Click buttons across the top of the preference pane to access various groups of settings.

TIP

Haven't I Been Here Before? To return to a preference pane you've just visited, click the left arrow at the top of the System Preferences window. The left and right arrows take you forward and back through the preference screens. ■

TIP

Asking for Directions Not sure which preferences pane to head for? Type a word or two into the search field in the upper-right corner of the System Preferences window, and you'll get a menu that takes you to the right place. ■

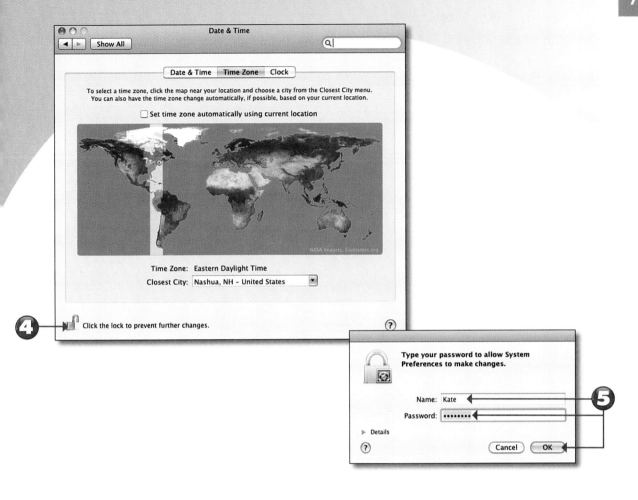

4 Lock or unlock a preferences pane by clicking the padlock button.

5 If the preferences are locked (indicated by a closed padlock button in the lower-left corner of the window), enter an admin name and password when prompted and click **OK**. The preferences will stay unlocked until you click the padlock again to lock them.

End

TIP

Down by the Dock If you make many trips to the System Preferences, the Dock can be a quicker way to get there than the Apple menu. Open your Applications folder, find System Preferences, and drag it to the left side of the Dock. ■

TIP

Now You Know Your ABCs If the System Preference categories don't make sense to you, choose View, Organize Alphabetically. This command reorders the buttons in good old alphabetical order, instead of dividing them by category. ■

CHANGING YOUR ALERT SOUND

The alert sound is that annoying beep you hear when you do something your Mac doesn't like or when you tell it to do something it can't do. The nice part about this is that you can change the sound that's played, as well as adjust its volume independently of the system's overall volume level.

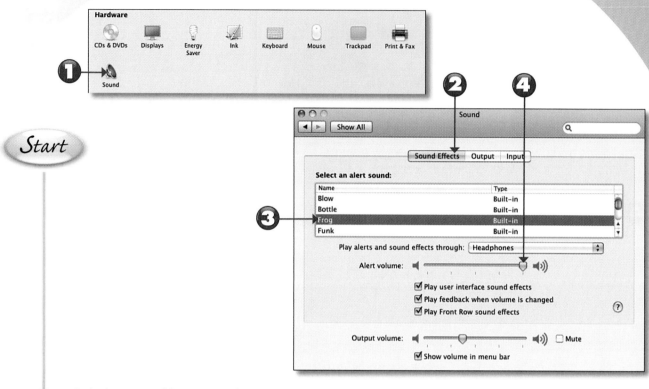

Start

Click the **Sound** button in the System Preferences window to display the sound preferences.

Click the **Sound Effects** button to see your choices.

Click a sound in the pick list to hear it.

Click and drag the **Alert volume** slider to set the volume level for alert sounds.

End

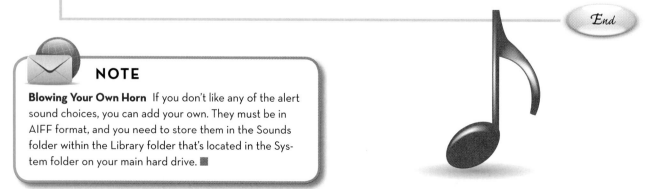

NOTE

Blowing Your Own Horn If you don't like any of the alert sound choices, you can add your own. They must be in AIFF format, and you need to store them in the Sounds folder within the Library folder that's located in the System folder on your main hard drive. ■

CHANGING DISPLAY SETTINGS

Your monitor's display resolution is the number of pixels it displays horizontally and vertically. You can change the resolution of most monitors. With a lower resolution, everything on the screen is bigger and you can't see as many windows at one time, and with a higher resolution everything is smaller, but you can fit more.

Start

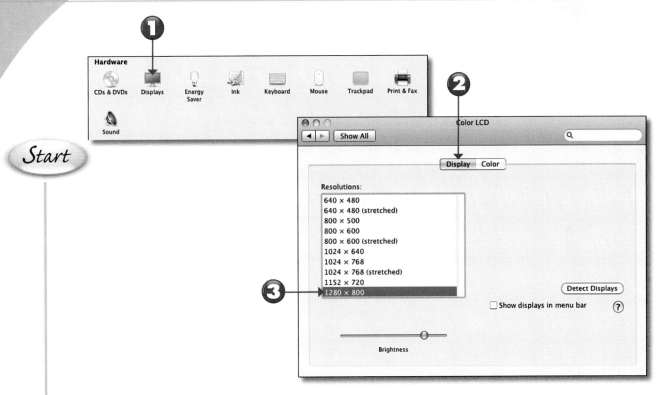

1 Click the **Displays** button in the System Preferences window to display monitor preferences.

2 Click the **Display** button to see your choices.

3 Click a setting in the **Resolutions** pick list to determine the scale of the images on your monitor. If the setting you choose doesn't work, click another.

End

TIP

Don't Keep Your Resolutions If you expect to change your settings often, click Show displays in menu bar in the Displays preference pane to add a menu that you can use to switch resolutions. ■

NOTE

The More, the Merrier Expert users generally choose the highest resolution that still allows them to read text onscreen. It makes onscreen objects seem small at first, but you get used to that quickly. You can fit more windows onscreen at higher resolutions. ■

CHANGING THE MOUSE SPEED

When you're in a hurry, there are few things more annoying than a slow mouse, or one that's so fast you can't keep track of it. Whether your mouse moves too slowly or too quickly for your taste, you can adjust its setting until it's just where you like it. You can also change the speed at which you must click for two clicks to register as an official double-click.

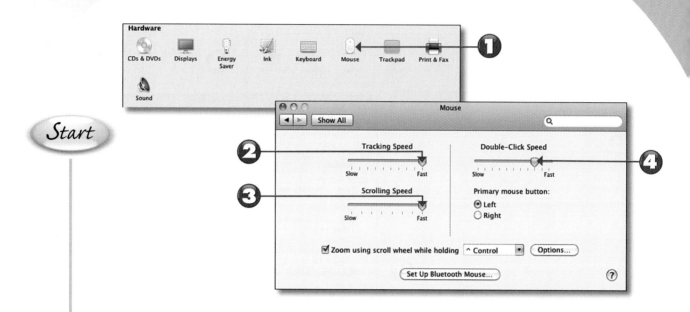

Start

① Click the **Mouse** button in the System Preferences window to display mouse preferences.

② Drag the **Tracking Speed** slider to change how quickly the mouse moves across the screen.

③ Drag the **Scrolling Speed** slider to change how fast windows scroll when you use a mouse with a scroll wheel.

④ Drag the **Double-Click Speed** slider to change the speed at which you must click in order for your Mac to recognize two clicks as a double-click.

End

NOTE

Scrolling, Scrolling, Scrolling If you haven't tried a mouse with a scroll wheel yet, you should make a point of checking one out. This handy little control makes scrolling through long documents or long web pages a breeze—and you can also use it to zoom in and out in graphics programs. Check the **Zoom using scroll wheel while holding** box at the bottom of the Keyboard & Mouse preferences, and then choose a modifier key that will invoke the zoom function.

CHANGING KEYBOARD SETTINGS

Most aspects of the way a keyboard works are determined by the hardware—in other words, the keyboard itself. However, there are a couple of keyboard settings you can adjust, having to do with how quickly your Mac repeats keys when you hold down a key.

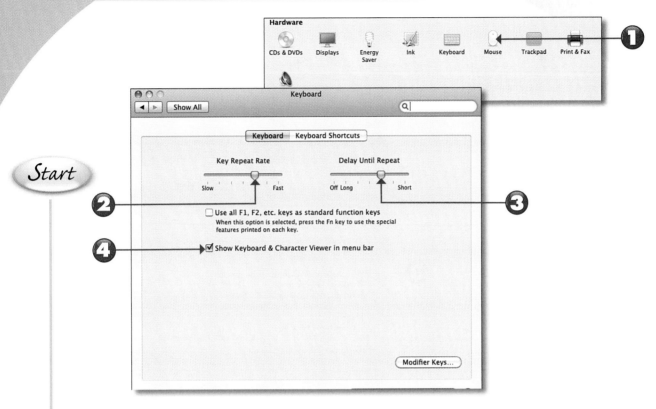

Click the **Keyboard** button in the System Preferences window to display keyboard preferences.

Drag the **Key Repeat Rate** slider to control how quickly keys repeat when you hold them down.

Drag the **Delay Until Repeat** slider to control how long the Mac waits before starting to repeat keys when you hold them down.

Click the **Show Keyboard & Character Viewer** in menu bar box to add a quick access menu for the Character and Keyboard Viewers, which help you type special characters.

End

NOTE

Taking a Shortcut You can use the Keyboard Shortcuts tab of the Keyboard & Mouse preferences to choose custom keyboard shortcuts for several Mac OS X system functions: taking screen shots; navigating the Finder using the keyboard; using the Dock, Exposé, and Dashboard; invoking Spotlight; and more. ■

SETTING ENERGY SAVER OPTIONS

You might not think your quiet little computer, sitting over there in the corner not even moving, could eat up that much electricity—but think again. That's why the Energy Saver settings are important; they enable you to reduce your Mac's power consumption during times when you're not using it. Be sure to take as much advantage of Energy Saver as possible.

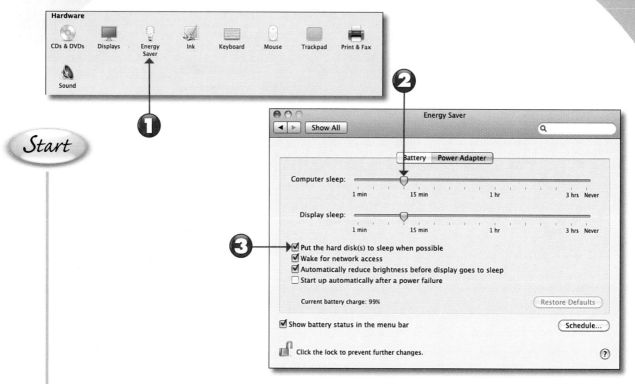

Start

① Click the **Energy Saver** button in the System Preferences window to display energy preferences.

② Drag the top slider to choose when your Mac will sleep and the bottom slider to set a separate time for when your monitor will sleep.

③ Click the check box if you want the hard drive to sleep.

Continued

NOTE

Hurry Hurry If you're always in a hurry when you come back to your computer, don't set the hard drive to sleep. The monitor wakes up from sleep instantly, but it takes a few moments for the hard drive to spin back up to speed when it wakes up. ∎

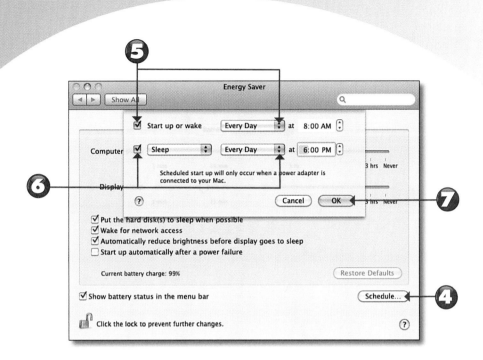

4 Click the **Schedule** button to display scheduled startup and shutdown options.

5 Check the box and choose when to start up the Mac automatically.

6 Check the box and choose when to shut down the Mac automatically.

7 Click **OK**.

End

TIP

Are You Getting Sleepy? Sleep is a state between powered up and powered down. A sleeping computer consumes much less power, but it's not completely turned off. Of course, it wakes up more quickly than it boots up from a powered-down state. ■

NOTE

Quick Start In step 6, you can also set your Mac to sleep at a particular time instead of shutting down. This is a good choice if you keep programs running all the time that you don't want to have to start up again every day. ■

SETTING THE TIME AND DATE

If you opt to set the date and time yourself, you can do it by clicking a calendar or dragging clock hands—no messy typing needed! If you have a constant or frequent online connection, you can choose instead to have your Mac's clock set automatically over the Internet.

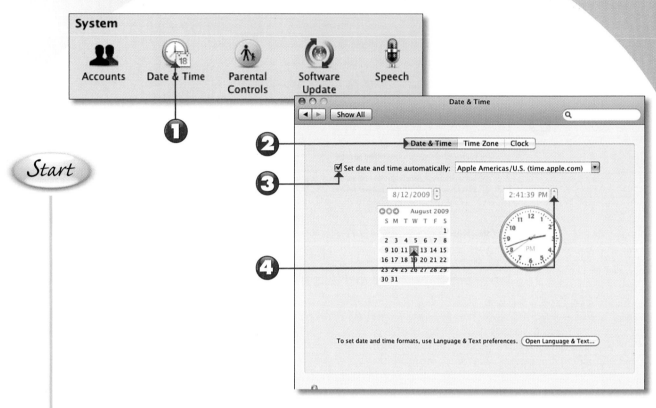

Start

1 Click the **Date & Time** button in the System Preferences window to display time and date preferences.

2 Click the **Date & Time** button to see your choices.

3 If the **Set date & time automatically** box is checked, click to remove the check mark.

4 Click a day on the calendar to set the date, or type in the date; drag the hands on the clock to set the time, or type in the time.

End

NOTE

Do You Have the Correct Time? If you use a timeserver to set your Mac's clock automatically over the Internet, be sure you've chosen the correct time zone in the Time Zone tab of the Date & Time preferences. ■

TIP

A Clockwork Preference The third button in the Date & Time preferences pane opens the Clock tab, where you'll find settings for the menu bar clock. You can even choose an analog clock with hands instead of the regular digital display. ■

ADJUSTING THE SYSTEM VOLUME

A small thing such as the volume of the sounds your Mac plays can have a significant impact on your experience while using the computer. You can always increase the volume when you're working in the next room or when you want to turn up the radio and sing along, or lower it when you don't want to wake the baby.

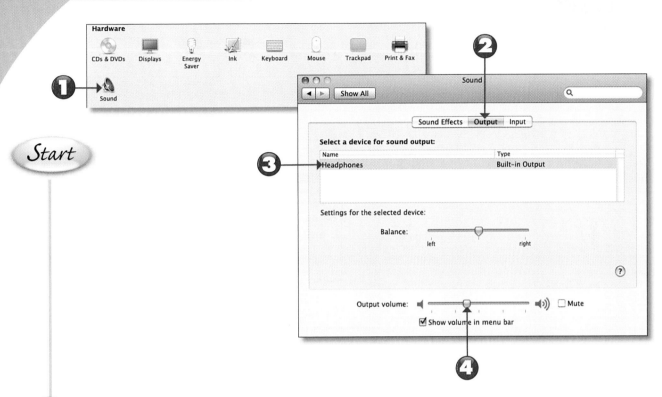

Start

1 Click the **Sound** button in the System Preferences window to display sound preferences.

2 Click the **Output** button to see your choices.

3 If you have more than one output method (internal speaker and external speakers), choose the device you want to use from the pick list.

4 Drag the **Output volume** slider to change the volume for all sounds produced by your Mac.

End

TIP

Muting for Discretion's Sake Click the Mute check box next to the Output volume slider if you want to turn the volume all the way down. ■

TIP

Getting Louder (or Softer) Faster Click the Show volume in menu bar check box to put an extra menu in your menu bar that's simply a volume slider. To use it, click its icon, release the mouse button, and click and drag the slider. Also, many keyboards now have volume controls at the top of the numeric keypad. ■

SETTING TRACKPAD PREFERENCES

Trackpads—those snazzy touch-sensitive pads laptops use instead of trackballs these days—are funny creatures. Because they don't feel the same as a mouse, you might want to use different speed and double-clicking settings than you would for a mouse. You'll need to experiment until you're comfortable with the settings.

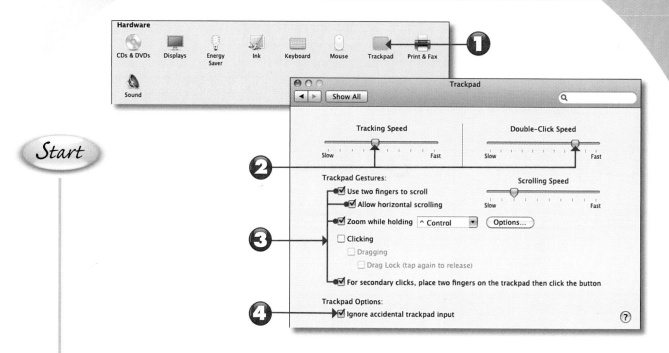

Start

 Click the **Trackpad** button in the System Preferences window to display mouse preferences.

Drag the **Tracking Speed** slider to set how fast the trackpad cursor moves; drag the **Double-Click Speed** slider to set how fast you must double-click.

Modify the settings in the **Trackpad Gestures** area to control your Mac with multi-finger gestures.

In the **Trackpad Options** section, click the check boxes to change your click and drag settings.

End

NOTE

Trackpad Settings Ignore accidental trackpad input reduces the sensitivity of the trackpad so you don't click or drag accidentally, and **Ignore trackpad when mouse is present** turns off the trackpad when you plug in a mouse. ■

NOTE

A Trackpad but No Laptop If you love trackpads but don't use a MacBook, you can still satisfy your craving. Try a standalone trackpad such as the Cirque Easy Cat—the USB version plugs right into your Mac—and your fingertips will be cruising along in no time. ■

MONITORING BATTERY USE

If you're a laptop user, you know how important it is to keep track of the charge in your PowerBook's battery. Running out of power at a crucial moment could be a disaster—you'll definitely want to keep an eye on the Battery menu to make sure the worst never happens to you.

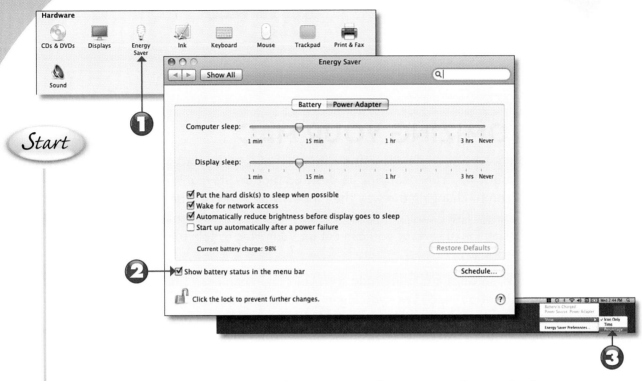

Start

1 Click the **Energy Saver** button in the System Preferences window to display energy preferences.

2 Click the check box to display a battery menu in your menu bar.

3 Click the battery status menu to change the way it displays how much battery charge is left.

End

NOTE

Saving More Power Look at the Energy Saver functions in the System Preferences—you can save a lot of power by setting the right preferences. See the task "Setting Energy Saver Options" earlier in this Part to learn more about Energy Saver settings. ∎

CUSTOMIZING YOUR MAC

It's your Mac—why not have some fun with it? There are myriad ways to make your Mac your own, from changing its desktop picture, its icons, and even your own login icon to changing the way the Finder works and responds to you. You can even change the Finder's language to any of a couple dozen alternatives, including Asian languages, or you can set up your Mac to talk to you—and listen for your responses.

Your custom settings are associated with your login name, so they're automatically put into effect each time you log in. When other users log in, their own settings are activated. That means a single Mac can offer each user a custom experience. Your custom settings can include useful preferences such as network locations and more fun preferences such as your desktop wallpaper.

In this chapter you'll learn how to customize the Finder, the Dock, the desktop, your screen saver, and your security preferences. You'll also learn how to make your own Dashboard widgets—tiny custom programs that you can build from pieces of your favorite websites. If you move your computer around or switch networks a lot, you'll benefit from the "Creating Custom Network Locations" task, which shows how to create custom location settings that change all your network preferences with a single click.

TAKING ADVANTAGE OF CUSTOM SETTINGS

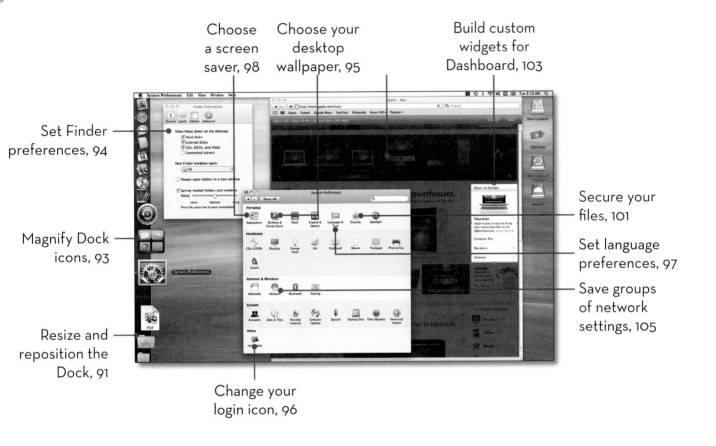

Choose a screen saver, 98

Choose your desktop wallpaper, 95

Build custom widgets for Dashboard, 103

Set Finder preferences, 94

Magnify Dock icons, 93

Resize and reposition the Dock, 91

Change your login icon, 96

Secure your files, 101

Set language preferences, 97

Save groups of network settings, 105

MOVING THE DOCK AROUND

Although the Dock normally lives at the bottom of your screen, it doesn't have to stay there. If you prefer, you can put it on the left or right side of the screen instead. No matter which edge of the screen it's on, the Dock works the same way and you can set its preferences to suit your tastes.

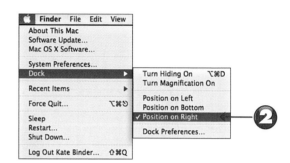

Start

① Choose **Apple menu**, **Dock**, **Position on Left** to move the Dock to the left edge of the screen.

② Choose **Apple menu**, **Dock**, **Position on Right** to move the Dock to the right edge of the screen.

End

TIP

Hide and Go Dock To hide the Dock, choose Apple menu, Dock, Turn Hiding On; now the Dock sinks off the edge of the screen whenever you're not using it. Move your mouse back to that edge, and the Dock pops back out. ■

NOTE

Dock Substitutes The Dock can get pretty crowded. Some users use the Dock strictly as an application switcher, with inactive programs and documents stored in a third-party Dock substitute such as DragThing (www.dragthing.com). ■

CHANGING THE DOCK'S SIZE

The more stuff you stash in the Dock, the more room it takes up on your screen. If it gets too full, you can shrink it to give you more room onscreen—or, if you prefer, you can make it larger so it's easier to see what it contains.

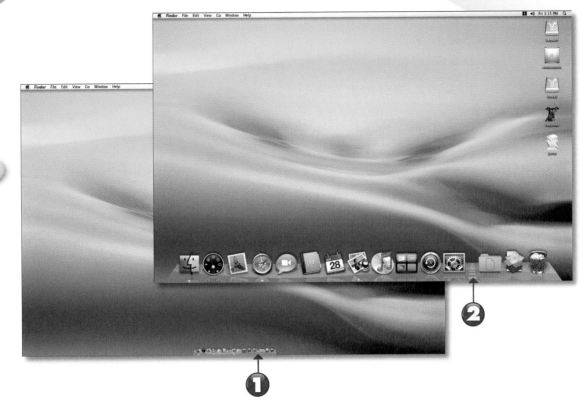

Start

1 Click the line between the two halves of the Dock and drag upward to enlarge the Dock.

2 Drag downward to reduce the Dock's size.

End

TIP

There's Always Another Way You can also use the Dock Size slider in the Dock preferences (choose the Apple menu, Dock, Dock Preferences) if you happen to be going there to change other preferences as well. ■

CUSTOMIZING THE DOCK'S BEHAVIOR

As if moving the Dock around and changing its size weren't enough, there's yet more you can do to make the Dock work just the way you want it to. The Dock preferences enable you to control the way the Dock moves—or, more precisely, the way its icons move and change size and the way windows enter the Dock.

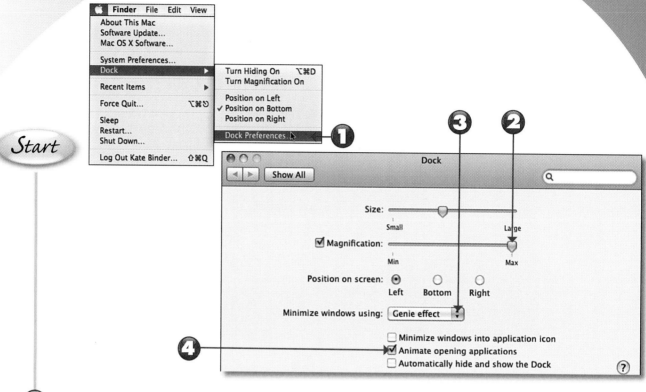

1 Choose **Apple menu**, **Dock**, **Dock Preferences**.

2 Click and drag the **Magnification** slider toward Max if you want Dock icons to be enlarged as you pass the mouse cursor over them.

3 Choose an option from the **Minimize using** pop-up menu.

4 Click the **Animate opening applications** check box to make Dock icons bounce as their programs start up.

End

TIP

Dock Behavior in Another Context You can control Dock Preferences by Ctrl-clicking the dividing line between the halves of the Dock. The contextual menu has controls for magnification, hiding, position, and the minimization effect, as well as a Dock Preferences command. ■

CHANGING THE WAY THE FINDER WORKS

The Finder—the program that generates the desktop and enables you to explore your hard drive and network drives visually via windows—is where you'll spend a lot of time while using your Mac. You have several choices about the way it operates; here's how to set up the Finder to suit your tastes.

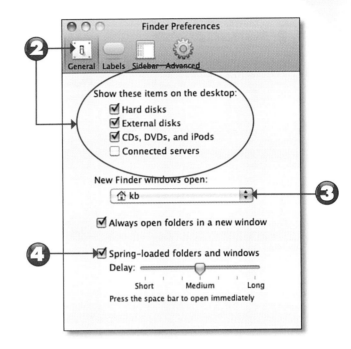

Start

1. In the Finder, choose **Finder**, **Preferences**.

2. Click the **General** button to see basic Finder preferences, and then click check boxes to set the kinds of disks to appear on the desktop.

3. Choose an option from the **New Finder windows open** pop-up menu to determine which folder or disk location appears in new Finder windows.

4. Click the check box to set whether each folder generates a new window.

End

TIP

Finding Files with the Finder The Finder got its name for its capability to find files. To find files in the Finder, choose File, Find or press ⌘-F and type in the information for which you want to search. ■

CHANGING YOUR DESKTOP PICTURE

Every time you sit down in front of your Mac, you're looking at your desktop—or, more specifically, at the picture displayed on it. Why not have some fun with it? You can change the desktop picture any time you like, using any photo, cartoon, or other graphic that catches your fancy.

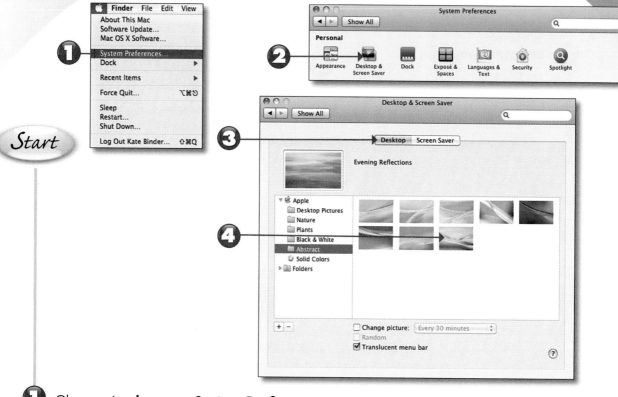

1 Choose **Apple menu**, **System Preferences**.

2 Click the **Desktop & Screen Saver** button to see your choices.

3 Click the **Desktop** button.

4 Click a folder and an image from within the folder to apply that image to the desktop.

TIP

Surprise Me If you want your desktop picture to change automatically, click the + button in the Desktop tab and pick a folder full of your favorite images. Then check Change picture at the bottom of the Desktop tab and choose a time interval. ■

NOTE

The Mother Lode Looking for more desktop pictures to relieve your boredom? You can download hundreds of high-quality desktop images at MacDesktops (www.macdesktops.com). ■

CHANGING YOUR LOGIN ICON

Your login icon represents your face within the world of your Mac. It's used as your buddy icon for online messaging in iChat, it appears next to your personal information in the Address Book, and you see it every time you log in. You can use one of the built-in pictures, or you can add any picture you like—your photo or anything else.

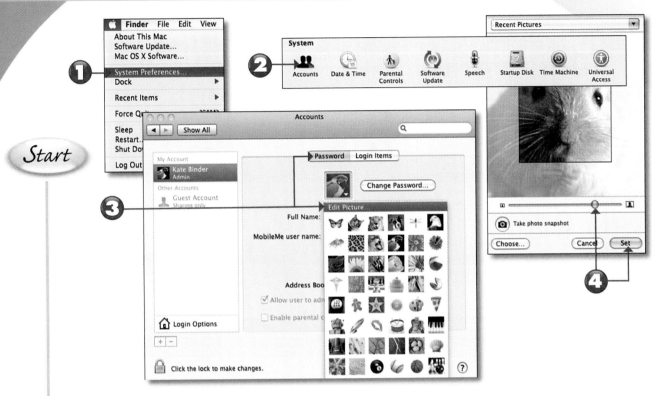

 Start

End

① Choose **Apple menu**, **System Preferences**.

② Click the **Accounts** button to see your choices.

③ Click the **Password** button; then click your picture and choose **Edit Picture** in the pop-up menu.

④ Drag or paste an image file into the Images window, drag the image and the scaling slider until the square shows the area you want for the icon, and then click **Set** to make it your login picture.

TIP
Using Your Own Picture If you're concerned about privacy, it might not be wise to use your own photo as a login icon. If people you don't know will see the photo—as an iChat icon, for instance—you might want to substitute a personal logo of some type. ■

TIP
I'm Ready for My Close-Up, Mr. Jobs If you have an iSight camera, either standalone or built into your Mac, you can use it to take a picture right from the Edit Picture dialog and turn that photo into an icon on the spot. ■

CHANGING YOUR MAC'S LANGUAGE

You might have thought that you would need to buy a special version of Mac OS X if you want your Mac's interface to use a language other than English. Actually, Mac OS X ships with the capability to display menus, dialog boxes, and other interface elements in a couple dozen languages, including those with non-Roman alphabets.

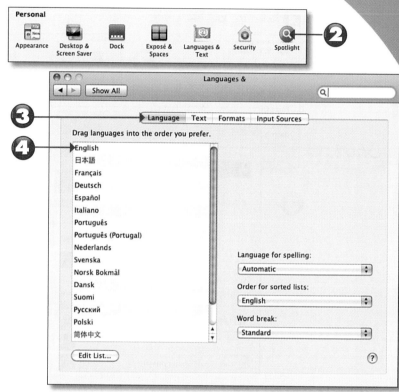

Start

1 Choose **Apple menu**, **System Preferences**.

2 Click the **Languages & Text** button to see your choices.

3 Click the **Language** button.

4 Click and drag your preferred language to the top of the pick list.

End

TIP

Making a Menu When you switch languages, you should also switch keyboard layouts to activate each language's special characters. In the International preferences' Input Menu tab, you can create a menu of the languages you use, then click the Show input menu in menu bar box so you can switch keyboard layouts quickly. ■

CHANGING YOUR SCREEN SAVER

Originally invented to stop the kind of screen burn-in that you see on automatic teller machines, screen savers are actually little more than a pretty entertainment these days. But that shouldn't prevent you from using them; screen savers provide some privacy, shielding your screen from casual observers, as well as being fun to look at.

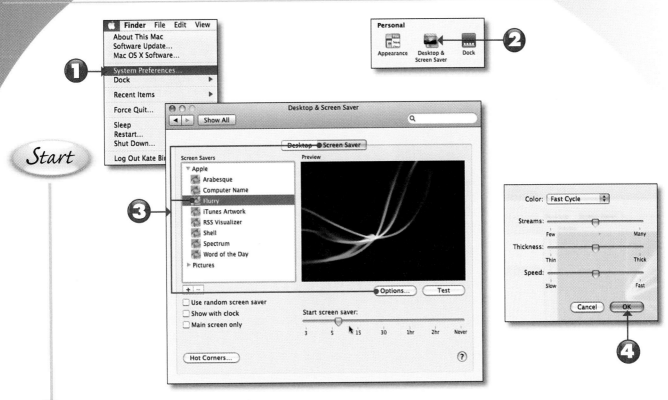

Start

End

1 Choose **Apple menu**, **System Preferences**.

2 Click the **Desktop & Screen Saver** button to see your choices.

3 Click the **Screen Saver** button, and then click a screen saver in the list to select it. Click the **Options** button.

4 Use the settings in this dialog box to change settings specific to each screen saver. Click **OK** when finished.

TIP

Got Savers? If you're not satisfied with the built-in selection of screen savers—or if you've run through them all and are desperately in need of new ones— check out www.macscreensavers.com. ■

TIP

A Screen Saver All Your Own For a custom screen saver, put your favorite photos in a folder and click the + button in the Screen Saver pane's pick list. Locate the folder you want to use and your Mac uses the "Ken Burns" effect to animate your photos. ■

CHANGING FILE ICONS

Mac OS X has wonderful graphics; it's a lovely looking operating system, and that's due in large part to its detailed, scalable icons. One of the easiest—and coolest—customizations you can perform on your Mac is to apply the system's dexterity with icons to your own homemade icons. You can turn any picture you like into an icon.

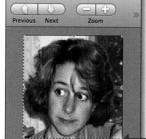

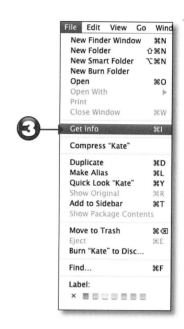

Start

1 In Preview or another graphics program, select part or all of an image to be the new icon. Press ⌘-**C** to copy the selection.

2 In the Finder, click to select the file whose icon you want to change.

3 Choose **File**, **Get Info** to see the file's Info window.

Continued

NOTE

More Fun with Icons You can copy and paste existing icons, too. For a great collection of free Mac icons you can download and apply to your files and folders, check out the InterfaceLIFT (www.interface-lift.com/icons-mac/). ■

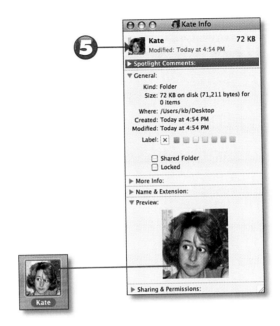

4 Click the icon shown in the Info window.

5 Press ⌘-**V** and the new image is pasted into the icon area.

End

TIP

For Best Results The bigger the picture you use to create an icon, the more detailed the icon will be when it's scaled to its largest size (512 pixels square). With that in mind, however, remember that at small sizes, simple, clear, less-detailed images are the easiest to identify. ■

INCREASING YOUR MAC'S SECURITY

Whether these settings are important to you depends on how vulnerable your Mac is to snoopy intruders. If your computer is in a dorm room or an open office, or if it's a laptop, you'll probably want to put at least some of these measures in place to ensure that unauthorized people can't use it.

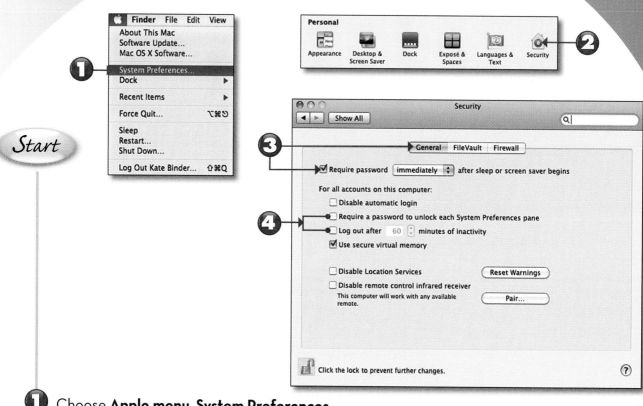

1 Choose **Apple menu**, **System Preferences**.

2 Click the **Security** button to see your choices.

3 Click the **General** button, and then click the **Require password** check box to make sure that only you can wake the computer up when it's sleeping.

4 Click the check boxes next to the other options to turn them on or off.

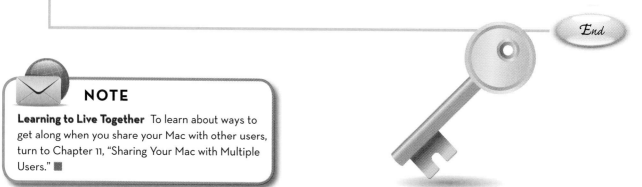

NOTE

Learning to Live Together To learn about ways to get along when you share your Mac with other users, turn to Chapter 11, "Sharing Your Mac with Multiple Users." ■

USING THE DASHBOARD

Naturally, the Dashboard is where you keep indicators, gauges, and other useful things. This handy feature enables you to quickly access helpful desk accessories and just as quickly sweep them out of the way when you're done using them.

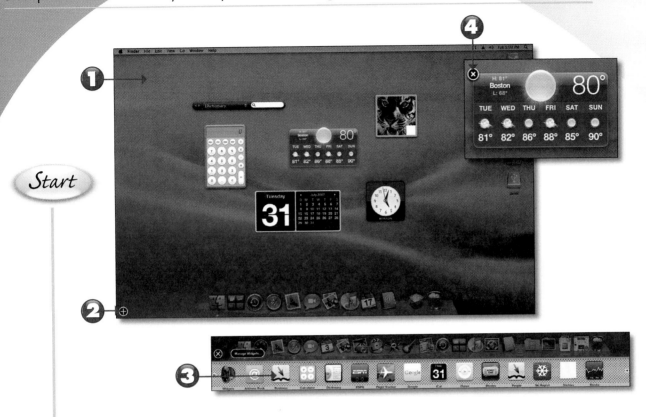

Start

1 Press **F12** to view or hide the Dashboard.

2 Click the **+** button to see the Dashboard shelf.

3 Drag a widget out of the shelf to place it on the Dashboard.

4 Click the **Close** button in the upper-left corner of a widget to put it back on the shelf.

End

TIP

Double Vision Some widgets can be in two places at once—you can drag more than one sticky or calendar out of the Favorites bar. Watch out, though; if you double-click a widget instead of clicking and dragging, you might unintentionally end up with two copies of it when you only wanted one. ■

MAKING YOUR OWN WIDGETS

If you frequently visit particular web pages, you'll be thrilled to hear that Leopard enables you to stick them right in your Dashboard so you can take a quick glance at them any time. It's very simple to turn your favorite web pages into Dashboard widgets, and you do it right from Safari.

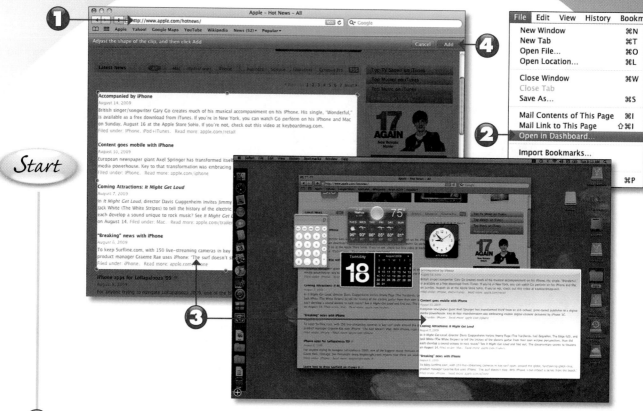

Start

1. In Safari, type the URL of the web page you want to turn into a widget.

2. Choose **File**, **Open in Dashboard**.

3. Select the area on the web page that you want to include in your widget.

4. Click **Add**; the new widget opens in Dashboard.

End

TIP

Make It Your Very Own To customize the appearance of your widget, click the i button in its lower-right corner. The widget flips neatly over and presents you with a choice of visual themes. Click the one you want to use. ■

TIP

The Widget Underground Want to be just a little bit subversive? Use Web Clip to avoid ads on web pages by turning the pages into widgets—and cropping out all the area occupied by ads. ■

AUTOMATICALLY UPDATING YOUR WIDGETS

If you use more than one computer, MobileMe now gives you a convenient way to make sure your favorite widgets are installed on *all* your Macs. If you're a MobileMe member, you need never again experience the frustration of not having just the widget you need.

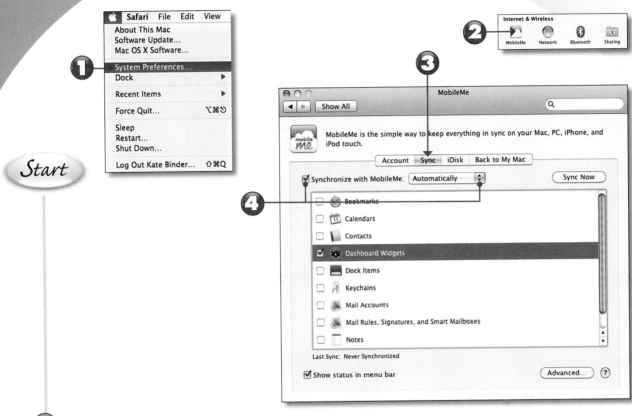

1 Choose **Apple menu**, **System Preferences**.

2 Click the **MobileMe** button in the System Preferences window to display the MobileMe preferences.

3 Click the **Sync** button.

4 Click the check box labeled **Synchronize with MobileMe** and then choose **Automatically** from the pop-up menu.

NOTE

Dotting Your Mac Apple's own online service, MobileMe, has lots of other benefits—your own website, synchronization of iCal, Address Book, and Safari's bookmarks, Internet backup for your important files, and much more. To learn how to set up a MobileMe account, turn to Chapter 9, "Living Online." ■

CREATING CUSTOM NETWORK LOCATIONS

Network locations are groups of network settings, each saved with a descriptive name so you can switch all your settings with a single click and get online or on the local network instantly no matter where you happen to be. After you've created a location, to use it all you have to do is choose it from a pop-up menu.

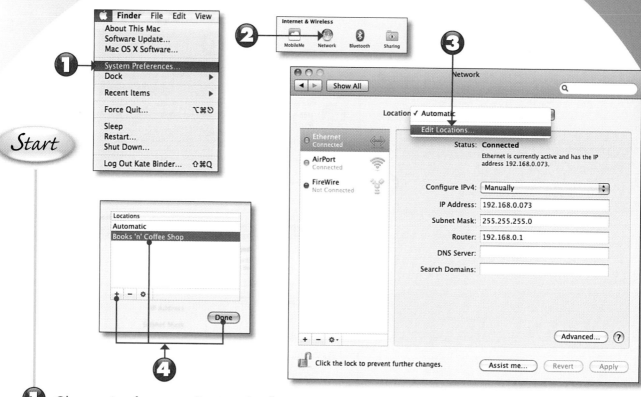

1 Choose **Apple menu**, **System Preferences**.

2 Click the **Network** button to see your choices.

3 Choose **Edit Locations** from the **Location** pop-up menu.

4 Click the **Add Location** button, give the location a descriptive name, and click **Done**.

Continued

NOTE

Naming Names Just to be sure we're all on the same page here, a descriptive name (see step 4) is something like "Joe's office Ethernet," rather than "New Location 4." It tells you where and under what circumstances the location setting is applicable. ■

TIP

What's in a Name? To change the names of your locations, choose Edit Locations from the pop-up menu again. ■

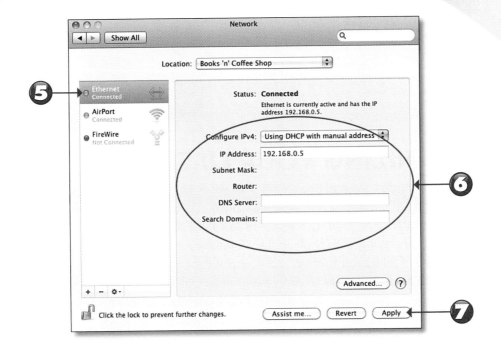

5 Choose the network interface you want to set up from the list at the left.

6 Make the appropriate settings for that network interface.

7 Click **Apply** to switch to the new location.

End

NOTE

A Time and a Place You can use locations to save settings for different situations as well as different places. For example, if you have both a cable modem and a dial-up account, create a location for each so you can switch to dial-up if the cable connection goes down.

ORGANIZING YOUR LIFE

Mac OS X includes several programs that work together to keep you organized: Address Book, iCal, and iSync. Address Book is a contact manager where you can store your friends', family members', and colleagues' names, addresses, and phone numbers along with their instant messaging IDs, websites, email addresses, and more. iCal keeps track of your appointments and a to-do list, and it can both publish and subscribe to online calendars so you can share them with others. And iSync makes sure that all the data in Address Book and iCal is available to your PDA, phone, or other device so you're never without it.

In this chapter you'll learn how to create and organize contacts in Address Book and how to use the program to view a map of a contact's address. iCal Tasks show how to create appointments and to-do lists and how to invite Address Book contacts to events; how to search calendars; and how to publish, subscribe to, and print calendars. Finally, you'll learn how to use iSync to keep all your information straight across devices, and how to turn email messages into items on your to-do list.

WORKING WITH CONTACTS AND SCHEDULES

Sync PDAs, iPods, and phones with iCal and Address Book, 129

View days, weeks, or entire months, 117

Organize your schedule in iCal, 116

Search your calendar, 123

Track notes and to-do items in Mail, 127

Keep track of contacts in Address Book, 109

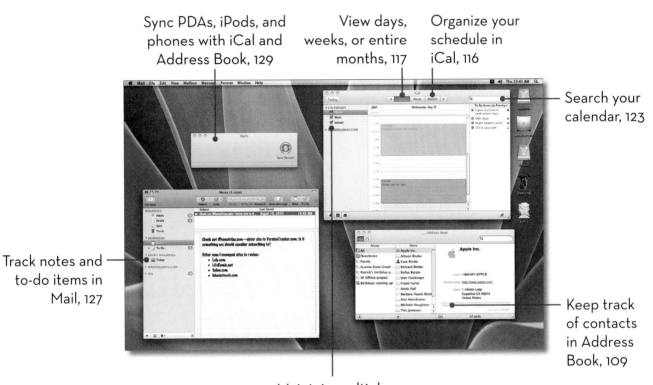

Maintain multiple calendars, 119

ADDING CONTACTS TO ADDRESS BOOK

Mac OS X's Address Book is accessible systemwide, meaning its information can be used by other programs such as iChat, Mail, and even Microsoft Word. Adding contacts and sorting them into groups is easy, and Address Book has an up-to-date selection of information fields, including places to stash online messaging IDs.

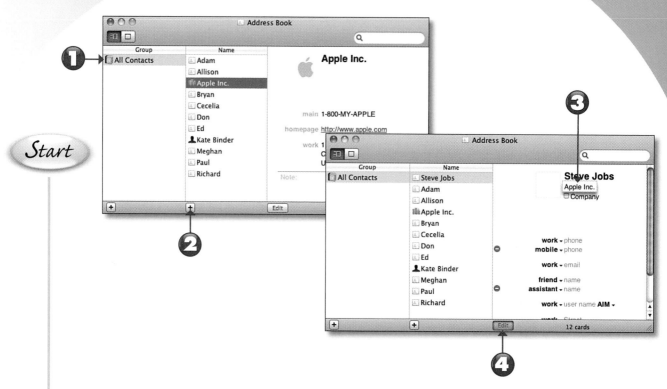

1 Click the group name to which you want to add the contact, or **All Contacts** if you don't have a group in mind.

2 Click the + button below the list of contacts in that group.

3 Type the person or company's name and other information.

4 Click **Edit** to complete the contact.

CREATING GROUPS OF CONTACTS

You can use Address Book's groups many ways. For example, you can create a group of people working on a current project so you can email them all at once. Or you can create a group of addresses for holiday cards so you can print address labels. Each contact can be in as many groups as you want to put it in; deleting it from a group doesn't delete it from Address Book.

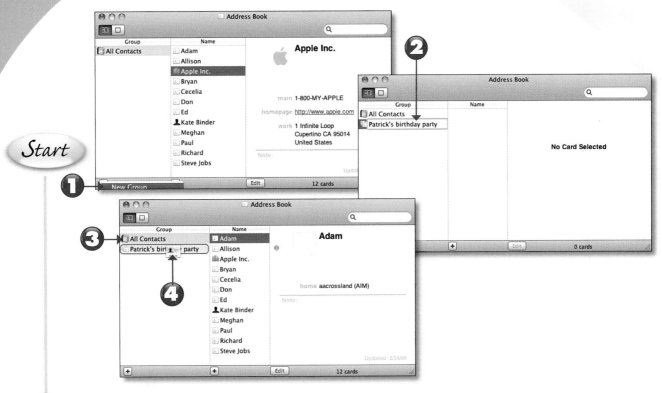

Start

1 Click the **+** button under the list of groups and choose **New Group** from the pop-up menu.

2 Give the new group a name.

3 Click **All Contacts** or a group that contains the contacts you want to add to the new group.

4 Drag the contacts into the new group.

End

TIP

A Two-Way Street Creating a new group can work backward, too. First, ⌘-click to select the contacts you want to put in the group; then choose File, New Group from Selection. ■

TIP

Edit This The Edit button is also where you should head (or, more precisely, click) when you want to make changes to an existing Address Book entry. To apply your changes, click Edit again, or you can just click another contact or group instead. ■

CREATING A SMART GROUP

You create smart groups in the Address Book, but your Mac maintains them. After you determine the criteria for a contact's inclusion in a smart group, the Mac makes sure that the right contacts are sorted into that group at all times, even after you've changed contact information or added new contacts.

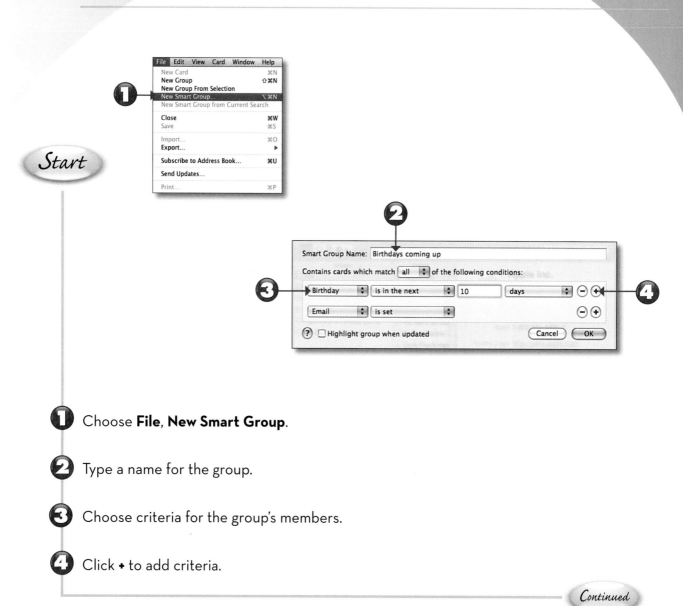

Start

1 Choose **File**, **New Smart Group**.

2 Type a name for the group.

3 Choose criteria for the group's members.

4 Click **+** to add criteria.

Continued

NOTE

Going Negative Don't forget that you can set most smart group criteria to negative values—meaning you can choose to include everyone in your Address Book who *doesn't* match a particular criterion. ■

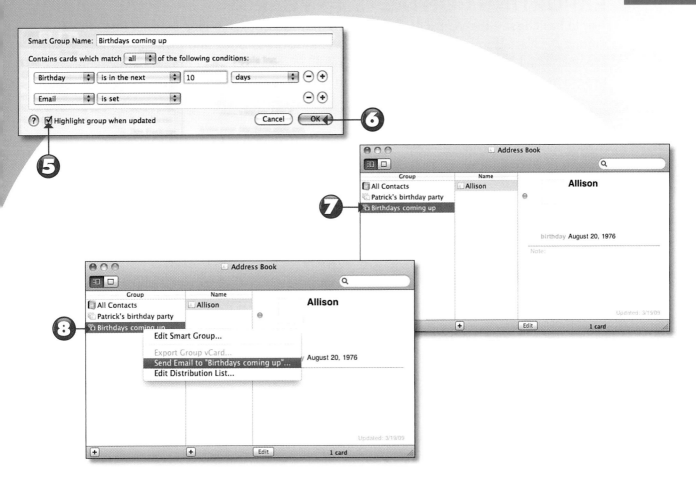

5 Click the box labeled **Highlight group when updated** to have Address Book highlight the group's name when it contains new members.

6 Click **OK** to create the group.

7 Click the group's name to see its members in the Name column.

8 Control-click the group's name to email its members or export their contact data.

End

NOTE

Setting Conditions You're not limited to just one criterion when creating a smart group. You can set as many conditions for inclusion as you like, and you can choose whether group members must satisfy all the conditions, or just some of them. ■

NOTE

What's It Good For? Use smart groups to track contacts' birthdays, anniversaries, or other important dates; collect all contacts from a particular company into a single group; or look up which friends and family members live near your next vacation spot. ■

EXPORTING CONTACTS AS VCARDS

Apple has chosen the vCard as its standard method of exchanging contact information among Address Book users as well as between Address Book and other programs. vCards are very small files that you can attach to email messages. Most contact management programs can read them, so they're a good way to send contact information to just about anyone, including Windows users.

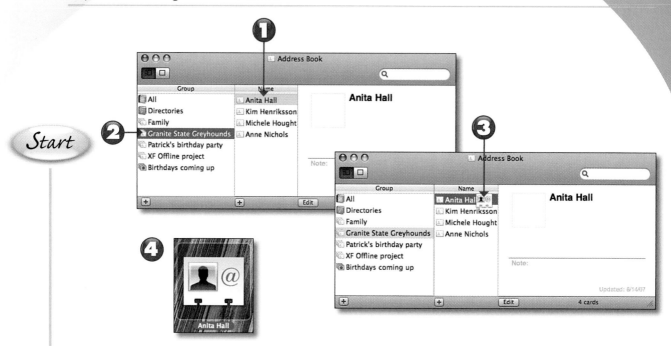

Start

1 Click a name in the contacts column to select a single person, or ⌘-**click** to select more than one person.

2 To create a vCard for an entire group, click the group's name in the first column.

3 Drag the group, contact, or contacts onto the desktop to create the vCard file.

4 The vCard appears on the desktop and can now be attached and sent via email.

End

NOTE

The Express Route You can find contacts quickly in Address Book by clicking the All group and typing a name, city, or other information into the Search entry field at the upper-left corner of the Address Book window. ■

IMPORTING A VCARD INTO ADDRESS BOOK

Getting vCards into the Address Book is just as easy as getting them out of the Address Book. When you receive a vCard attached to an email as a sort of electronic business card, you need to locate the file in your attachments folder—you'll recognize it because of its .vcf filename extension and its address card icon.

Start

1 Drag the vCard file from the desktop into the Address Book window.

2 Click **Add** in the confirmation dialog box.

End

NOTE

The Case of the Missing Attachment vCard files typically end up in your email attachments folder—the location and name can vary depending on which email program you use. To get at these files easily, try clicking their names or icons in the email window and dragging them onto the desktop, or even directly into the Address Book window. ■

MAPPING A CONTACT'S ADDRESS

If you have an instant-on or constant Internet connection, you're going to love this Address Book feature. You can view a map (and from there, driving directions) for an address in your contact list. It all starts with a simple click to a pop-up menu. Just remember, it won't work if you're not online.

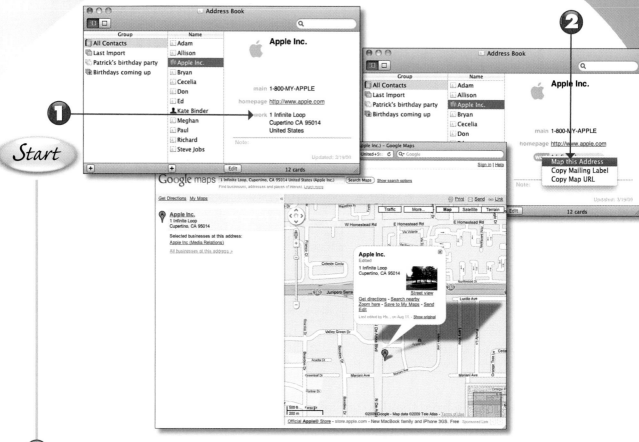

Start

① Click the address label next to the address to display a pop-up menu.

② Click **Map this Address**.

③ The map is displayed in your web browser.

End

NOTE

Just the URL, Please If you want to pass a map along to a friend, rather than just use it yourself, take advantage of another choice in the address pop-up menu: Copy Map URL. After you choose this command, click in any text document or email window and press ⌘-V to paste the map's URL so the reader can click it to see the map. ■

ADDING A TO-DO IN ICAL

Using a calendar to keep track of events is very important (turn to the next task to see how it works in iCal), but for many people, tracking a to-do list is an even more vital function. In iCal, you can assign each to-do item to a specific calendar, so you can distinguish among work, home, and hobby- or club-related tasks.

Start

1 Click the **Show/Hide To-Do List** button to display to-do items to the right of the calendar.

2 Click the calendar to which you want to add the to-do item.

3 Double-click in the blank space in the **To Do items** area.

4 Enter the to-do text.

End

TIP

Making To-Do Items Disappear Choose **iCal, Preferences** to change how long items stay on your calendar after they're completed and to determine how to-do items are sorted: by priority, by due date, or alphabetically. ■

ADDING AN APPOINTMENT IN ICAL

iCal is compact and easy to use, but don't underestimate it. This little calendar program has a surprising amount of power. Its primary purpose, of course, is keeping track of your appointments. Adding new ones couldn't be simpler, and reading iCal's neatly color-coded calendar is as easy as it gets.

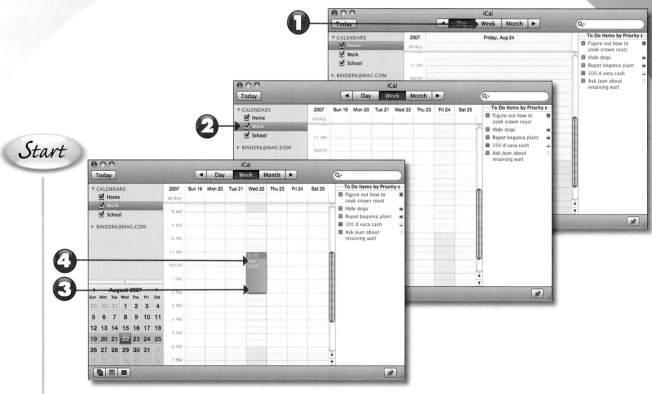

Start

End

① Click the **Day** or **Week** button to switch to Day or Week view.

② Click the calendar to which you want to add the appointment.

③ Click and drag on the hour grid for the day of the appointment to define the time span for the appointment.

④ Type in the appointment text.

TIP

Filling in the Details To refine your appointment entry, double-click the appointment and then click the **Edit** button at the bottom-right corner of the iCal window. Enter a location, add an alarm notification, set the appointment to repeat regularly, and more. You can also change the event's calendar here. ■

MODIFYING AN EVENT IN ICAL

The more things change, well, the more confused you get. Unless you have iCal, that is—it's easy to make changes to events you've scheduled previously. You can, of course, change an event's day and time by simply dragging it to another place on your calendar. Here you'll learn how to make other changes.

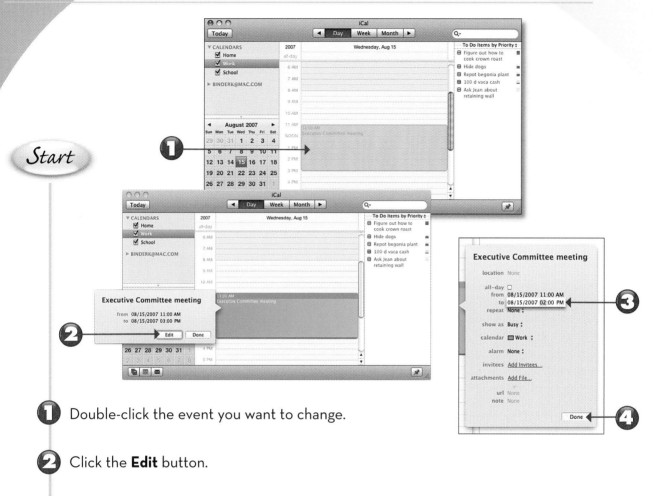

1. Double-click the event you want to change.

2. Click the **Edit** button.

3. Make changes to the event's time or other attributes.

4. Click **Done**.

Start

End

SWITCHING CALENDAR VIEWS IN ICAL

Whether you want to zero in on each hour of the day or back off and take in a month at a time, iCal can accommodate you. You can view your calendar by the day, week, or month. Meanwhile, mini-months off to the side enable you to keep track of the months surrounding today's date.

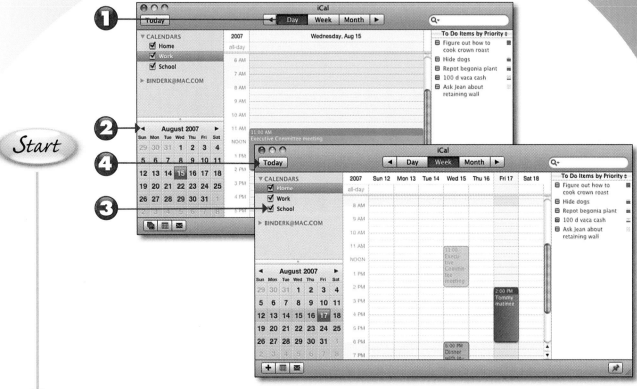

Start

1 Click the **Day, Week,** or **Month** button at the top of the iCal window to switch views.

2 Click the arrows to view different mini-months at the left side of the iCal window.

3 Click the check box next to each calendar to show or hide its appointments and to-do items.

4 Click the **Today** button to return to viewing today.

End

TIP

Customizing Day and Week Views Choose iCal, Preferences to set the number of days displayed in Week view and choose on which day the week should start. You can also choose how many hours are shown in Day view and set start and end times for the day. ■

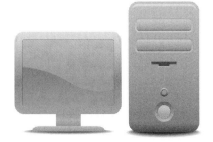

SETTING UP AN ALARM IN ICAL

If you want to be reminded before an appointment, you can set up an alarm that will get your attention to let you know the appointment is coming up. iCal alarms take several forms: displaying a dialog box, displaying a dialog box and playing a sound, sending an email, or opening a specified file.

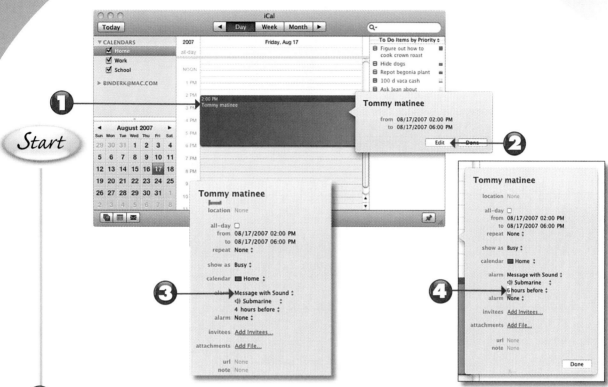

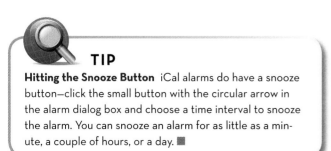

1. Double-click the appointment to which you want to add an alarm.

2. Click **Edit**.

3. Click the **alarm** pop-up menu and choose an alarm type; then specify a sound, a file, or an email address to use, if necessary.

4. Set the time for the alarm to appear and then click **Done**.

End

TIP

Hitting the Snooze Button iCal alarms do have a snooze button—click the small button with the circular arrow in the alarm dialog box and choose a time interval to snooze the alarm. You can snooze an alarm for as little as a minute, a couple of hours, or a day. ■

INVITING CONTACTS TO EVENTS IN ICAL

If you use Apple's Mail as your email program, you can invite people to scheduled events right from iCal, and even update information about the event as it gets closer. You'll just need to know the email addresses of the people you want to invite to your event.

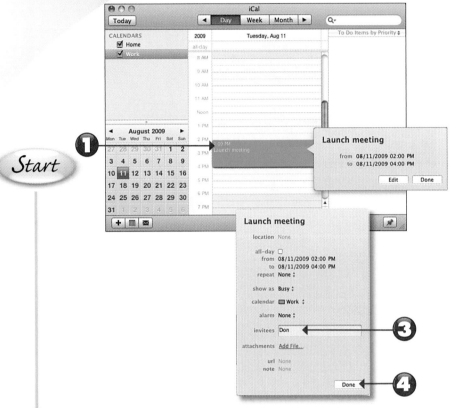

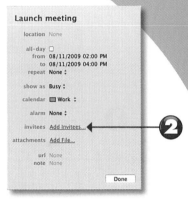

 Double-click the appointment to which you want to invite others and then click **Edit**.

 Click **Add Invitees**.

Click next to **invitees** and type the names or email addresses of the people you want to invite; iCal inserts email addresses for names that are in the Address Book.

Click **Done** to send email invitations.

Start

End

NOTE

Separate Names To invite more than one person to an event, type a comma after each name before you type the next name. Otherwise, iCal isn't sure where one name ends and the next begins. ■

TIP

Getting People in the Door Another way to add people to the attendees list for an event is to choose Window, Address Panel and drag names from the list to the event's listing in the calendar. ■

PUTTING CONTACTS, BOOKMARKS, AND CALENDARS ONLINE

If you have a MobileMe membership, you can sync your contact information, web bookmarks, calendars, and other information between two computers—or more. You can also access this information from the web when you're using a computer that's not synced up, such as a public terminal or a friend's PC.

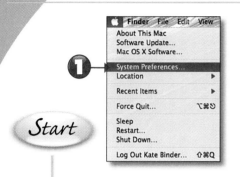

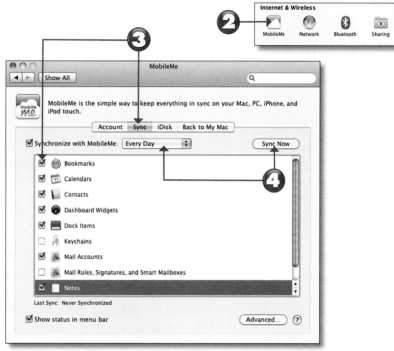

Start

1 Choose **Apple menu**, **System Preferences**.

2 In System Preferences, click **MobileMe**.

3 Click the **Sync** tab and check the boxes for the items you want to sync.

4 Choose a frequency option from the pop-up menu and click **Sync Now**.

End

TIP

In Touch Anywhere To see your information using a web browser on any computer, go to www.me.com and log in using your MobileMe name and password. Then click one of the links on the left side of the page, such as Address Book. ■

NOTE

Seeing Double If you're using the same iCal calendar on two or more Macs, you'll receive duplicate event reminders. That's fine if the reminder is a simple dialog box. But if you use duplicate email reminders, it can be a bit annoying. ■

SEARCHING CALENDARS IN ICAL

You know you put Aunt Blanche's birthday in iCal, but you can't even remember the month, much less the day. Never fear: iCal will find the date for you. Just search for "Blanche," and your trusty calendar will offer you a list of every event containing her name, including that elusive birthday.

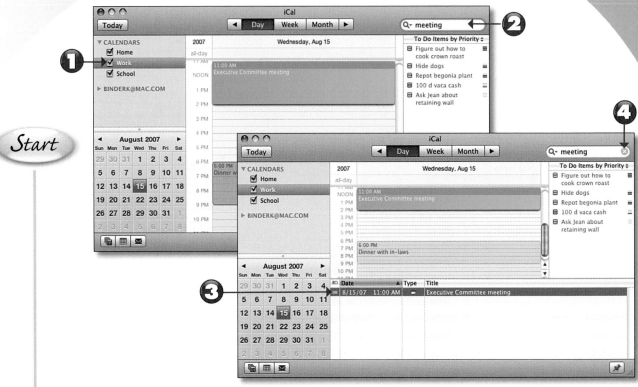

Start

1 Click the check boxes next to the calendars you want to search.

2 Type the text you want to search for in the **search** field.

3 Click an event or to-do in the **Search Result** list to go to it.

4 To clear the search field and get rid of the Search Result list, click the **X**.

End

SUBSCRIBING TO AN ICAL CALENDAR

Perhaps iCal's coolest feature is its capability to share calendars online. This means you can subscribe to calendars created by other people, whether their day-to-day events (your spouse's schedule, perhaps) or special events (your favorite football team's season schedule, maybe).

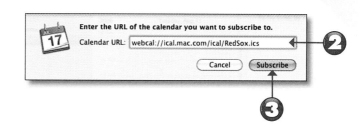

Start

1 Choose **Calendar**, **Subscribe**.

2 Enter the URL for the calendar to which you want to subscribe. The calendar's owner provides this information.

3 Click **Subscribe**.

4 Choose a frequency in the **Auto-Refresh** pop-up menu for iCal to check the calendar for changes, and click **OK**.

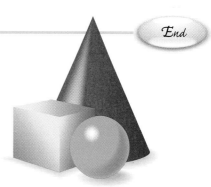

End

TIP

Where to Find Calendars Apple has compiled a list of carefully selected public iCal calendars on its website (www.apple.com/ical/library/). Another great site for finding public calendars is iCalShare.com (www.icalshare.com). ■

PUBLISHING AN ICAL CALENDAR

What can you publish? Well, you can choose to share your home or work calendar with your family or colleagues. Or you might decide to be the keeper of the birthdays among your friends and publish a calendar showing everyone's special days. You can use your MobileMe account or a free web service to publish calendars, as you prefer.

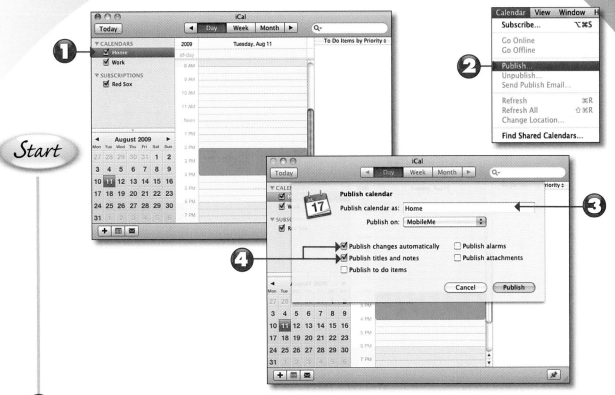

Start

1 Click the calendar you want to publish.

2 Choose **Calendar**, **Publish**.

3 Type a name for the published calendar.

4 Click the check boxes to publish changes automatically and to publish both the title and notes for an event (rather than just its title).

Continued

TIP
Changing Your Mind If you decide to stop publishing a calendar, click its name in the Calendars list and choose Calendar, Unpublish. iCal warns you that people will no longer be able to subscribe to the calendar; just click Unpublish to take your calendar offline. ■

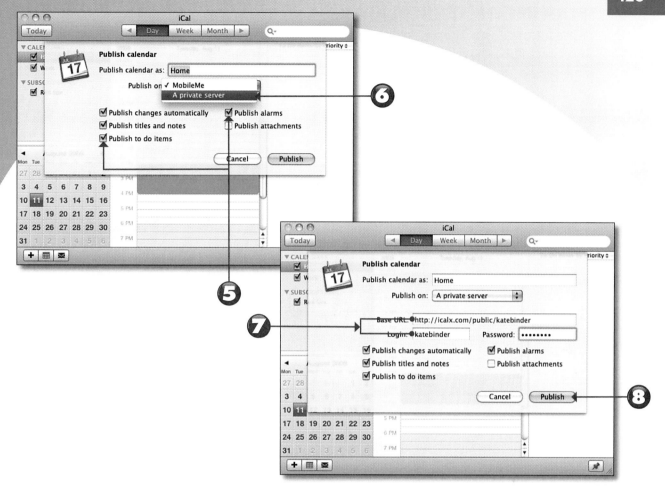

5 Click the check boxes to publish alarms and to-do items.

6 Choose an option from the **Publish on** pop-up menu for where you're publishing the calendar: using MobileMe or using an independent server.

7 If you're using an independent server, enter its URL and your login name and password.

8 Click **Publish**.

End

NOTE

Becoming a Publisher If you want to publish your own calendars but don't have a MobileMe account, go to iCalExchange.com (icalx.com). It offers free access to the WebDAV servers you need to publish calendars. ■

NOTE

Automatic Updates or Not? Publishing calendar changes automatically requires a constant online connection. Don't choose this option if you use a dial-up Internet service because you might find your computer dialing in unexpectedly. ■

MAKING NOTES IN MAIL

For a lot of people, their email is the most organized thing about them. It's in folders! Sorted by date! Labeled! How many of us can say that about our random notes—lists of movies to see, recipes to try, gift ideas for Grandma? Now Mail makes it possible for you to organize your notes right alongside your email.

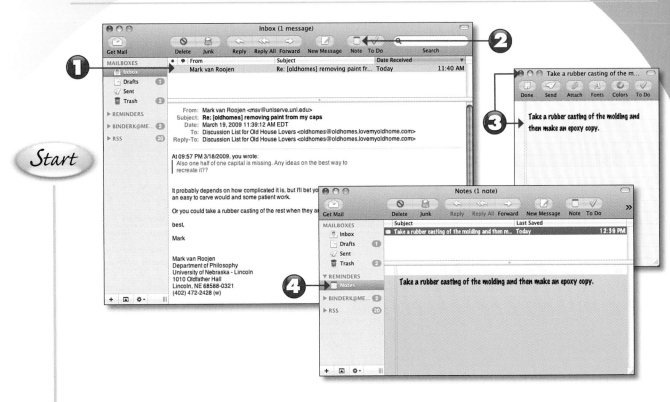

Start

1 Click to view the email about which you want to make notes.

2 Click the **Note** button.

3 Enter your notes and close the Note window to save the note.

4 To view notes, click arrow next to the Notes entry in the **Mailboxes** column.

End

NOTE

Take Your Notes with You A note is really just a specially formatted email message, which means it can be stored online with the rest of your mail. That, in turn, means that you'll be able to check your Mail notes from any computer with a web connection, as long as your email account has web mail access. ■

TURNING AN EMAIL INTO A TO-DO ITEM

If you're anything like me, many of the items on your to-do list are based on emails. Your boss wants you to do this, your mom says you should remember that, you really need to call your girlfriend. Now you can create a new to-do right in Mail, based on the content of an email message, and it's automatically added to iCal as well as being accessible in Mail.

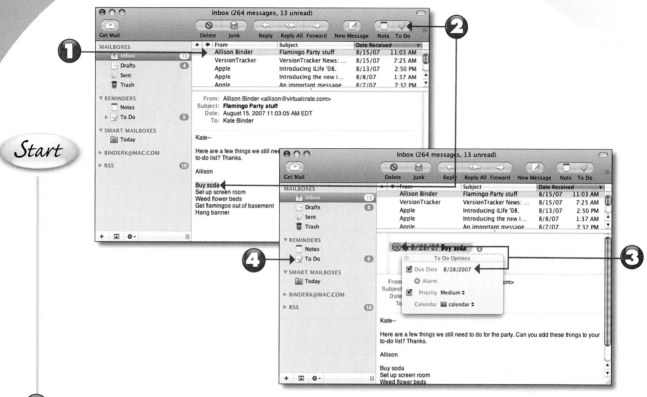

 Start

1. Click to view the email containing your to-do items.

2. Select the text you want to turn into a to-do; then click the **To Do** button.

3. To set options such as a deadline, click the **Options** button and make your changes.

4. To view to-dos, click the **To Do** entry in the **Mailboxes** column.

End

TIP

Step by Step Mail makes one to-do item per click on the To Do button, so be sure to select just one item on your list to convert at a time. ■

SYNCING A PDA, AN IPOD, OR A PHONE WITH YOUR MAC

If you use an iPhone, a Palm, or another device that can interact with your Mac, you're definitely going to want to sync that device with iCal and Address Book. The procedure is a bit different for Palms than it is for other devices, but in either case it takes only a few steps. Here's how to get started.

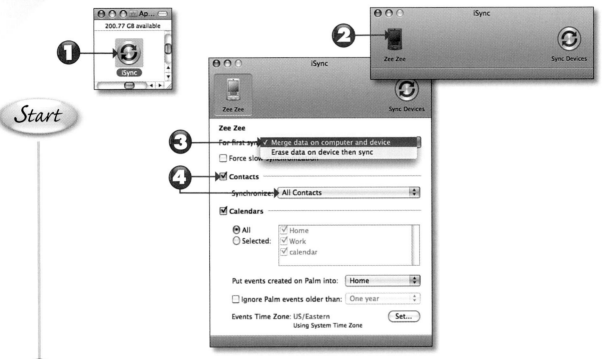

Start

1. Start up iSync (located in the Applications folder).

2. Click the icon for the device you want to sync.

3. If this is the first time you're syncing, click each device icon and choose an option from the **For first sync** pop-up menu.

4. Click the **Contacts** check box to include contacts in the sync, and choose which groups to include from the **Synchronize** pop-up menu.

Continued

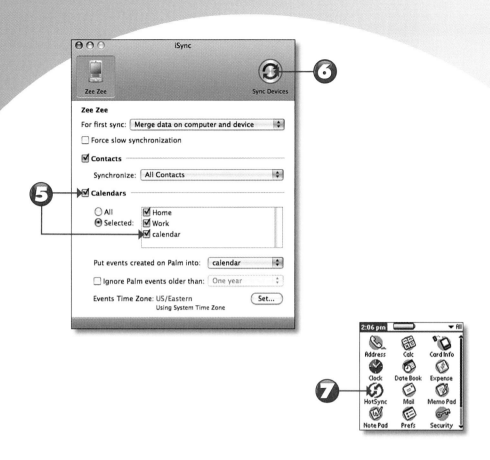

5 Click the **Calendars** check box to include calendars in the sync, and choose which calendars to include.

6 To sync all devices other than a Palm device, click **Sync Devices** to begin the sync process.

7 To sync all devices, including a Palm PDA, start a HotSync by tapping the Palm's **HotSync** button.

End

TIP

When Little Changes Add Up If more than 5% of your data will be modified by the sync process, iSync lets you know what the percentage of change is and offers you the option of canceling the sync. Choose iSync, Preferences to change the percentage that triggers this warning. ■

TIP

Getting Hooked Up with iSync You can download iSync at www.apple.com/isync/. To add a device to iSync, hook it up to your Mac and start iSync. Choose Devices, Add Device. Double-click the new device when it appears in the Add Device window. ■

Chapter 7

PRINTING, FAXING, AND SCANNING

Mac OS X makes it easy to use your printer, fax modem, and scanner. All three functions are built in to the system, so you don't need to worry about buggy, incompatible software that slows you down when you're trying to get things done. You have lots of options for printing, faxing, and scanning that enable you to get the most from your devices, but if you're in a hurry each function can be accomplished with just a few clicks.

Before printing a document, you can preview to make sure it looks the way you want it to, and preview documents can be saved as PDFs that you can exchange with others who don't have the software you used to create the document; so they can see the document exactly the way you designed it, and print it on their own printers.

Faxing happens the same way and in the same place as printing—the Print dialog box—so if you have a modem, you can fax any document you can print. And a small, simple, but powerful program called Image Capture is responsible for scanning duties.

USING PRINTERS, FAX MODEMS, SCANNERS, AND FONTS

Set up
printers, 133

Switch
printers, 135

Scan documents
and pictures, 141

Cancel
printing, 138

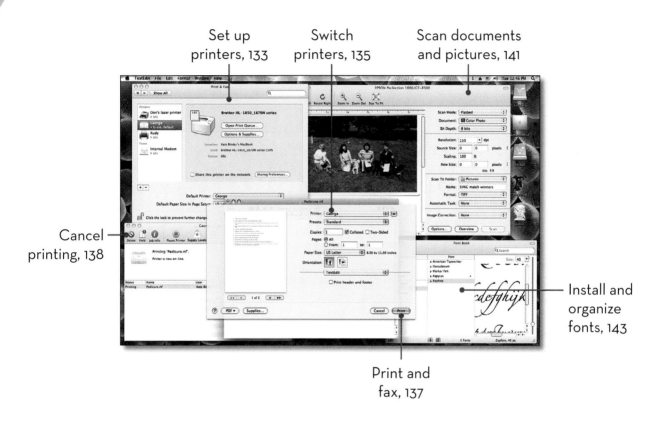

Install and
organize
fonts, 143

Print and
fax, 137

SETTING UP A PRINTER

First, you need to know at least one thing about your printer: how it's connected. It might be a USB printer plugged in to the Mac itself, or it could be a network printer. When you get that figured out, the Mac's Printer Setup Utility can go out and find the printer for itself.

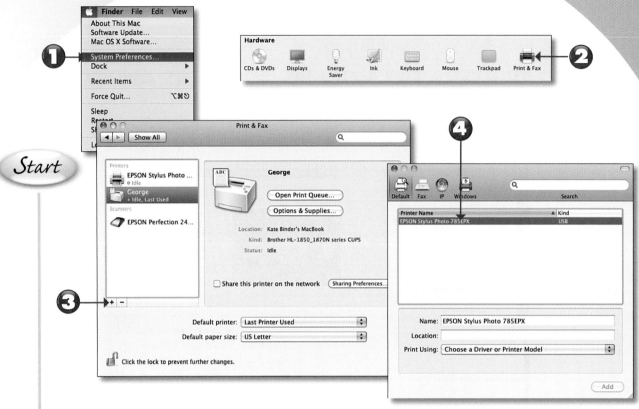

Start

1 Choose **Apple menu**, **System Preferences**.

2 Click the **Print & Fax** button to see your choices.

3 Click the **Add** button below the **Printers** list.

4 Choose a printer from the pick list.

Continued

TIP

Missing Pieces To work with your printer, the Mac has to have access to the printer drivers (the software) that came with the printer. If you don't have these on disc or if they're out of date, visit the printer manufacturer's website to download the latest drivers. ■

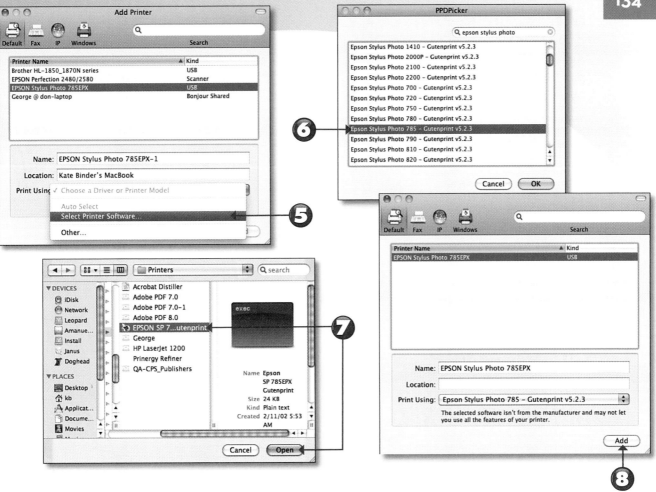

5 If the system isn't able to figure out which model your printer is, choose **Select a Driver** from the **Print Using** pop-up menu.

6 Click your printer model in the pick list.

7 If you don't see your printer model in the list, choose **Other** from the **Print Using** pop-up menu; then navigate to the printer driver that came with your printer and click **Open**.

8 Click **Add**. If you see a dialog box asking about your printer's options, choose the appropriate equipment or settings and click **Continue**.

End

NOTE

Close Enough If you don't have the correct printer driver for your printer, you can usually get away with using one that's similar. Just choose the closest model available. ∎

TIP

Two for One If your printer doesn't have its model name and number on the front, check the manual that came with it. Sometimes multiple similar models share a driver, and in that case all the similar models should be listed in the manual. ∎

SWITCHING PRINTERS

If you have more than one printer, you want to make sure you send each document to the right printer. You can choose a printer each time you print, or you can change the default printer to ensure that the next time you click Print the desired printer will be chosen. Start by choosing **File**, **Print** in any program and then follow these steps.

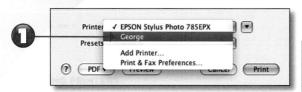

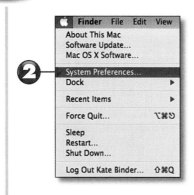

To change printers on-the-fly as you prepare to print, choose a different printer from the **Printer** pop-up menu at the top of the Print dialog box.

To change default printers ahead of time, choose **Apple menu**, **System Preferences**.

Click the **Print & Fax** button to see your choices.

Choose a printer from the **Default Printer** pop-up menu.

TIP
Who's Who? If you're not a fan of printer names like "Su-perPrint PhotoJet XL67825 Pro v8.5.1c," click your printer in the Print and Fax preferences, then click **Options & Supplies** to change its name to whatever you like. ■

TIP
Printing Success If a friend or family member will be using your computer and you're not confident of that person's ability to select the right printer on-the-fly, set the default printer ahead of time so the right printer is preselected in the Print dialog. ■

PREVIEWING A DOCUMENT BEFORE PRINTING

Mac OS X's printing system lets you easily see what a document will look like when it's printed before you commit it to paper. Using this system feature, you can preview any document you can print, right from the Print dialog box.

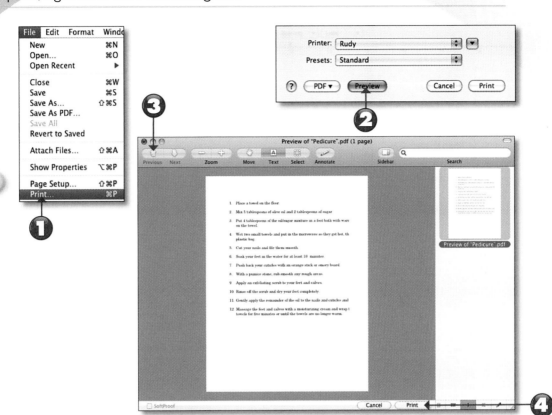

Start

1. With the document open, choose **File**, **Print** (or press ⌘-**P**) to **display** the Print dialog box.

2. Click the **Preview** button; the system creates a PDF of the document and opens the PDF in the Preview program.

3. Scroll through the document in Preview by clicking the **Previous** and **Next** buttons on the toolbar.

4. Click the **Cancel** button to return to the original application, or click **Print** to print the document.

End

NOTE

Spreading the Wealth When you click Preview, Mac OS X creates a new document from your original and opens it in Preview. You can save the preview document in PDF format, which also opens in Adobe Reader, to share with others who don't have the program you used to create it. ■

PRINTING A DOCUMENT

For all practical purposes, the actual process of sending a document to the printer works the same in Mac OS X as it has in previous generations of the Mac OS. You can exert greater control if you want by inspecting each pane of the Print dialog box and adjusting the settings you find there, or you can just click **Print** and go.

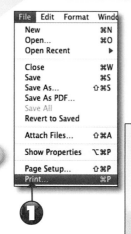

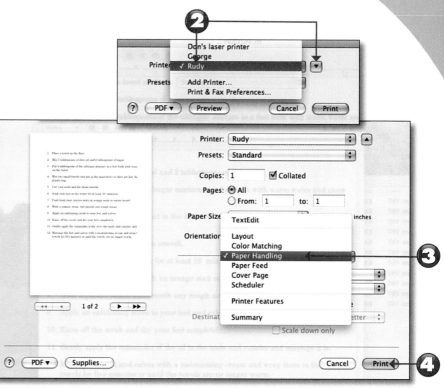

Start

1 Choose **File**, **Print** (or press ⌘-**P**) to display the Print dialog box.

2 Choose a printer from the **Printer** pop-up menu and then click the arrow button to reveal more settings menus.

3 Check the settings in each pane of the Print dialog box using the pop-up menu and make changes as needed.

4 Click **Print**.

End

TIP

The Print Dialog Box The Print dialog box's panes vary according to the printer, but they always include Layout (how many pages to print on each sheet of paper), Paper Handling (which paper tray the printer should use), and one for program-specific features. ∎

CANCELING A PRINT JOB

It happens to the best of us: You send a received fax or a rough draft of your term paper to the printer, only to realize that you're printing the document on $1/page glossy photo paper. Cancel that print job—now! Here's how.

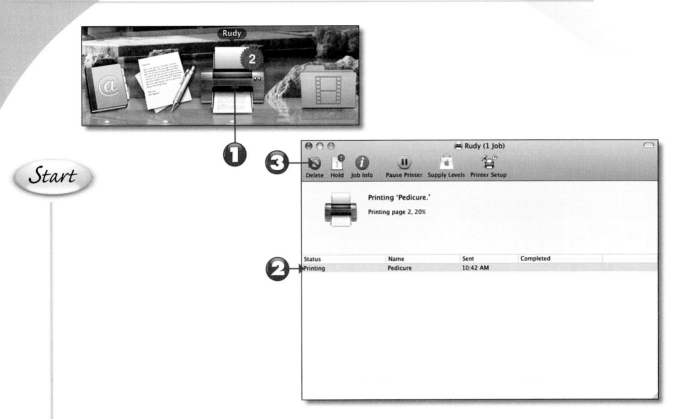

Start

① View the printer's print queue by clicking the printer icon in the Dock.

② Click the job you want to cancel.

③ Click the **Delete** button in the toolbar.

End

TIP

Not Now, But Later If you want to stop a job from printing now but you plan on allowing it to print later, don't delete it from the queue. Instead, click the Hold button in the print queue's toolbar to put all the documents that are currently printing on hold. When you're ready to restart printing, click Resume. ■

SENDING A FAX

If you have a fax modem, you've probably spent some time wrestling with third-party fax software, which never seems to work right with either the system software or all the programs from which you want to fax. Those days are over; fax sending capability is built in to Mac OS X, and it's as close as the Print command.

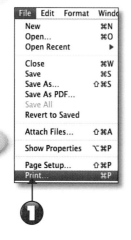

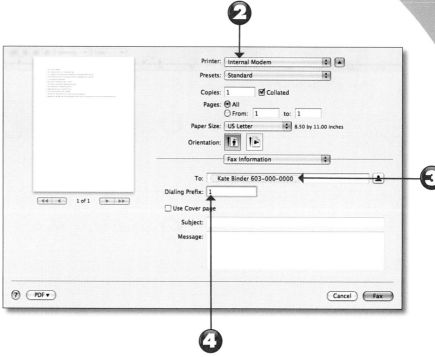

Start

1 Open the document and choose **File**, **Print**.

2 Choose your fax modem from the **Printer** pop-up menu.

3 Type the name and fax number of the person you want to fax. If the fax recipient's name is in the Address Book, the fax number is filled in automatically.

4 Type a dialing prefix (such as 1 for long distance or a long distance access code).

End

TIP

Choosing Fax Recipients To select fax recipients from your Address Book, click the Address Book button to the right of the To field. The Address pane appears—here, you can click to select a single person or ⌘-click to select multiple people. ∎

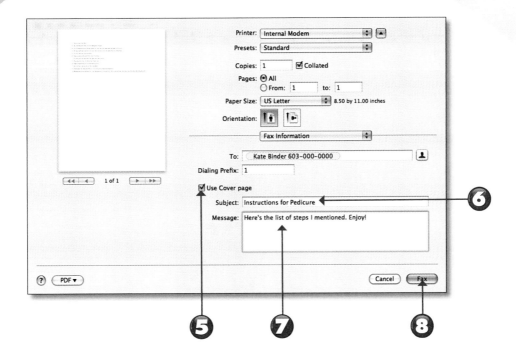

5 Click **Use Cover page**.

6 Enter a subject for the fax's cover page.

7 Enter any message you want to add to the fax's cover page.

8 Click **Fax**.

End

TIP

What Goes Out Can Come In, Too To receive faxes on your Mac, choose Apple menu, System Preferences and then click Print & Fax. Choose your fax modem from the pick list and click Receive Options. Click the check box labeled Receive faxes on this computer. Then set options for what your Mac is to do when a fax is received. ■

USING A SCANNER

Your scanner is the way to get pictures inside your Mac, whether you need to copy a document, email a photo, or produce a web-ready image of a flat item you're selling at auction online. First, install the scanner and its software according to the instructions that came with it. Then you're ready to get scanning.

Start

1 Double-click **Image Capture** in the Applications folder.

2 Click and drag in the window to select the portion of the image you want to scan.

3 Choose a source type from the **Scan Mode** pop-up menu, and select a document type from the **Document** pop-up menu.

Continued

NOTE

Sticking to the Safe Side You should be conservative in selecting the scan area. If you scan a larger area than you need, you can trim it when you edit the image in Adobe Photoshop or another program. If you don't scan enough, you'll have to rescan the image. ■

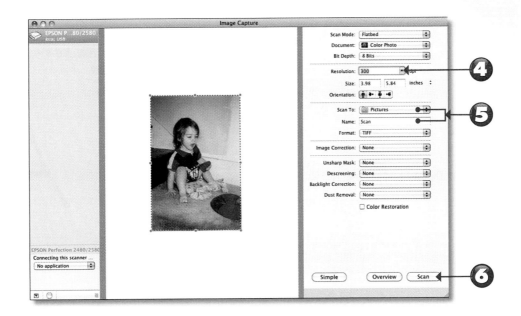

4 Set the **Resolution**.

5 Choose a location for the image file and give it a name.

6 Click **Scan**. The image is saved in the selected folder.

End

TIP

Making It Better If you don't plan to edit your scanned image in an image editor such as Photoshop, you can adjust it using the controls located at the bottom of the dialog box, directly over the Scan button. ■

NOTE

More Scanner Options Click **Options** to change some of the scanner's global settings, such as the resolution at which it makes overview scans and which programs start up when you press the buttons on the front of the scanner. ■

ADDING FONTS

There's no such thing as a font collection that's too big. Don't take that the wrong way—using all the fonts you have in one document is usually a very bad move, design-wise. But having a lot of fonts to choose from when you're creating graphics or printed documents is a luxury that's available to anyone with a Mac. Here's how to install a new font.

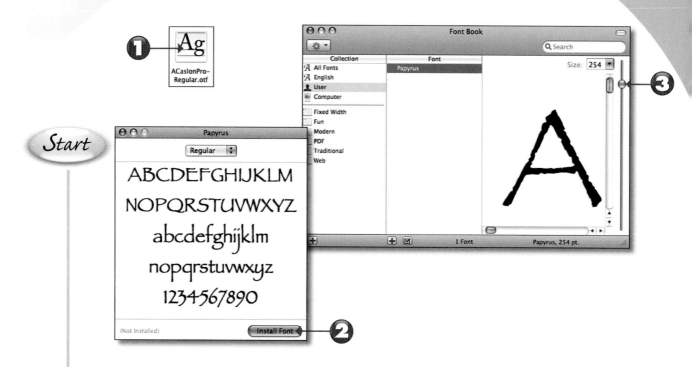

1. Double-click the font's icon. Font Book starts up and displays the font.

2. Click **Install Font**. The font is installed in your home folder's Library folder.

3. Drag the **Size** slider in the Font Book window to preview the font at different sizes.

TIP

Shopping Time Where do fonts come from? One place to start is Apple's Macintosh Products Guide (www.guide.apple.com). Click **Productivity & Utilities** in the left navigation bar on the web page and click **Fonts** from the Sub-category pop-up menu; then click search. ■

ORGANIZING FONTS

If your font collection has been growing, you'll love the capability to group the installed fonts into collections. Collections keep your fonts organized so you can quickly apply the fonts you're using for a given project. Mac OS X comes with a few predefined collections, but feel free to create as many collections as you want.

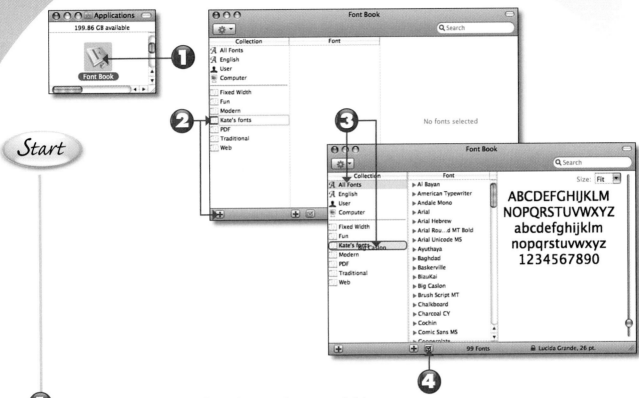

1 Double-click **Font Book** in the Applications folder.

2 Click the + button below the Collection column to create a new collection and then type in a name.

3 Click **All Fonts** in the Collection column and drag a font from the Font column into the new collection.

4 Click a collection name or a font name and click **Disable** to remove that font from the Font panel. If you see a confirmation dialog box, click **Disable** again.

TIP

Putting Fonts Back on the Menu Disabling a font doesn't delete it—you can always return to Font Book, select the font from the All Fonts collection, and click the same button to make the font available again. ∎

GETTING ONLINE

Before you can do anything online, you have to actually get online. Fortunately, with Mac OS X getting online couldn't be easier. In fact, your Mac might have completed some of these tasks for you already based on the information you gave it when you first started up Mac OS X. If not, don't worry—nothing here will take you more than a couple of minutes to complete, and then you'll be ready to go.

In this chapter you learn how to set up an Internet connection and how to get online using those settings. Although the details vary somewhat depending on your connection type, the setup process is similar no matter how you connect. Don't be intimidated by the techie terminology—after you have your settings in place, you won't need to worry about any of the details again. You might need to get some information from your Internet service provider, but if that's the case, you'll receive this information when you sign up with the provider.

You'll also learn about Mail accounts: how to set them up and use them to send and receive email. And you'll learn ways to keep your email spam-free, organized, and easy to deal with—no matter how much email you receive each day. You can even automate some organizational tasks so Mail takes care of them for you, such as filing your email in the proper mailboxes according to sender, recipient, or subject; this chapter shows you how.

SETTING UP AN INTERNET CONNECTION AND YOUR EMAIL

Configure your Mac
to get online, 147

Get rid of
spam, 163

Connect to
your ISP, 150

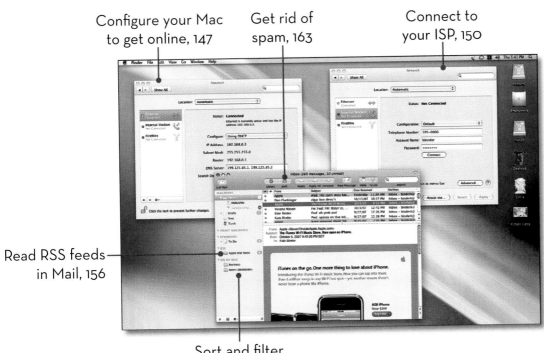

Read RSS feeds
in Mail, 156

Sort and filter
email messages,
161

SETTING UP YOUR CONNECTION

To set up your Internet connection, you'll need to find out a few things from your Internet service provider (ISP): your login name and password, possibly the ISP's DNS (Domain Name System) server addresses, and definitely the preferred configuration method.

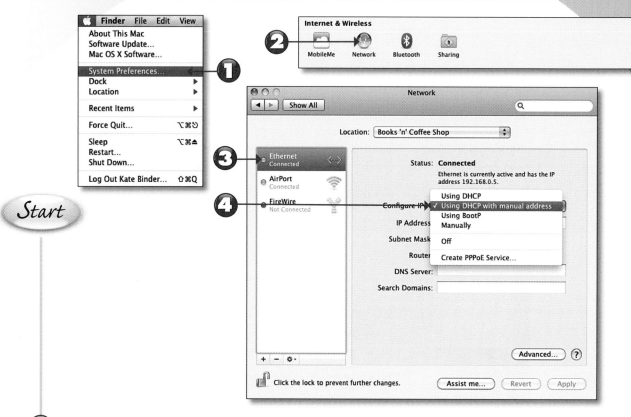

Start

① Choose **Apple menu**, **System Preferences**.

② Click the **Network** button to see your connection settings.

③ Choose your connection type from the column at the left of the window.

④ Choose your ISP's configuration method from the **Configure** pop-up menu: usually **Using PPP** for phone modems, **Manually** for LAN connections, or **Using DHCP** for cable and DSL modems.

Continued

NOTE

Talk to Me Transmission Control Protocol/Internet Protocol (TCP/IP) is the language in which your Mac communicates with the other computers on the Internet. The choices in the Configure IPv4 menu are different ways of setting up a TCP/IP connection. PPP (Point-to-Point Protocol) is used for phone line connections, and DHCP (Dynamic Host Configuration Protocol) is used for broadband connections and internal networks. If your ISP doesn't use DHCP, you need to enter settings manually. ■

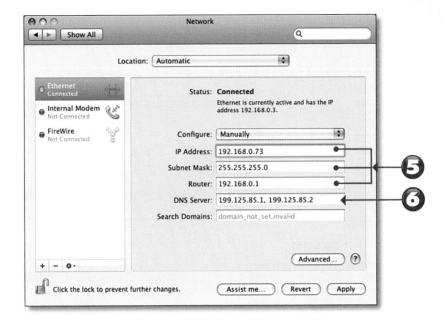

5 If your configuration method is **Manually**, enter your IP address, the subnet mask, and the router address for your network.

6 Enter your ISP's DNS server in the **DNS Server** field.

Continued

NOTE

Getting Help When You Need It If any of these settings don't make sense to you, get in touch with your ISP's tech support people. It's their job to help you make the connection, so stick with it until you have what you need. ■

NOTE

Don't Worry, Be Happy You might notice different tabs in the Network preferences pane, but don't worry. For example, when you're configuring Ethernet, you see PPPoE settings that don't appear when you're configuring a phone modem. ■

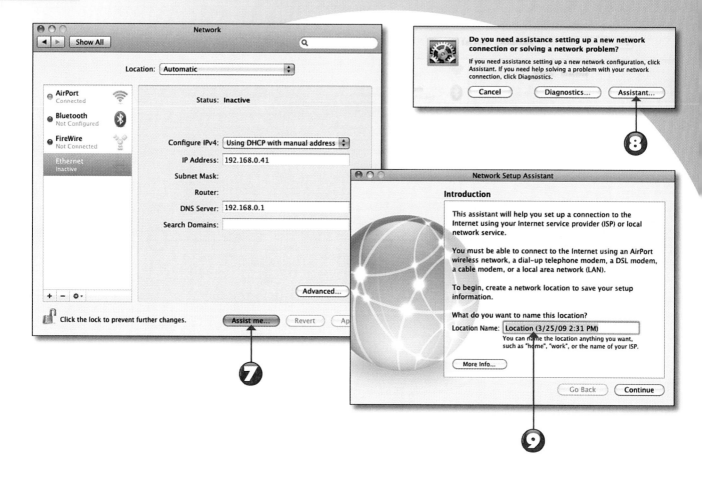

7 Click **Assist Me** if you're having trouble and want your Mac to walk you through the steps to set up your network.

8 Click **Diagnostics** if your existing network settings aren't working; click **Assistant** if you want help making the settings.

9 Follow the remaining steps in the Network Setup Assistant.

End

NOTE

If Your Mac Is a Laptop If you connect using different methods in different places, you should definitely
look into creating custom locations so you don't have to
change all these settings every time you switch connections (see Chapter 5, "Customizing Your Mac"). ■

NOTE

Status Quo After your network settings are in
place, you shouldn't need to change them unless
you buy new hardware (such as a router for Internet connection sharing) or your service provider
changes the way its service is set up. ■

CONNECTING TO YOUR ISP

If you use a phone modem or a DSL modem with PPPoE, you need to initiate a connection when you want to go online. You can store more than one configuration, in case you connect in different ways at home, at work, and on the road. System Preferences always remembers the last connection you made.

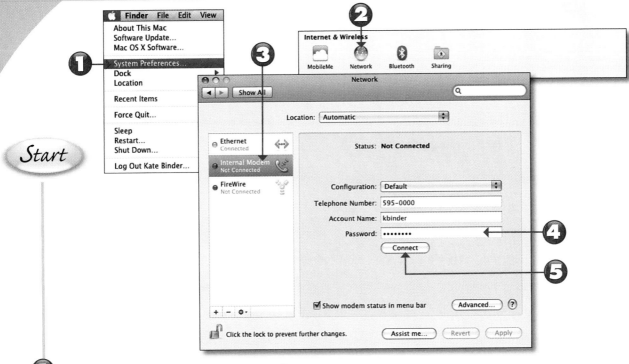

 Choose **Apple Menu**, **System Preferences**.

2 Click the **Network** button to see your correction settings.

3 Click to choose your modem.

4 Type in the connection data, including your username and password.

5 Click **Connect**.

Start

End

TIP

Getting Offline You need to disconnect when you're done surfing and checking your email. Go back to System Preferences and you'll find that the **Connect** button has changed to a **Disconnect** button. Click that and you're offline again. ■

TIP

Status Symbol In System Preferences, check the box labeled **Show modem status in menu bar** to add a Modem Status menu to your menu bar. And in the **Modem Status** menu, choose **Show time connected** to display how long you've been online. ■

SETTING UP EMAIL ACCOUNTS

Setting up new email accounts works the same way whether you're using Mail for the first time or adding an umpteenth different email address for yourself. You'll go through a series of dialog boxes that ask you for your username, password, server names, and other information.

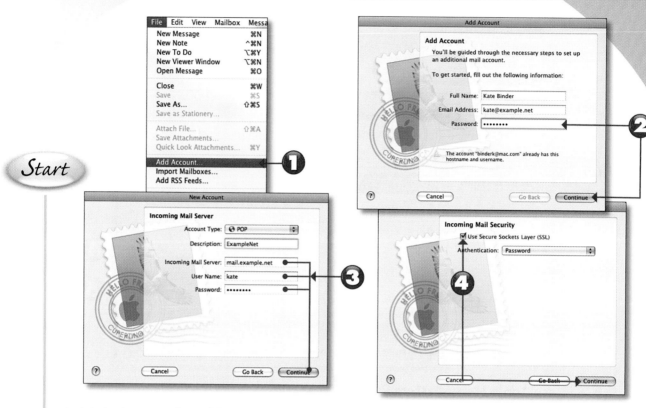

1 In Mail, choose **File**, **Add Account**. (If you're starting Mail for the first time, you're taken directly to this series of dialog boxes.)

2 Fill in your name, email address, and password; then click **Continue**.

3 Type your incoming mail server's address, your username, and your password; then click Continue.

4 Check **Use Secure Sockets Layer (SSL)** (if your provider supports it) and then click **Continue**.

Continued

NOTE

More Fun with Mail Accounts You can set up as many Mail accounts as you have email addresses. Mail automatically filters your incoming email into a separate mailbox for each address, so you can keep your messages organized. ■

TIP

Different, but the Same If you choose **MobileMe** from the Account Type pop-up menu in the first dialog box, your choices will be slightly different. Mail knows how MobileMe is configured, including the server addresses, so it fills in a lot of information itself. ■

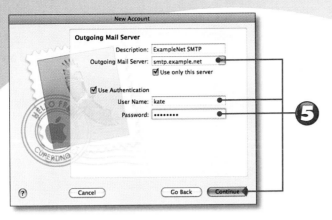

5 Type your outgoing mail server's address and (if necessary) your username and password; then click **Continue**.

6 Check **Use Secure Sockets Layer (SSL)** and then click **Continue**.

7 Double-check the settings you made; click **Go Back** to change them or **Create** to accept them.

End

NOTE

Pop Goes the Email! POP and IMAP, the two Account Type choices that you are most likely to use, refer to the way your email is handled on the server, the computer that receives your email over the Internet and forwards it to your Mac. Most commercial ISPs use POP, but university systems, for example, often use IMAP. If you're not sure which account type your email uses, check with your network administrator or technical support department. ■

SENDING EMAIL WITH MAIL

The steps given here assume that you're composing a new message. If you click a received message in one of your mailboxes, you'll see toolbar buttons for replying and forwarding; just click the appropriate button and then add your message text and an email address if you're forwarding the message.

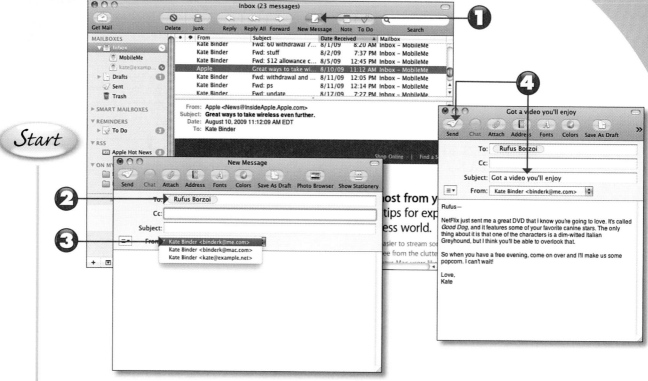

Start

End

1 Click the **New Message** button in the toolbar.

2 Type the name of the person you want to email. If the email address doesn't appear automatically, type the email address in angle brackets after the name.

3 If you've set up multiple email accounts, choose the one from which you want to send in the **From** pop-up menu.

4 Type a subject in the **Subject** line and your message in the message area. Click **Send**.

TIP

Jazzing Up Your Emails To attach a file, click the **Attach** button in the toolbar and navigate to the file you want to attach. To make your email text colored, click the **Colors** button and choose a color in the Colors panel. ■

RECEIVING EMAIL WITH MAIL

There's nothing quite like that friendly chime (or beep, or other sound) from your computer indicating that you, yes you, have email. By default, Mail drops all of your new, unread email into your In Box each time you check for new messages.

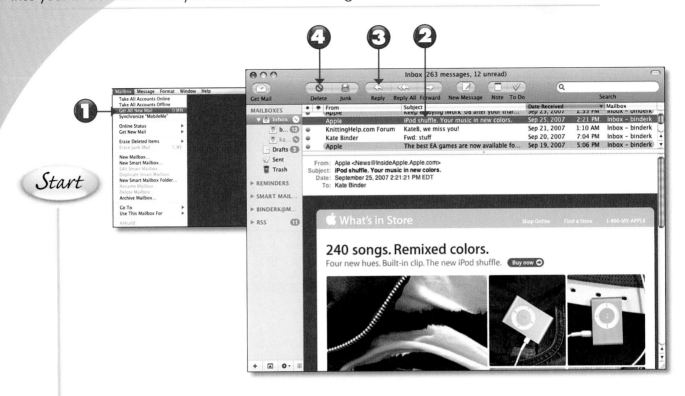

Start

1. Choose **Mailbox**, **Get All New Mail**.

2. Click a message listing in the In Box to see the message's contents.

3. Click **Reply** to answer the current message.

4. Click **Delete** if you want to send the message to the Trash.

End

TIP

I've Got Mail? Mail can retrieve your email messages automatically on a schedule you determine. Choose **Mail**, **Preferences** and click **General**. Choose a time interval from the **Check for New Mail** pop-up menu. ■

TIP

More Ways to Reply To answer an email message, click **Reply** to send your answer to just the original sender. Click **Reply All** to send it to everyone who originally received the email. And click **Forward** to send it to another recipient. ■

USING STATIONERY TEMPLATES

Email is a lot more than just text these days. Yes, back in the day, your geek IQ was measured by the complexity of the ASCII art in your mail signature, but we've moved on. Now, with beautifully designed stationery templates, Mail makes it easy for you to turn your emails into 21st-century masterpieces.

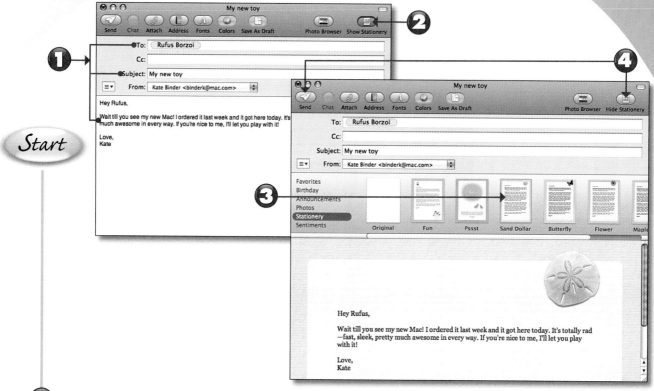

Start

End

1 In Mail, enter the subject of your message; then address and compose it.

2 Click the **Show Stationery** button.

3 Click the stationery template you want to use.

4 Click the **Hide Stationery** button and send your message.

TIP

Over and Over and Over If you find yourself using the same stationery template a lot, drag it into the Favorites category, which will show up first each time you click the **Show Stationery** button. ■

TIP

The Order of Things If you don't compose your email message before choosing a stationery template, you'll find that Mail has inserted placeholder text into your message area. To get rid of it, select the text and type your own text over it. ■

SUBSCRIBING TO RSS FEEDS IN MAIL

RSS is a technology for putting website content wherever you want it: on your screensaver, in your Dock, or even in Mail. If you check a particular website frequently for updates, try subscribing to its RSS feed so you can keep an eye on the site without having to switch to your web browser every few minutes.

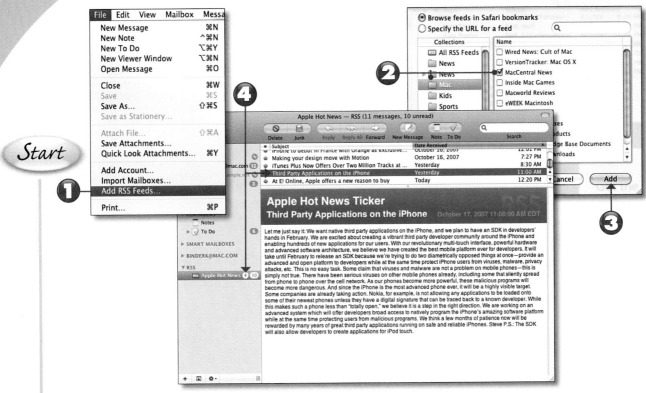

Start

1. In Mail, choose **File**, **Add RSS Feeds**.

2. Click a category on the left; then choose the feeds to which you want to subscribe.

3. Click **Add**.

4. In your new RSS mailbox, click an RSS message to read it.

End

TIP

Feeding Yourself If the feed you want isn't listed, it's easy enough to add it. In Step 2, click and enter the URL for the feed you want. This information should be located on the site's home page. ■

TIP

A Word to the Wise When you're choosing RSS feeds, check the **Show in Inbox** box if you want to be sure you see all messages from a feed right away. Be warned, though—your Inbox may soon be chock-full of RSS messages. ■

ORGANIZING MAILBOXES

If you get a lot of email, you'll quickly find your Inbox filling up. Creating a system of mailboxes in which you can file all that email will save you time in the long run because it makes finding what you want when you need it easier. You can nest mailboxes within other mailboxes to set up as complex a system as you need.

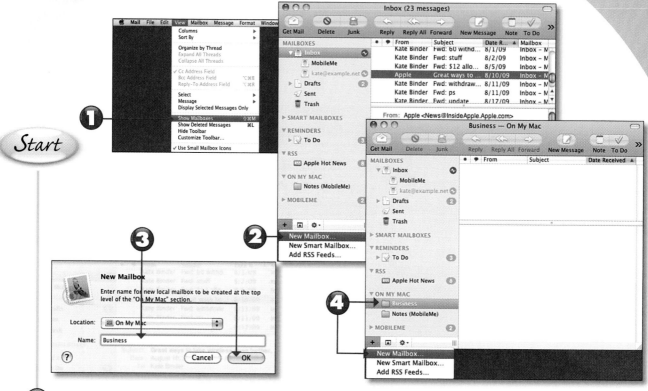

Start

1 In Mail, select **View**, **Show Mailboxes** if mailboxes are not visible.

2 Click the + button at the bottom-left corner of the window to create a new mailbox.

3 Enter a name for the mailbox and click **OK**.

4 To create a mailbox inside another mailbox, click a mailbox name and then click the + button.

Continued

TIP

Like Parent, Like Child If a mailbox is selected when you click the + button, the new mailbox is created as a child of the selected mailbox—in other words, it is within the selected one. ■

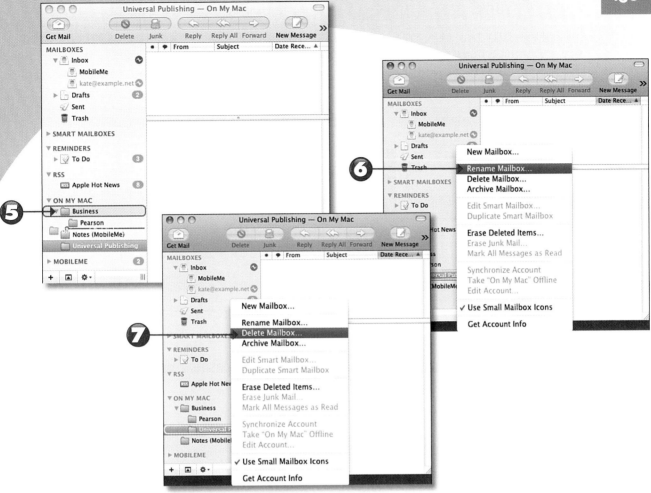

5 To move a mailbox inside another mailbox, drag and drop it into position.

6 Control-click a mailbox and choose **Rename Mailbox** from the contextual menu to change its name.

7 Control-click a mailbox and choose **Delete Mailbox** from the contextual menu to remove it.

End

NOTE

You Can't Go There You can't add mailboxes inside the default mailboxes (In, Out, Drafts, and Sent). However, Mail automatically creates mailboxes within your Inbox to segregate mail received at different email addresses. ■

TIP

Another Way to Get There The same commands you see in the contextual menu are available in the Action menu at the bottom of the Mailbox drawer—click the gear button to see the menu. ■

CREATING A SMART MAILBOX

Like smart groups in Address Book, smart mailboxes in Mail are maintained by your Mac. After you determine the criteria for a message's inclusion in a smart mailbox, the Mac takes over to sort messages into that mailbox as you receive new mail. Because messages can exist in both a regular mailbox and a smart mailbox, smart mailboxes don't interfere with your usual filing scheme.

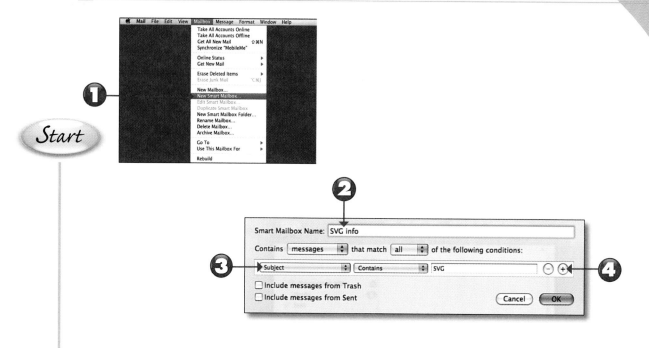

1. Choose **Mailbox**, **New Smart Mailbox**.

2. Type a name for the mailbox.

3. Choose criteria for which messages should be sorted into the mailbox.

4. Click + to add more criteria.

Continued

NOTE

What's It Good For? Use smart mailboxes to track messages related to a particular project or from people who share a company or ISP. For example, you can have Mail sort all messages about your upcoming Flamingo Party into a smart mailbox. ■

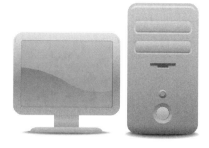

60

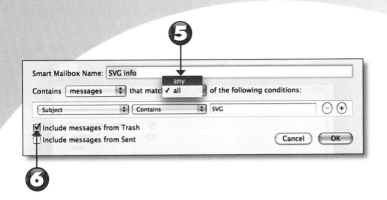

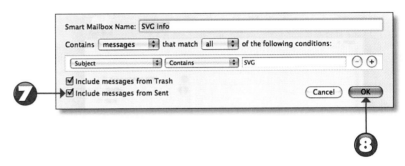

5 Select **any** or **all** from the pop-up menu to determine whether messages must meet all the criteria or any single criterion.

6 Click the box labeled **Include messages from Trash** to file messages that are in the Trash folder.

7 Click the box labeled **Include messages from Sent** to file messages you send along with ones you receive.

8 Click **OK** to create the smart mailbox.

End

TIP

Any or All Use **any** to collect messages that fulfill one criterion or another (if the subject contains "Paris" or "Grand Canyon," file it under Vacation Plans). Use **all** to collect messages that fulfill both criteria (if the message sender's name is "Claus" and the email address contains "northpole.com," file it under Christmas). ∎

FILTERING EMAIL IN MAIL

The more email you get, the more you'll appreciate having Mail help you with the filing. Mail can analyze each message you receive based on who sent it, where it was addressed, what it says, or several other criteria, and it can file that message in the appropriate mailbox. Mailboxes with unread messages are shown in bold type.

Start

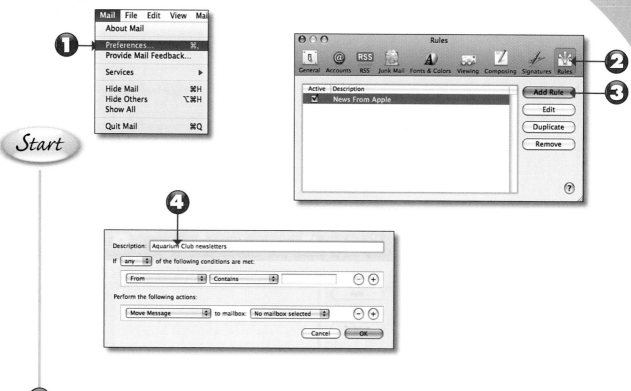

1 In Mail, choose **Mail**, **Preferences**.

2 Click the **Rules** button to see the filtering options.

3 Click **Add Rule**.

4 Give the rule a name in the **Description** field.

Continued

TIP

Excluding Messages from Rules You can make a set of rules that acts on all email messages but a particular group. First, create a rule that filters the group you don't want to act on into the Trash or a mailbox. Then create another rule to apply your action to Every Message; this rule acts on all the messages remaining after the first rule is executed. ◼

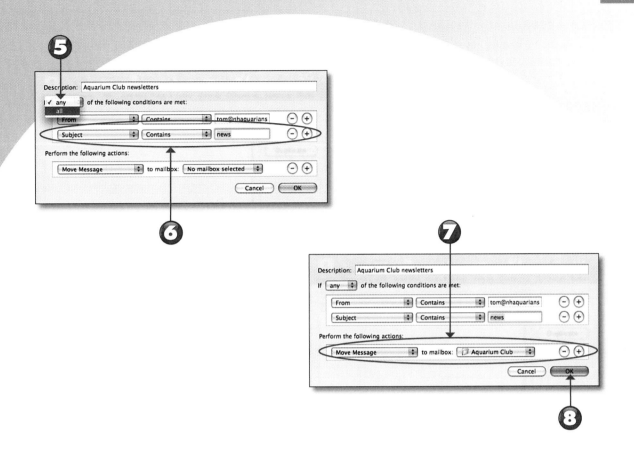

5 Choose **any** or **all** from the pop-up menu; with any, the rule is activated if one or more condition is met, and with all it's activated only if they're all met.

6 Set up the condition you want to filter on; click the **+** button to add more conditions.

7 Set up the action to be invoked if the conditions are met; click the **+** button to add more actions.

8 Click **OK**.

End

TIP

Explore Your Options There are many ways to select messages for special treatment. You can tag all messages sent to a particular address with a red label, or you can put messages from anyone in an Address Book group into a specific mailbox. ■

TIP

Watching for Rule Interactions The last action step in most rules should be Stop evaluating rules. That way, a message properly filed according to one rule won't be refiled by another. You can also drag and drop rules to change the order they're executed in. ■

INTERCEPTING SPAM IN MAIL

Spam (or junk mail or unsolicited commercial email) is everywhere, and it's increasing by the moment. Email users are constantly looking for new ways to deal with the deluge, and Apple has done its part by including a built-in, smart junk mail filter in Mail. With your help, the filter learns to better recognize spam day by day.

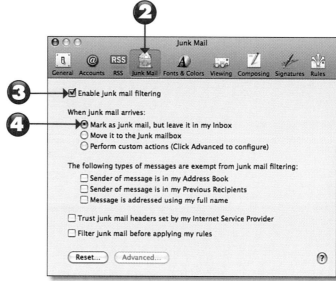

Start

1. In Mail, choose **Mail**, **Preferences**.

2. Click the **Junk Mail** button to see the spam options.

3. Click the **Enable junk mail filtering** check box.

4. Click a radio button to tell Mail what to do with junk mail it receives.

Continued

NOTE

How Does It Work? Mail recognizes junk mail using what Apple calls "latent adaptive semantic analysis." The program scans email messages for certain word patterns—not typical spam keywords such as "make money," but speech patterns spammers tend to use. ∎

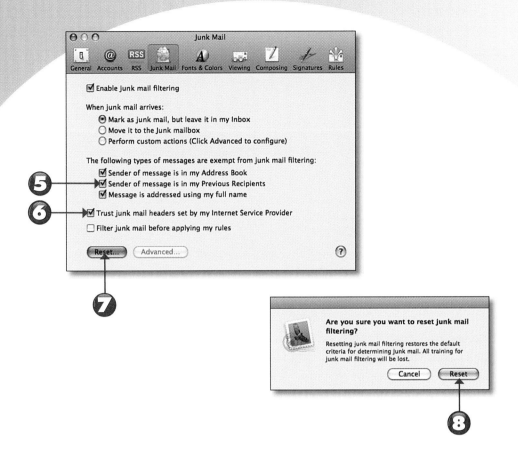

5 Click the check boxes to indicate which types of email shouldn't be considered spam.

6 Click the check box to take advantage of junk mail prefiltering done by your ISP.

7 If you want to make Mail forget the list of known junk mail senders and subjects it has compiled, click **Reset**.

8 Click **Reset** again to confirm that you want Mail to forget its list of junk mail senders and subjects.

End

TIP

Teaching Mail More About Spam Mail marks junk mail with a brown label. If a message is brown but isn't spam, click it and choose **Message, Mark As Not Junk Mail**. If you get spam that's not labeled brown, choose **Message, Mark As Junk Mail**. ■

TIP

Where to Put Spam To put all your junk mail in a special mailbox, choose **Mail, Preferences** and click **Junk Mail**. Click **Move it to the Junk mailbox (Automatic)**. You can get rid of all the spam you've received by choosing **Mailbox, Erase Junk Mail**. ■

LIVING ONLINE

So much of modern life happens online. Despite some people's complaints that a sense of community is disappearing from our society, it's thriving on the Internet. That's what the Internet is all about—a network of people sharing a network of information—and your Mac is your passport to that network.

In this chapter you learn how to set up iChat and begin exchanging messages with others. iChat works with AOL, .Mac, and Jabber screen names, but if you don't have a screen name already you'll learn how to create one for free. With iChat, you can set up your own chat rooms in which multiple people can exchange messages; in this chapter you also learn how to create a chat room and how to take advantage of iChat's video and audio chat features to actually talk with your buddies or even see them over a video feed. For those features, of course, your Mac must have a microphone and a webcam (a small digital video camera).

Other tasks introduce you to surfing the web with Apple's very own web browser, Safari—a fast, compact browser that you'll quickly learn to love. You'll learn how to create bookmarks and use the History so you can return to your favorite sites, as well as how to keep those bookmarks organized and accessible. And you'll see how to download files, view RSS feeds, save a Safari web page, and enable Safari to automatically fill out web forms for you—a great time-saving feature if you do a lot of online shopping.

HANGING OUT ON THE NET

Control kids'
computer use, 195

Use tabbed
browsing, 189

Surf the web
with Safari, 181

Chat online
with iChat, 171

Edit your
buddy list, 169

SETTING UP AN ICHAT ACCOUNT

iChat works with either your MobileMe username or an America Online Instant Messenger (AIM) screen name. If you don't have either, get a AIM screen name—it's free. The steps below walk you through getting a screen name and then entering your name and password in iChat so you can get online and start chatting.

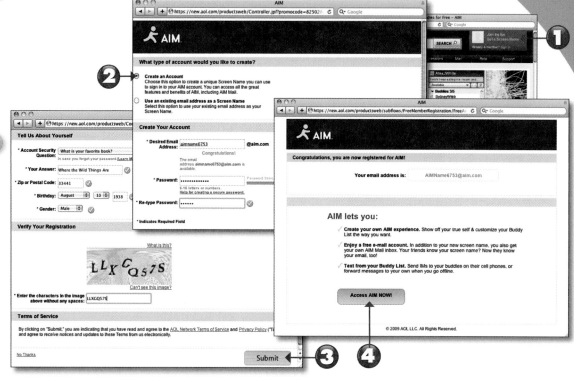

① If you need to get an AIM screen name, go to the AIM website (www.aim.com). Click the **Get a Screen Name** link.

② Click **Create an Account** and enter the screen name and password that you want to use.

③ Enter the rest of the requested information and click **Submit**.

④ Click **Access AIM NOW!** below the Congratulations! message.

Continued

TIP

Chat This iChat's not just for chatting—you can use iChat to transfer files as well. Click a person in your buddy list and choose Buddies, Send File to open a dialog box where you can choose the file. ◼

NOTE

What's in a Name? When choosing a screen name, think about how you want to appear. If you'll be using iChat with clients and colleagues, you probably don't want to choose "FluffyBunny." And if you'll be chatting mainly with friends, "AcmeInc" isn't the best choice. ◼

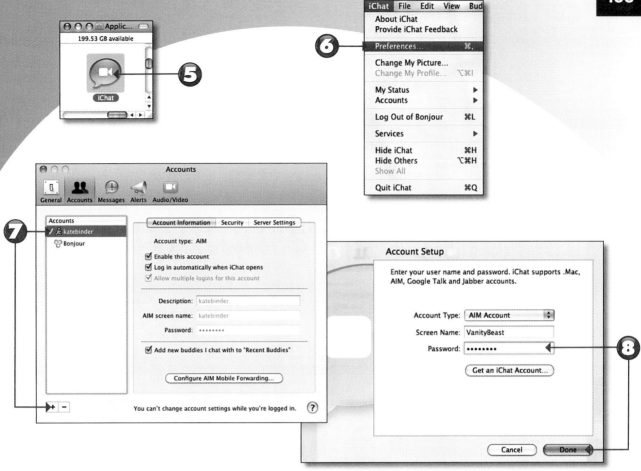

168

5 Double-click the **iChat** icon in your Applications folder.

6 Choose **iChat**, **Preferences**.

7 Click the **Accounts** button, and then click the **Add** button.

8 Choose **AIM Account**, and then enter your AIM screen name and password. Click **Done** to save your changes.

End

TIP

Chatting on the Menu Choose **iChat, Preferences** and click the **General** button to enter global iChat settings. The most useful one is **Show status in menu bar**, which enables you to start a chat with an online member of your buddy list without even starting up iChat first. ■

NOTE

First Time for Everything If it's the first time iChat has been started on your Mac, you'll see a series of dialog boxes in which you can enter your screen name and password. ■

EDITING YOUR ICHAT BUDDY LIST

If iChat finds your buddies' screen names in your Address Book, it can attach their real names to them and display those in the Buddy List window. The most convenient thing you can do with the buddy list is set it to show only buddies who are online at the moment.

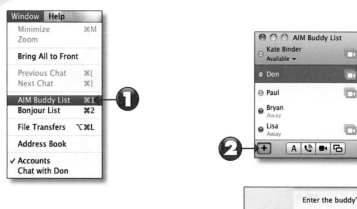

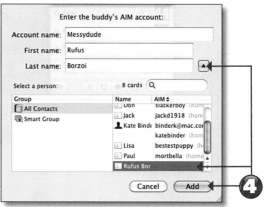

Start

1. Choose **Window**, **AIM Buddy List** (or the name of your AIM account).

2. To add a buddy, click the **+** button.

3. To create a new listing, enter the contact's name and screen name and click **Add**.

4. If the person is already in your Address Book, click the reveal arrow, choose a listing, and click **Add**.

Continued

TIP

Nice to Meet You If you're adding a completely new person to your buddy list, you must enter the screen name. If you want, you can also add the person's first and last name and email address. When you're done, click Add. ■

TIP

Bye-Bye To remove a buddy, click to select the name and choose **Buddies, Remove Buddy**. ■

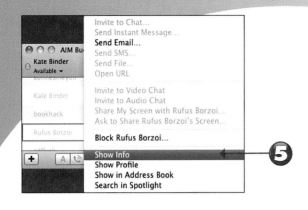

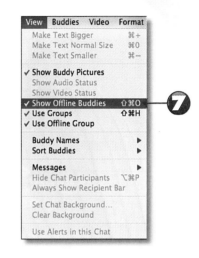

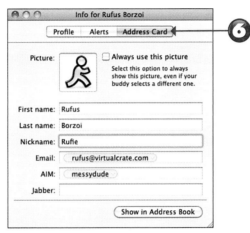

To change a buddy's screen name or other information, **Control-click** the name and choose **Show Info** from the contextual menu.

Click the **Address Card** tab and make your changes.

To show only buddies who are currently online, choose **View**, **Show Offline Buddies** to remove the check mark next to it.

End

TIP

Everything's in Order   You're also in control of the order in which your buddies are displayed in the Buddy List window. Choose a **Sort Buddies** option from the **View** menu: **By Availability, By First Name, By Last Name,** or **Manually**. ■

MESSAGING WITH ICHAT

Chatting with iChat requires two things: You must sign on to AIM with iChat and you must know the screen name of the person you want to reach. Conveniently enough, your buddy list is stored on AOL's servers, so it follows you around—you'll always see your own buddy list even if you log in on a computer other than your own.

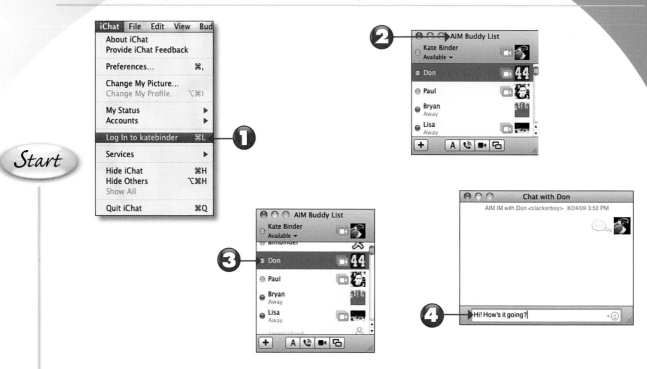

Start

End

① Open iChat from the Applications folder and (if not already logged in) choose **iChat**, **Log In to AIM** (or the name of your AIM account).

② Choose **Window**, **AIM Buddy List** (or the name of your AIM account) if your buddy list isn't visible.

③ Double-click the name or screen name of the person to whom you want to send an instant message.

④ Type your message at the bottom of the message window and press **Return** to send the message.

NOTE

On the Record You can save transcripts of iChat conversations: Choose **iChat, Preferences** and click the **Messages** button. **Click Save chat transcripts to**; then choose a folder from the pop-up menu. ■

TIP

A Two-Way Street You don't have to be an AOL member to use iChat. Whether you use an AOL screen name or a MobileMe screen name, iChat works the same. However, you can use an AOL screen name with AOL Instant Messenger, but you can't use a MobileMe name with AIM. ■

TALKING OVER THE INTERNET IN ICHAT

With iChat and a microphone, you can enjoy voice conversations over the Net with anyone similarly equipped. All MacBooks have built-in microphones, and mics for other Macs are very inexpensive—so it's time to say hello to iChat and goodbye to your long-distance phone bill.

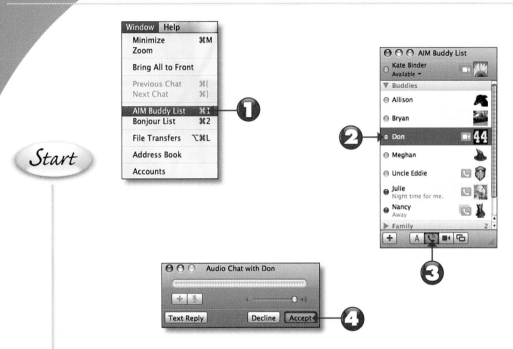

Start

① In iChat, choose your buddy list from the Window menu if your buddy list isn't visible

② Click the name or screen name of the person to whom you want to talk; a phone icon tells you that person has audio capabilities, and a movie camera icon indicates someone who has both audio and video capabilities.

③ Click the **Start Audio Chat** button at the bottom of the Buddy List window.

④ If you receive an audio chat invitation, click **Accept** to begin the conversation.

End

NOTE

Going One Way If the person you want to talk to has iChat but no microphone, you can still have one-way audio along with two-way text. This feature is great for calling up your microphone-less friends via iChat and singing "Happy Birthday" to them. ■

NOTE

One-Way Street What if you have a camera and your friend doesn't, or vice versa? Well, you can still do video chat with iChat—just one-way. Hey, it's better than nothing! ■

HOLDING A VIDEOCONFERENCE

Who needs a videophone? You don't—you have your Mac. If you also have a high-speed Internet connection and a webcam, you're good to go. First, make sure your camera is plugged in to your Mac and working correctly. Then check your iChat preferences to ensure that iChat realizes the camera is there.

Start

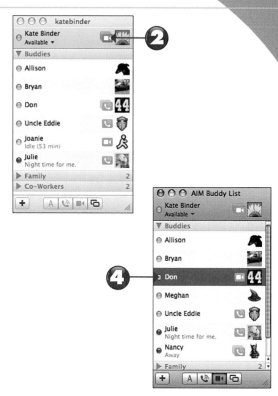

(1) In iChat, choose **Window**, **AIM Buddy List** if your buddy list isn't visible.

(2) Click the **camera** button next to your own icon.

(3) Looking at the preview window, adjust your camera angle and height until you're happy with your appearance.

(4) Click the name or screen name of the person to whom you want to talk.

Continued

TIP

In a Rush? A quicker way to begin a videoconference is to click the camera button next to the name of the person with whom you want to chat. You can start an audio chat session quickly by clicking the microphone button next to a buddy's name. ■

TIP

Let's Have a Party To conference with multiple people, ⌘+click to select their names in the Buddy List window; then click the **Start Video Chat** button. To add a participant during a chat, click the + button in the chat window. ■

5 Click the **Start Video Chat** button at the bottom of the Buddy List window.

6 The video window opens and you can see yourself; when your buddy answers, you can see both your buddy and yourself in the window.

7 Click the **Full Screen** button to expand the window to fill your screen.

8 Click the **Mute** button to freeze the video and mute the audio of yourself.

End

TIP

Knock Knock If someone initiates a video or audio chat with you, you see a dialog box telling you so. As soon as you've combed your hair, you can click **Accept** to begin chatting. ■

NOTE

No Webcam? No Worries If you haven't got a webcam but you do have a digital camcorder, you can use that instead. You'll find a small tripod helpful in positioning the camera so it can "see" your face; try looking for one at the dollar store. ■

APPLYING SPECIAL VIDEO EFFECTS

This isn't your father's iChat, that's for sure. These days, video chats can make use of some of the same special effects found in Photo Booth (turn to "Applying Fun Photo Effects" in Chapter 10 to learn more). As long as you and the people you're chatting with are all using Leopard or Snow Leopard, you can go to town with these cool effects.

1. In your iChat buddy list, click the **camera** button next to a buddy's name to begin a video chat.

2. Click **Effects** to open the Video Effects window.

3. Click the arrows to scroll through the different effects that you can use.

4. Click the thumbnail of an effect to apply it to your video image.

TIP

Don't Overdo It Using special effects takes a lot of processing power, and even more when more than one chat participant is using effects. If your video gets slow and jerky, or parts of the picture are dropping out, try removing the effects for better performance. ■

5 Click the **Original** thumbnail to remove the video effect from your image.

End

NOTE

Special FX Video effects only work if all the participants in a chat are using Leopard or Snow Leopard. If that's not the case, you can try a little third-party program called ChatFX (www.scriptsoftware.com). It's a $20 shareware that offers even more features than the video effects you see here, such as the ability to replace your background with a video in a chat window. ■

GIVING A PRESENTATION OVER ICHAT

Instant messaging is cool, true. Video chat is even cooler. And when you want to show off a file on your Mac to someone you're chatting with, you can now use the ultimate cool iChat feature: iChat Theater. You'll be able to run photo slideshows, flip through documents, play videos, and more, all visible to both you and anyone you're chatting with.

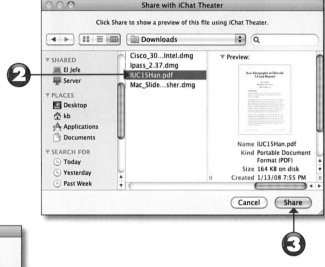

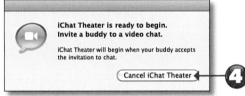

Start

1 In iChat, choose **File**, **Share a File With iChat Theater**.

2 Choose the file you want to show.

3 Click **Share**.

4 A dialog box tells you to begin a video chat.

Continued

NOTE

Just a Quick Look iChat Theater works with any file that you can view using Quick Look in the Finder (see "Previewing a File," in Chapter 2). So if you want to see how a file will look in iChat Theater, try it out using Quick Look first. ■

TIP

Take a Look at This If you want to present an iPhoto album as a slide show, choose **File, Share iPhoto With iChat Theater** in step 1. ■

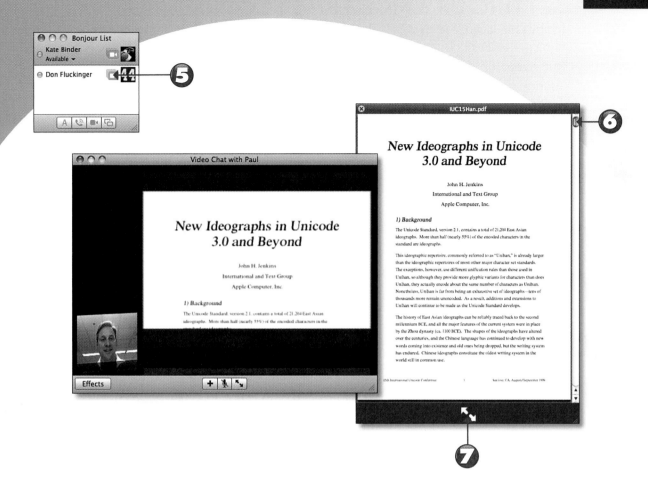

5 Click the **Video Chat** button next to a buddy's name in the Buddy List.

6 When the presentation begins, use the Quick Look window to navigate through the file you're sharing.

7 Click the **Full Screen** button to view the file on the entire screen.

End

NOTE

Skipping a Step If you already have a video chat going, you won't see the dialog box in step 4—instead, your presentation will start immediately. And if you're really in a hurry, you can bypass the File menu and start the presentation by simply dragging the file you want to show into the video chat window. ■

SETTING UP A MOBILEME ACCOUNT

MobileMe is Apple's own set of web services, including email, a custom website, online storage space (iDisk), and more. It costs $99 per year, but the first two months are free—so why not give it a try? Many MobileMe services are accessible directly from your Mac desktop—such as file storage on your iDisk—and others are based on the MobileMe website.

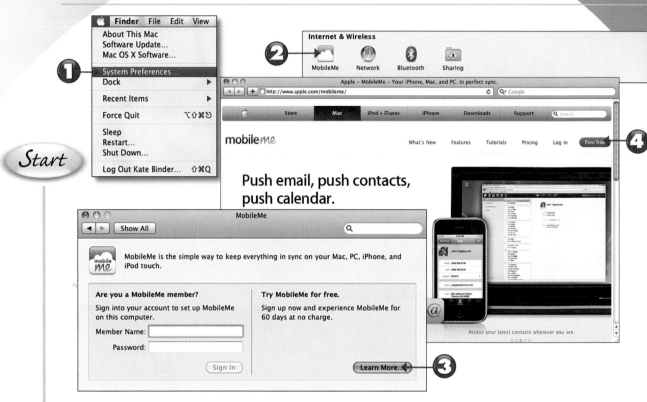

Push email, push contacts, push calendar.

1 Choose **Apple menu**, **System Preferences**.

2 Click the **MobileMe** button to open the MobileMe preferences.

3 Click **Learn More** to go to the MobileMe web page.

4 Click **Free Trial** to see the sign-up page.

Continued

NOTE

What's an iDisk? An iDisk is your hard drive on the Internet. It's storage space on an Apple server that belongs just to you. You can use it to store pictures for your MobileMe web page, for backing up your important files, or to hold anything you want. ■

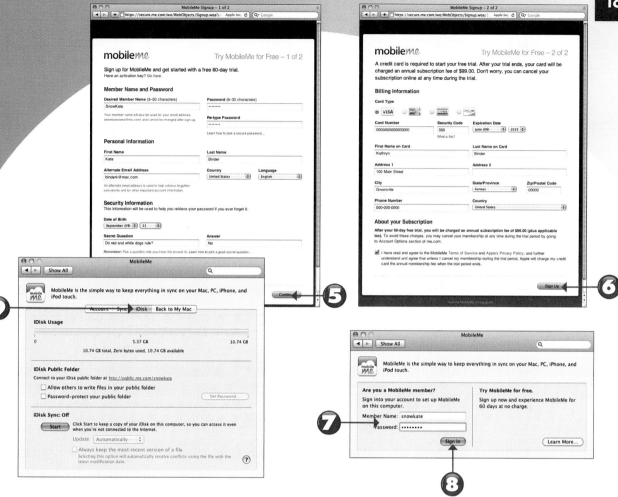

5 Enter the requested information and click **Continue**.

6 Enter your credit card information and click Sign Up.

7 Make a note of your account settings; then return to System Preferences and enter your new MobileMe username and password.

8 Click the **Sign In** button.

9 Click the **iDisk** tab, and then click Start to create a copy of your iDisk on your hard drive.

End

TIP

I Just Don't Remember If you've forgotten your MobileMe password, go to the MobileMe website (www.me.com) and click **Forget password**, then follow the directions to get your password back. ■

NOTE

Why a Local Copy? If you don't feel like waiting around on your online iDisk, you can rearrange a local copy of your iDisk instead; then your Mac updates the real iDisk later. If you're short on disk space, turn off this option. ■

SURFING IN SAFARI

For many years, Mac web surfers had a simple choice of web browsers: Netscape or Internet Explorer. Then Apple trumped everyone with its very own, Mac-only browser, Safari. It's fast, it's smooth, and—best of all—it's designed from the ground up to work the way a Mac should.

Start

1. Start up Safari (in the Applications folder).

2. Click a link on your home page to go to another page.

3. Choose **View**, **Show Toolbar** if the toolbar isn't already visible.

4. Type the URL in the address field on the toolbar for the site you want to visit.

Continued

TIP

Two for the Price of One If you want to view a new web page without getting rid of the one you're looking at now, press ⌘-**N** or choose **File, New Window** to begin surfing in a new window while leaving the current window open in the background. ■

Click the **Previous Page** and **Next Page** buttons to go back and forward through the web pages you've visited.

Click **Reload** to have Safari redisplay the page from scratch; this is how you can update pages that change every few minutes, such as online auction listings.

Type search terms in the **Google Search** field and press **Return** to go to the Google site and initiate the search.

End

TIP

Checking Your Status Safari's Status bar shows you when it's contacting a web server, and it shows you the address behind any link you hold the mouse cursor over. To see the Status bar, choose **View, Show Status Bar**. ■

MAKING A BOOKMARK IN SAFARI

Whether you're used to calling them *bookmarks* or *favorites*, they mean the same thing: Your web browser notes a website's address so it can get you there again the next time you ask for that page. Bookmarks have two components: the web address (called a *URL*) and a name.

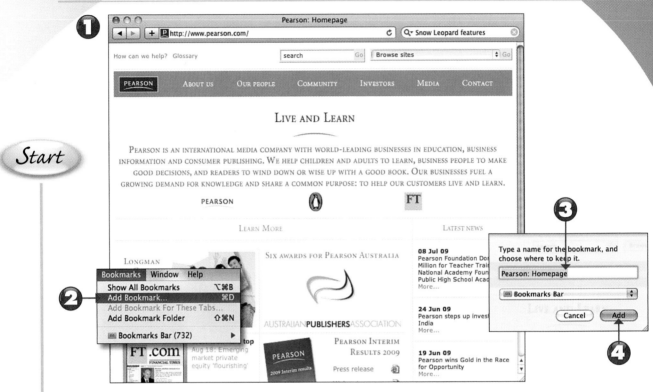

Open Safari (in the Applications folder) and go to the site for which you want to create a bookmark.

Choose **Bookmarks**, **Add Bookmark** (or press ⌘-**D**).

Enter a name for the bookmark (the page title is inserted by default) and choose a location for it.

Click **Add**.

TIP

Bookmarks Here, There, and Over There Safari stores bookmarks in three places: the Bookmarks menu, the Bookmarks bar, and its main Bookmarks collection. If you create a bookmark but don't put it in the Bookmarks menu or bar, go to your Bookmarks collection to find the bookmark. To see your Bookmarks collection, click the **Bookmarks** button on the Bookmarks bar or choose **Bookmarks, Show All Bookmarks**. ■

VIEWING AN RSS FEED

RSS stands for "really simple syndication," and it's an easy way for news organizations, bloggers, and others to offer a constantly updated stream of content. Safari can display RSS feeds for any website that offers one—you can tell by the RSS button next to the site's web address.

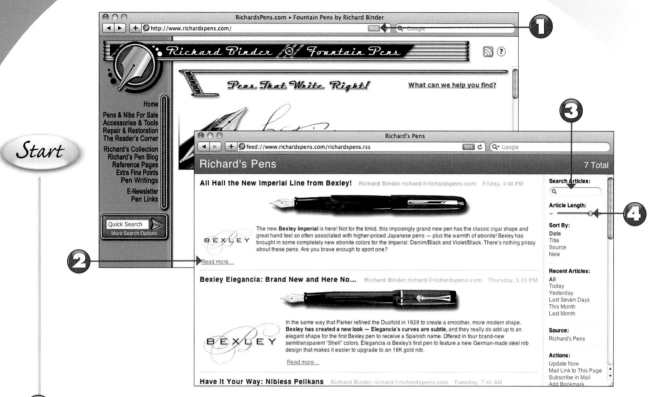

1 Click the **RSS** button to see the site's RSS feed.

2 Click **Read More** to see the rest of an article if it's not all visible.

3 Type words in the **Search Articles** field to search for those terms in the site's RSS articles.

4 Drag the slider to determine how much of each article shows in the window.

TIP

That's the Way I Like It You can further customize your RSS display by choosing a different Sort By option (Date is the default) and by choosing which articles to view (All is the default). ■

TIP

Time and Again When you have a feed's settings just the way you like them—including article length and sort order—you can bookmark it so that when you return, the display will be just the same. Click **Add Bookmark** under Actions. ■

ORGANIZING BOOKMARKS

Some people never bookmark anything. Others are sensible enough to bookmark only sites they know they'll need again. And still others—naming no names here—bookmark just about everything. If you're in that third group, chances are you could stand to spend some time organizing your bookmarks.

Start

① Choose **Bookmarks**, **Show All Bookmarks** (or click the **Bookmarks** button in the Bookmarks bar).

② Click a collection in the **Collections** column to see the bookmarks it contains.

③ Drag bookmarks up or down to change their order.

④ Click a bookmark and press **Delete** to remove it.

Continued

NOTE

More Bookmarks You can fit a lot more bookmarks in the Bookmarks bar by using submenus. Create a folder for each bookmark category, and then drop your bookmarks inside. Back in the main window, click a category name to see the submenu of bookmarks. ■

5 To add a bookmark to the Bookmarks bar, drag it into the **Bookmarks Bar** collection.

6 To add a bookmark to the Bookmarks menu, drag it into the **Bookmarks Menu** collection.

7 To add a submenu to the Bookmarks menu, add a folder by clicking the **Add** button, give it a name, and then drag bookmarks into the folder.

8 To change the name of a bookmark or folder, click it again, type the new name, and press **Return**.

End

TIP

More Address Book Integration If you keep your contacts' website URLs in the Address Book, you can add them to the Bookmarks bar or menu automatically. Choose **Safari, Preferences** and click the **Bookmarks** button; then click the appropriate check box to add Address Book items. ■

USING THE HISTORY IN SAFARI

Safari's History listing is just what you need when you need to go back to a website you visited recently but forgot to bookmark. It keeps track of the last several days of your surfing exploits, neatly listing the websites you visited in folders labeled by date.

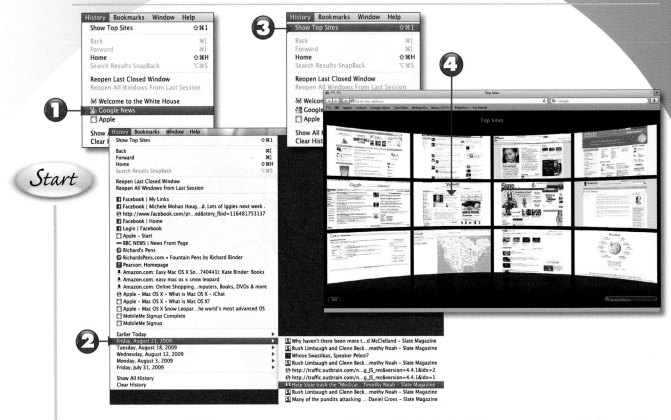

1. To return to one of the pages you've visited recently, click the **History** menu in Safari and choose the page's name.

2. To go back to an earlier page, click the **History** menu and choose the appropriate submenu; then choose the page's name.

3. Choose **History, Show Top Sites** to see thumbnails of the sites you visit most often.

4. Click a thumbnail to visit that site.

End

TIP

A Fresh Start for History If you've been surfing a lot and you're finding the History list a bit too crowded to let you find what you want, choose **History, Clear History** to start over with a blank History. ■

TIP

Automatic SnapBack When you use Safari's Google search field, search results are automatically marked for SnapBack. After clicking to view a page in the results, click the orange **SnapBack** button in the search field to return to that page. ■

AUTOMATICALLY FILLING OUT FORMS

Every time you buy something from a web store, create a new account with a website, or sign up to receive some service from a website, you have to input the same information. Wouldn't it be nice if Safari could remember that information and type it in for you? Guess what? It can.

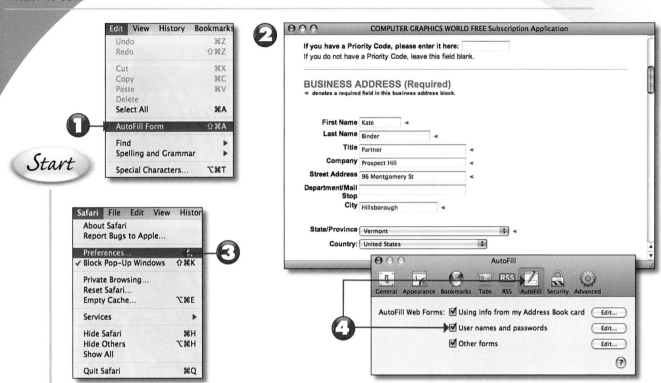

Start

1 On a page with a form that requires this information, choose **Edit**, **AutoFill Form** (or press ⌘-**Shift-A**).

2 The information is automatically filled in.

3 To enable AutoFill to work with other types of forms, choose **Safari**, **Preferences**.

4 Click the **AutoFill** button and check **User names and passwords** and **Other forms**.

End

TIP
When Safari Gets It Wrong Safari tints the fields yellow where it's inserted information. If Safari guesses wrong and inserts incorrect data, just click in the field and type the correct information to fix it. ■

NOTE
First Things First Before using AutoFill, make sure your address, phone numbers, fax number, and other information are correct in your Address Book (which you'll find in the Applications folder). ■

USING TABBED BROWSER WINDOWS

Neatniks will love this feature. If you like to flip from one web page to another and back again, here's how you can keep from cluttering up your screen with a zillion Safari windows: tabs. Keep all your pages open in one window, and move from one to another by just clicking the tab at the top of the window.

Start

① To create a new tab in the current window, choose **File, New Tab**.

② Enter the address for the new page or choose a bookmark.

③ Click a tab to view the page it contains.

④ To change the order of the tabs in a window, click a tab's handle and drag it to its new locations.

Continued

TIP

Don't Stop Now If you're in a hurry, you'll appreciate knowing the quickest way to open a web page in a separate tab: Press ⌘ while you click the **Back** or **Forward** arrows or as you click a link. ∎

NOTE

Not the Only One Cool as it is, tabbed browsing isn't unique to Safari. Apple uses the concept elsewhere, such as in iChat (it's great for managing multiple conversations), and other web browsers, including Firefox, Opera, and Camino, support it as well. ∎

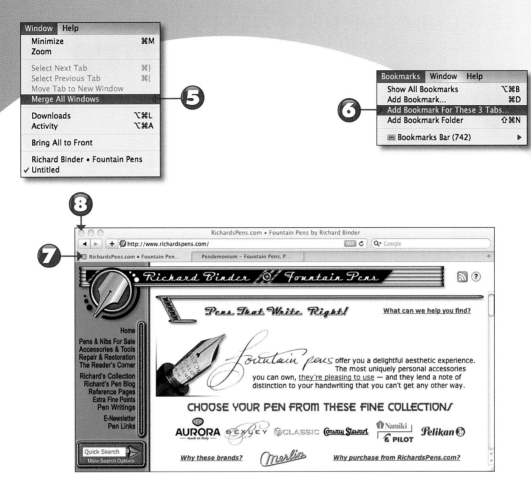

5 To turn multiple open windows into tabs in a single window, choose **Window**, **Merge All Windows**.

6 Choose **Bookmarks**, **Add Bookmarks for These Tabs** to add a bookmark set that contains a bookmark for each tab in a window.

7 Click the **X** next to its name to close a tab.

8 Click the **Close** button at the top of the window to close the window and all its tabs.

End

TIP

Tab, Window; Window, Tab Drag a tab to the desktop to transfer its contents into a new window. To create a new tab from an open window, click the URL and drag it to the **New Tab** button in that open window or another one. ■

SEARCHING WITHIN A WEB PAGE

Sure, Spotlight finds anything on your computer, and Google finds anything on the web (and pretty much anywhere else), but sometimes you've gotten to the right web page and you *still* can't find what you want. That's when it comes in handy to be able to search through the text on the page itself.

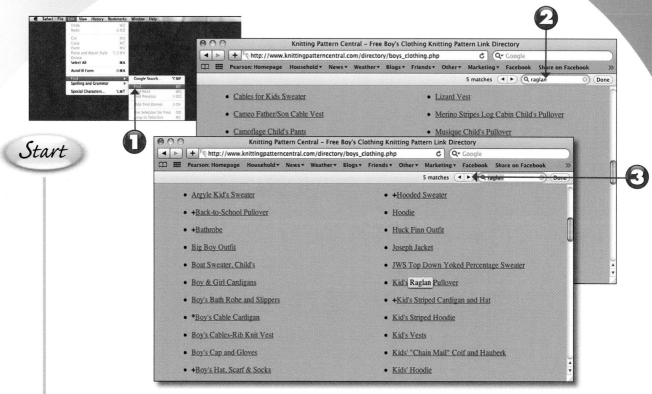

Start

1. Choose **Edit**, **Find**, **Find**, or press ⌘-**F**.

2. Type the word for which you want to search.

3. Click the arrow buttons to highlight each instance of the search term.

4. Click **Done** to hide the Find banner.

End

NOTE

It Counts! Note that when it finds your search terms on the page, Safari also tells you how many matches it found. This is a great way to get a quick count of, for example, the number of employees named "Paula" in a company directory. ■

BROWSING SECURELY

Not a week goes by that we don't hear about another frightening case of identity theft or data theft in the news. One way to protect yourself is to make sure that no one else can see where you've been on the Web and what you did there. To accomplish this feat, Safari features Private Browsing.

Choose **Safari**, **Private Browsing**.

Click **OK** to turn on Private Browsing.

TIP
Keeping It Really Safe If you're concerned about online safety, you can take more precautions. Choose **Safari, Preferences** and click **Security** to see a range of options for disabling features like JavaScript, managing cookies, and turning on high-end encryption so that if intercepted, your personal information still can't be deciphered. Of course, some websites won't work if you turn on the strongest security options—life is all about trade-offs. ■

ACCESSING YOUR MAC REMOTELY

Wouldn't it be cool if you could just grab a file from your home Mac while you're at the office? You know right where the file is, if you could only.... With Leopard or Snow Leopard, you can connect to any Mac that's logged in to MobileMe with your user name and password and control it just as though you were sitting in front of it. Here's how.

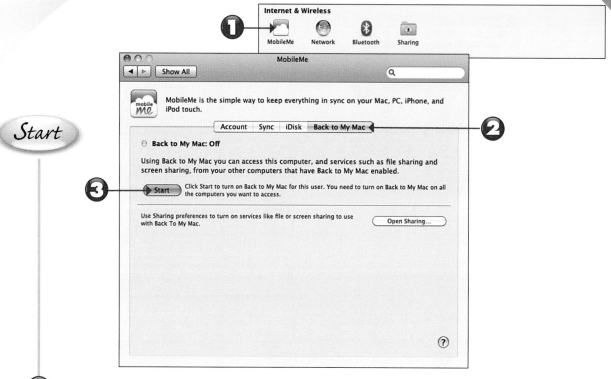

1 In System Preferences, click the **MobileMe** button to view preferences for MobileMe.

2 Click **Back To My Mac**.

3 Click **Start** to turn on Back To My Mac.

Continued

NOTE

I Gotta Be Me For Back To My Mac to work, both Macs must have your MobileMe member name and password entered on the Account pane in MobileMe System Preferences. Be sure to click **Sign In** if you haven't already. ■

TIP

Something to Share If you don't see the Screen Sharing or Connect As buttons, you probably haven't turned on any sharing services. In System Preferences, click **Sharing**, and then click next to the services you want to activate, such as File Sharing or Screen Sharing. ■

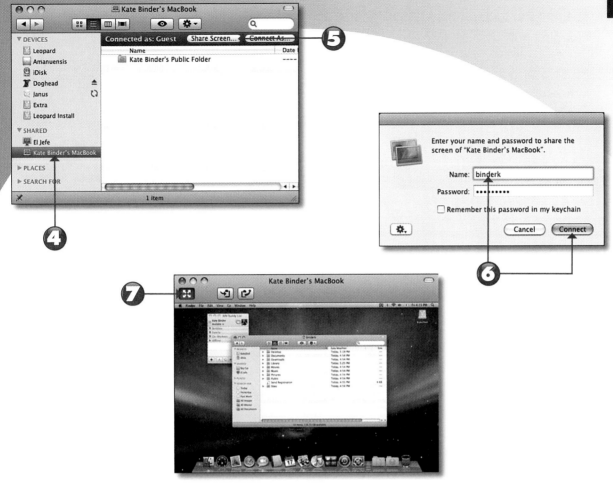

4 In a Finder window, click your other Mac in the sidebar under Shared.

5 Click **Share Screen** to control the other Mac's screen.

6 Enter your user name and password and click **Connect**.

7 Click the **Full Screen** button to see the other Mac's screen at full size.

End

NOTE

The Bad News Back To My Mac only works with MobileMe, so if you haven't joined yet, you're out of luck.
You can still use a separate program to control remote
computers, such as Timbuktu (www.netopia.com), which
works both over the Internet and on a local network. ■

CONTROLLING KIDS' COMPUTER USE

Learning how to work with computers is important—in fact, for today's kids it's pretty much unavoidable—but no parent wants kids sitting in front of the computer all day and all night. Mac OS X's Parental Controls enable you, as an admin user, to set limits on how much your kids use your Mac and what they can use it to do.

Start

1 Choose **Apple menu**, **System Preferences**.

2 Click **Parental Controls**.

3 Click the name of the user for whom you want to set controls, then click the lock button to unlock the Parental Controls preferences. Click **Enable Parental Controls**.

4 Enter an administrator account's username and your password and click **OK**.

Continued

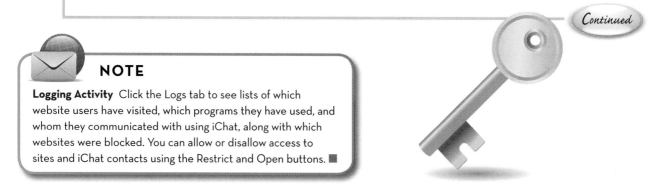

NOTE

Logging Activity Click the Logs tab to see lists of which website users have visited, which programs they have used, and whom they communicated with using iChat, along with which websites were blocked. You can allow or disallow access to sites and iChat contacts using the Restrict and Open buttons. ■

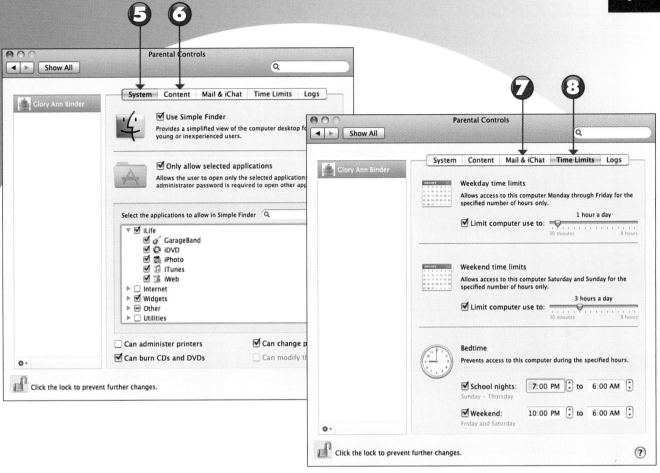

5 Click the **System** tab and set restrictions on access to the Finder, the programs installed on your Mac, and hardware configuration.

6 Click the **Content** tab to hide adult content in the Mac OS X Dictionary and on the web.

7 Click the **Mail & iChat** tab to limit use of email and instant messaging to specified users.

8 Click the **Time Limits** tab to set time limits for computer use.

End

NOTE

More Than the Internet Parental Controls aren't just about the Internet. Check out the settings at the bottom of the System tab: You can control whether a user can burn discs, administer printers, modify the Dock, and change his or her password. ■

TIP

Mother, May I? To receive automatic notice that a restricted user is attempting to contact someone who's not on your approved list, go to the **Mail & iChat** tab, check **Send permission requests to** and enter your email address. ■

BACKING UP TO YOUR IDISK

Backing up your important files is a good thing, but you won't appreciate how good it is until you need that backup someday. In the meantime, take the experts' word for it—set up a backup routine and stick to it. If you're a MobileMe member, you can automate backups to your iDisk with Apple's own Backup software, which you'll find in your iDisk's Software folder.

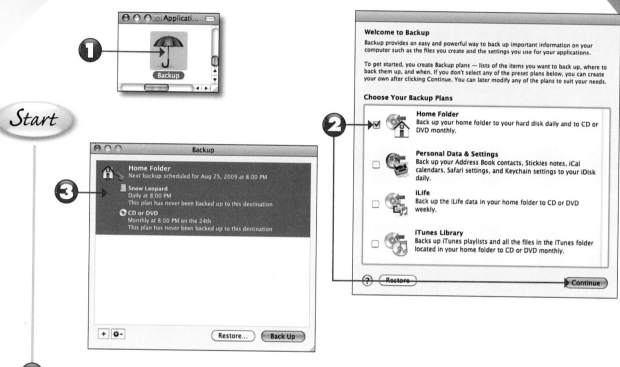

Start

1 Double-click **Backup** to open it.

2 Check the backup plan that you want to use, and then click **Continue**.

3 Double-click the backup plan to make changes to it.

Continued

NOTE

Backing Up the Big Files If you have a built-in CD-R drive, CD-RW drive, or SuperDrive, you can back up to CDs or DVDs. They hold more information than your iDisk, and backups go faster. ■

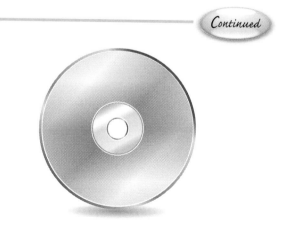

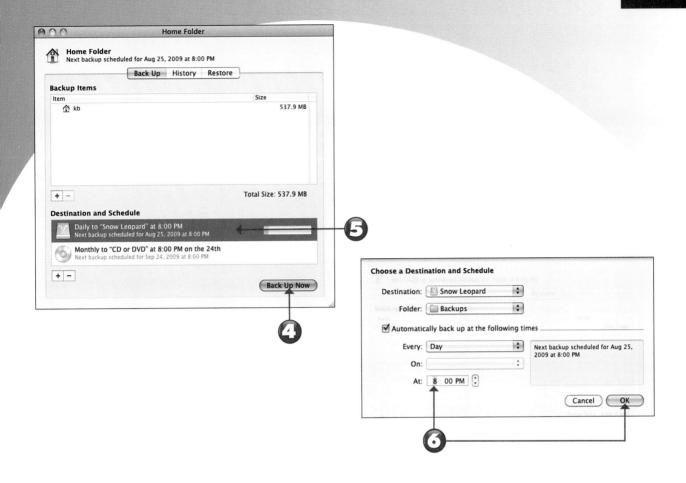

4 Click **Back Up Now** to begin copying your files to the specified backup location.

5 Double-click an entry in the **Destination and Schedule** list to change the schedule for automatic backups.

6 Select a frequency, time, and day and click **OK**. Backup starts automatically at that time and backs up the files currently selected.

End

NOTE

When to Upgrade Backup is great for home users or very small businesses that don't need to back up a lot of data. If you need to back up your entire hard drive daily, however, you should look into an industrial-strength backup program, such as Retrospect (www.dantz.com). ■

CAUTION

For the Stubborn Ones Still not backing up? Remember, you're the one with the most to lose if your hard drive crashes irretrievably. And statistics show that a major crash will happen to every computer user sometime in his or her life. ■

CREATING A MOBILEME HOME PAGE

Apple's easy Web design program, iWeb, features built-in templates for photo albums, file sharing, iMovies, résumés, new baby announcements, invitations, and more—each category comes with anywhere from a few to a couple dozen page templates you can customize to suit your needs.

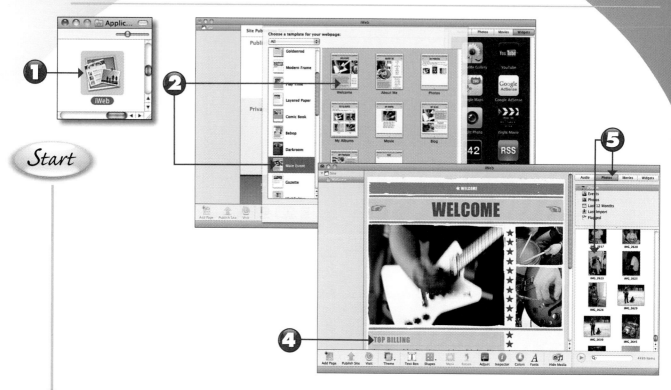

Start

1. Start up iWeb (you'll find it in your Applications folder).

2. Choose a template and a page type in the template chooser.

3. Click **Choose**.

4. Select sample text in the page and type over it to add your own text.

5. To add photos from iPhoto, click the **Photos** tab and drag images onto the page.

Continued

TIP

Rolling Your Own If you're already a web wizard, you can create your own web pages in any program. Just drop them into the Sites folder on your iDisk and make sure the main page is called index.html; your pages will be published just like ones created in iWeb. ■

NOTE

Being Choosy The first time you use iWeb, the template chooser shows up automatically, as shown on this page. After that, it only shows up when you click Add Page or when you delete the only page in your site. To delete a page, click it in the sidebar and press **Delete**. ■

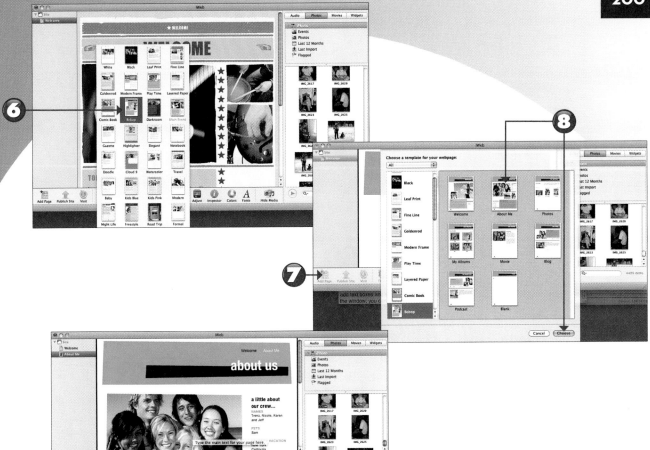

6 Choose a different option from the Theme pop-up menu to change the design of your whole site.

7 Click **Add Page** to insert another page into the site.

8 Choose a page type, then click **Choose**.

9 When you're ready, click **Publish Site** to upload your pages to MobileMe.

End

TIP

Letting the World Know If you want to let your friends know about your new website, click the **Announce Site** button at the top of the page that appears after you click **Publish**. You'll be guided through creating an e-card that will be emailed to your friends to publicize your new home on the web. ■

Chapter 10

GETTING AN ILIFE

iLife is Apple's name for its collection of five "digital hub" i programs: iPhoto, iWeb, iMovie, Garageband, and iDVD. Along with iTunes, this software represents the company's effort to empower Mac users to create and control their own entertainment media. With iLife and iTunes, you can manage, edit, and share your digital photos; acquire and mix music; make your own music; produce digital movies; create a website in seconds; and create professional-looking DVDs that combine movies, music, still images, and more.

In this chapter you'll learn how to get your pictures into iPhoto and organize them into albums. When you have albums, you can print your photos, share them on the web, and design real coffee-table-style books of photos. You'll also learn how to import music from your CD collection into iTunes, create custom mixes called *playlists*, and burn your own CDs. With a visit to the iTunes Music Store, you'll pick and choose from the latest tunes on the market—at about a buck a pop.

With iMovie, you'll learn how to import video from your camcorder and add scene transitions and fun special effects to turn your footage into a masterpiece. Finally, you'll be introduced to iDVD; with this program, you'll create a new DVD project, preview it to make sure it's just the way you want it, and then burn it to a DVD disc so you can play it in your DVD player.

MANAGING PHOTOS, VIDEO, AND MUSIC

Organize songs in playlists, 212

Turn playlists into CDs, 213

Rip CDs to your hard drive, 211

Organize photos in albums, 204

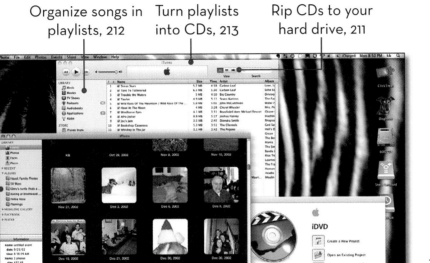

Turn home video into professional-quality DVDs, 222

Design and buy bound photo books, 205

IMPORTING PHOTOS INTO IPHOTO

iPhoto can do a lot of things, but its most important function is simply providing a place to keep all your digital photos. Think of it as a super-duper photo album, or maybe a filing cabinet for your photos (if you take a lot of them). So, the first step in doing anything with iPhoto is getting your photos into its database.

Start

Delete Photos on Your Camera?

156 photos were successfully imported into iPhoto.

Delete Photos   **Keep Photos**

1. Plug your camera into your Mac's USB port, turn it on, and start up iPhoto (in the Applications folder).

2. Click **Import All**.

3. Click **Delete Photos** if you want to clear the original images off the camera; otherwise, click **Keep Photos**.

End

TIP

You Can Get There from Here To import image files from your hard drive, a removable disk, or camera media you've mounted on the Desktop, drag and drop the files directly onto the Photo Library entry in the Albums list. ■

NOTE

Found, Not Lost If you can't find the latest photos you brought into iPhoto, check out the Last Import album in the **Recent** heading in the sidebar. That's where the most recent group of images you imported is always stored. ■

CREATING IPHOTO ALBUMS

Rather than being exactly parallel to a real-world photo album, an iPhoto album is really just a way to group photos together so iPhoto knows which photos you want to print, display, or export. Albums are the way you organize your photos so you can find the ones you want. Creating an album is also the first step in creating a book or web page.

Start

① In iPhoto, click the **Create New Album** button.

② Type a name for the new album and click **Create**.

③ Add photos to the new album by dragging and dropping them from the preview area to the album's name.

④ Click the album's name, and then drag and drop the album's photos in the preview area to change their order.

End

TIP

Information Please You can add descriptive information to the photos in your albums. Click the **Show Info** (i) button below the Album column to display Title, Comments, and Date fields that you can fill out. ■

PRINTING PHOTOS

It's not a paperless world yet, so you're bound to want to print your photos at some point. iPhoto offers several printing layouts so you can create standard prints, picture packages like the ones photo studios offer, or just plain printouts in your choice of size and number.

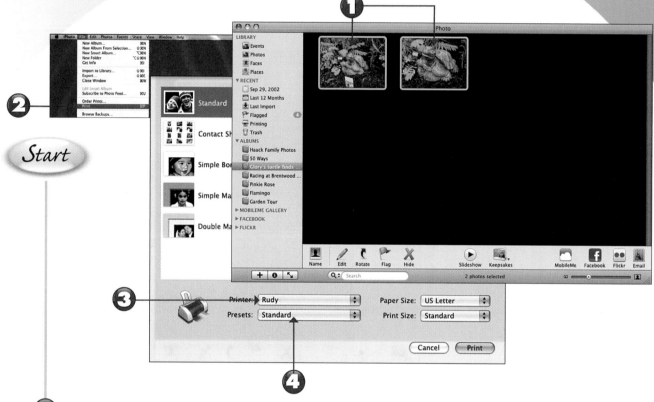

Start

1 ⌘-**click** in the preview area to select individual photos.

2 Choose **File**, **Print**.

3 Choose a printer from the **Printer** pop-up menu.

4 If available, choose an option from the **Presets** pop-up menu to set the output type.

Continued

TIP

Fine-Tuning Print Settings Although your printer driver probably includes presets for photo and plain paper, you might need to fine-tune the settings for your printer. Click **Advanced** in the final iPhoto Print dialog box to get to a Print dialog box with the usual options, including color and media. ■

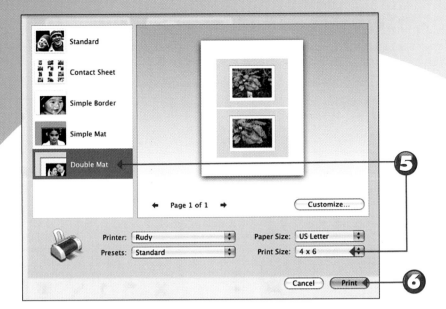

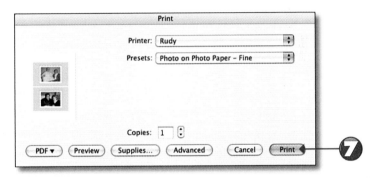

5 Choose a **Style** option and a **Print Size** option, and make sure the Paper Size setting is correct for your printer.

6 Click **Print**.

7 Click **Print** again.

End

NOTE

Proxy Preview The proxy preview area in iPhoto's Print dialog box shows you how your printouts will look with the selected printer's paper size and the selected Style option. The proxy preview updates on-the-fly as you change the settings for the selected style. ■

TIP

Custom for the Customers If you want to change the settings for a style, such as the order in which the photos print or their size on the page, click **Customize** in the lower-right corner of the proxy preview area. ■

SHARING PHOTOS ON THE WEB

The best way to share your photos with friends and family all over the country or the world is to put them on the web. iPhoto makes creating a web picture gallery easy, even if you're not a MobileMe member. To share pictures, all you have to do is put the files that iPhoto generates on your web space and let everyone know the URL.

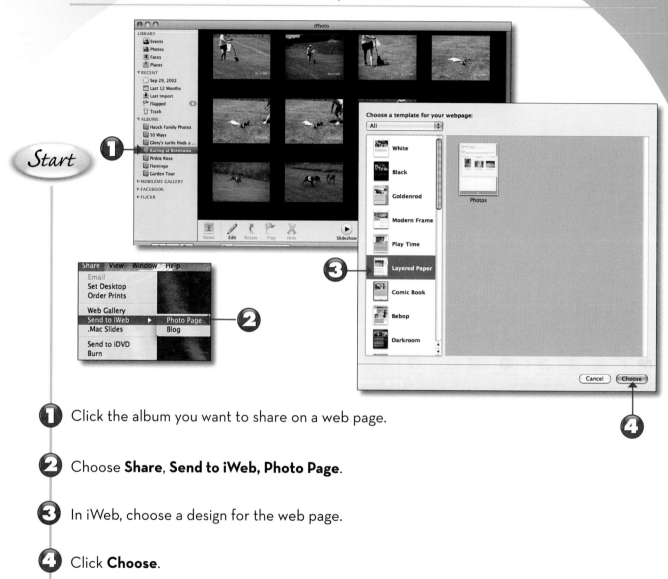

Start

1 Click the album you want to share on a web page.

2 Choose **Share**, **Send to iWeb**, **Photo Page**.

3 In iWeb, choose a design for the web page.

4 Click **Choose**.

Continued

 NOTE

Even Easier If you do have a MobileMe account, your job just got much, much simpler! Instead of Send to iWeb, choose **Web Gallery** from iPhoto's **Share** menu. With this command, iPhoto uploads the whole shebang straight to your MobileMe site. ■

 NOTE

What's in a Name? iPhoto inserts the album's name in the Title field, but you can change that page title to anything you want. ■

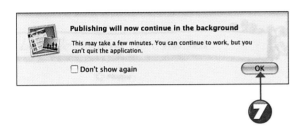

5 In iWeb, Choose **File**, **Publish to a Folder**.

6 Click **Continue** if you have the legal right to publish the text and photos in your site.

7 Click **OK** to allow iWeb to continue publishing your site.

8 Click **Announce** to send an email to your friends letting them know about your new site.

End

NOTE

Big and Little iPhoto creates all the full-size and thumbnail images your web album needs, but you must specify sizes. Thumbnail images are small versions of the photos on which viewers can click to see the full-size versions. ▪

APPLYING FUN PHOTO EFFECTS

Ever spent time in one of those mall photo booths, messing around to produce a strip of funny photos? Now there's no trip to the mall needed; just use Photo Booth to take pictures of yourself using your webcam. You can also add cool special effects and even change the background so it looks as though you're sitting in, say, the mall.

Start

1 Start up **Photo Booth** (you'll find it in the Applications folder).

2 Adjust your position within the photo frame and click the **Effects** button.

3 Use the arrow buttons to scroll through the available effects.

4 Double-click on the thumbnail image for the effect you want to use.

Continued

NOTE

Wait! There's More Photo Booth's Effects include lens effects—such as fisheye—and backdrops that you can put behind your image. You can even add your own backdrops: Just drag a photo into one of the blank spaces in the Effects pane of the Photo Booth window. ■

NOTE

Flickring Photos If you use Flickr to share photos with friends and family, you'll love FlickrBooth (www.otierney.net/flickrbooth). It's a plug-in for Photo Booth that lets you send your photos directly to Flickr, no Web browser required! ■

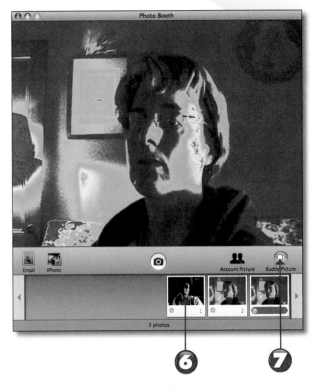

5 Click the **camera** button when you're ready to shoot a picture. Photo Booth counts down and then takes the photo.

6 Click one of the photos shown at the bottom of the window to use it.

7 Click a button to indicate what you want to do with the photo: email it, send it to iPhoto, use it as your login picture, or use it as your buddy icon in iChat.

End

TIP

More in Store When you feel that you've exhausted Photo Booth's possibilities, hold your horses. You can also take quick bursts of four pictures (which are then displayed four-up, rather than singly), and you can take videos as well. Click the **Burst** button in the lower-left corner of the Photo Booth window to shoot a burst, and click the **Video** button to shoot a movie. ■

RIPPING SONGS FROM A CD

You'll be amazed at how much more use you get from your CD collection after you get the music off CDs and into iTunes. The songs on CDs are already digital files; *ripping* them consists of transferring them to your hard drive and resaving them in MP3 format.

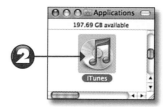

1 Insert the CD.

2 If iTunes doesn't start up automatically, open the Applications folder and double-click to start up **iTunes**.

3 Click to remove the check marks next to any songs on the CD that you don't want to add to your library.

4 Click **Import CD**.

TIP
The Sounds of Silence iTunes plays songs while it's importing them, but if you don't want to listen to them, you can click **Pause** to stop the playback. iTunes continues importing the songs. ■

TIP
Mind the Gap If you want consecutive songs to play with no pause between them, choose **Advanced**, **Join CD Tracks** before clicking **Import**. ■

MAKING A NEW PLAYLIST

Playlists are simply groups of songs, containing just one song or hundreds. You can use them to create party mixes, plan mix CDs, or categorize your music by genre or any other criterion. Building playlists is a simple drag-and-drop operation.

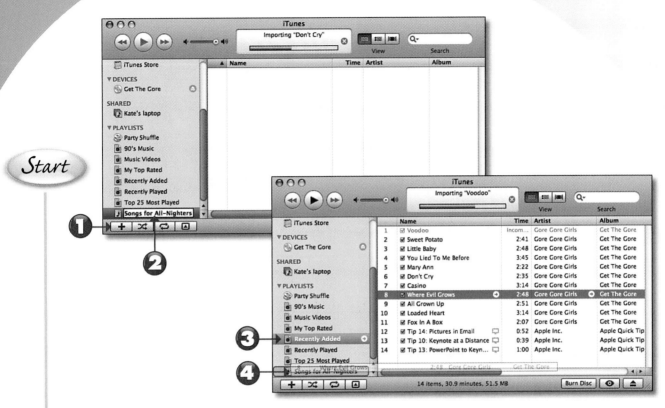

Start

1 In iTunes, click the **Create Playlist** button.

2 Type a name for the playlist.

3 Click the **Library** entry in the **Source** column to see all your songs, or click the name of another playlist.

4 Drag songs from the **Name** column and drop them into the new playlist.

End

TIP

Finding What You Want To locate a specific song in the Library or in a playlist, click in the **Search** field and type part of the song name. As you type, the list of songs shortens to include only the songs that match your search term. ■

TIP

Changing Your Mind To remove a song from a playlist (but not from your Library), click to select it and press **Delete**. ■

BURNING A MUSIC CD

You can take your music with you in the form of custom mix CDs for parties, for gifts, or just to use in the car. Before you burn a CD, you need to create a playlist containing the songs you want to use on the disc. And, of course, you need to have a CD drive that can write CDs as well as play them.

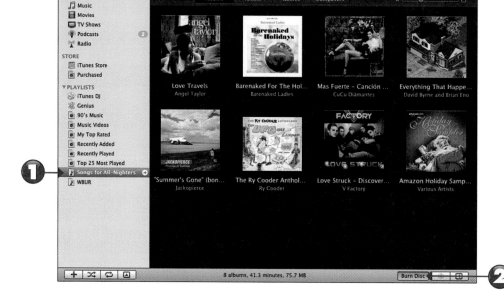

1 Click to select the playlist you want to make into a CD.

2 Click the **Burn Disc** button.

Continued

TIP

Picture This Any song you buy from the iTunes Store (see the next task) comes with cover artwork. When you burn a compilation, iTunes creates a custom mosaic of the songs' cover art and drops that into a template to create an insert for the CD case. ■

TIP

The Right Media Make sure you use CD-R media, rather than CD-RW media, if you plan to play your CD in a regular CD player (meaning, on your stereo) rather than in a computer CD drive. ■

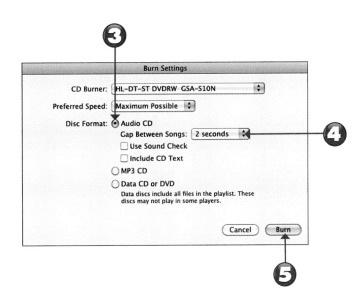

3 Click **Audio CD**.

4 Choose a time from the **Gap Between Songs** pop-up menu.

5 Insert a blank CD-R disc and click **Burn**; iTunes burns your playlist onto the disc.

End

TIP
Avoiding a Small Annoyance If you insert a blank CD before clicking **Burn Disc** in the iTunes window, your Mac asks you what you want it to do with the CD. Clicking **Burn Disc** before putting the CD-R in the drive bypasses this dialog box. ■

TIP
Stop Right There To stop the CD burner after you click Burn Disc, click the **X** next to the progress bar. You can use your CD drive again immediately, but the CD you canceled is no longer usable. ■

PURCHASING SONGS THROUGH ITUNES

The iTunes Store offers thousands of tunes in all genres at very reasonable prices. You can download entire albums or one song at a time. Your purchases are charged to your credit card, and the songs are downloaded directly into iTunes, where you can play them on your computer, transfer to them to an iPod, or burn them to a CD.

Start

1. In iTunes, click **Music Store** in the Source column.

2. Click **Sign In**.

3. Type your Apple ID and password and click **Sign In**.

4. If you haven't bought songs before, a dialog box tells you that this ID hasn't been used with the Music Store; click **Review**.

Continued

TIP

Getting an iTunes Account If you already have an Apple ID, you're all set—just enter that username and password to sign in to the iTunes Store. If you have a paid subscription to MobileMe, use that username and password for the Music Store. If you don't have either, follow the Store's prompts to create a new ID and supply your credit card information for purchases. ■

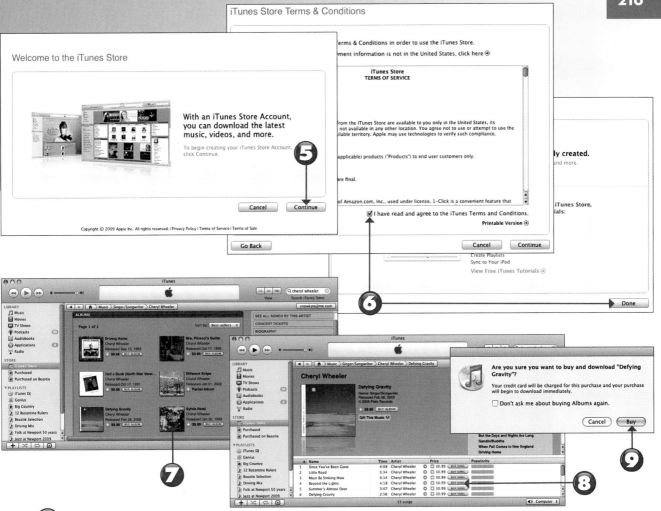

5 Click **Continue**.

6 Read the Terms and Conditions and click the checkbox and **Continue**; then click **Done**.

7 Click a song or album title to see more information about it.

8 Click **Buy Song** or **Buy Album** to purchase music.

9 Click **Buy**. The song downloads into iTunes and appears in a new playlist called Purchased Music.

End

TIP

Quick and Clean Searching You can search the iTunes Store quickly for any text by entering the search text in the regular iTunes search field at the top of the iTunes window. Type the song or artist name you want to look for and press Return. ■

TIP

Just a Taste When you're browsing the iTunes Store, click iTunes' **Play** button to hear a high-quality, 30-second snippet of a selected song. ■

IMPORTING VIDEO FOOTAGE INTO IMOVIE

With iMovie, your home movies will reach new heights. You can add titles and credits, special effects, music and sound effects, and more. Then you can save your finished creations as small QuickTime files for emailing, high-quality DVD movies, or anything in between. The first step is to bring video from your video camera into iMovie.

Start

In iMovie, choose **File**, **New Project**.

Give the new movie project a name, choose a theme, and click **Create**.

Choose **File**, **Import from Camera**.

Choose a location for the imported footage and click **OK**.

Continued

NOTE

Trouble in iMovie Paradise Can't seem to get the camera to respond to iMovie's controls? Check to make sure the camera is in playback mode (VTR or VCR mode) rather than recording mode. ■

Capture...

6

5 Click **Fast Forward** or **Rewind** to move the tape to the section you want to import.

6 Click **Capture** to start importing footage.

7 Click **Stop** when you've imported the footage you want. The video is added to the Clip Shelf.

End

NOTE

On the Safe Side Be conservative when importing video—always import a bit extra on either end of the section you want. You can trim extra footage in iMovie to end up with just the right scene, but if you cut off the scene you'll need to import it again. ■

TIP

Sound and Vision Drag the slider next to the playback controls if you want to adjust the volume level of the tape's audio while you watch it import. Doing this doesn't affect the recording level on the tape or in the final movie. ■

INSERTING TRANSITIONS

After you've assembled your movie's raw footage by dragging clips from the Clip Shelf into the Clip Viewer, you can spice up the production by adding *transitions* between clips.

Start

1. To see the available transitions, click the **Transitions** button.

2. Hold the cursor over a transition to see how it looks in action.

3. Drag the transition to the Clip Viewer and drop it into the point in the movie where you want it.

Continued

NOTE

Creative Transitioning Unfortunately, iMovie restricts you to using one transition between each pair of clips. But don't forget that you can also use transitions before and after titles, photos, and other elements. ■

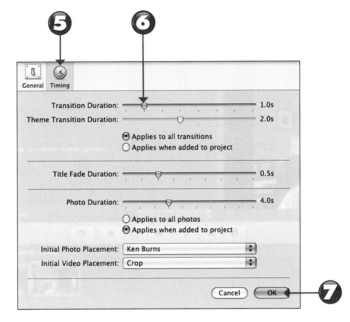

4 To change settings for your transitions, choose **File**, **Project Properties**.

5 Click the **Timing** tab.

6 Drag the **Transition Duration** slider to determine how long each transition takes.

7 Click **OK**.

End

NOTE

Transition Timing Be sure to pay attention to the duration of your transitions as you preview your movie. What seemed like a perfectly reasonable amount of time when you put in the transition can stretch to an awfully long time when you're watching. ■

SAVING A MOVIE

When your magnum opus is complete—or at least when you're ready to share it with the outside world—you'll need to export it to a real movie format. This is an easy process, with only a few options to set.

Start

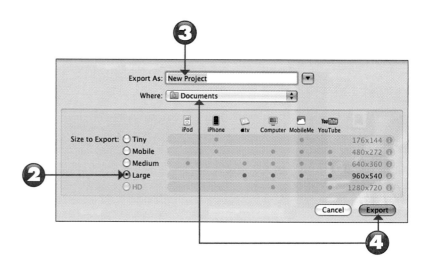

1 Choose **Share**, **Export Movie**.

2 Choose a size for the movie, based on what you want to do with it.

3 Enter a name for the file.

4 Choose a location for the file and click **Export**.

End

TIP

Saving Your Work When you quit iMovie, your project is saved in iMovie's special project format, and when you start iMovie again, you'll see everything right where you left it. You don't need to export the movie until you're done working on it. ■

CREATING A NEW IDVD PROJECT

Like iMovie, iDVD always opens the last project you worked on. You can open another project by choosing **File**, **Open**, or you can begin a new project from scratch. Here's how to do that.

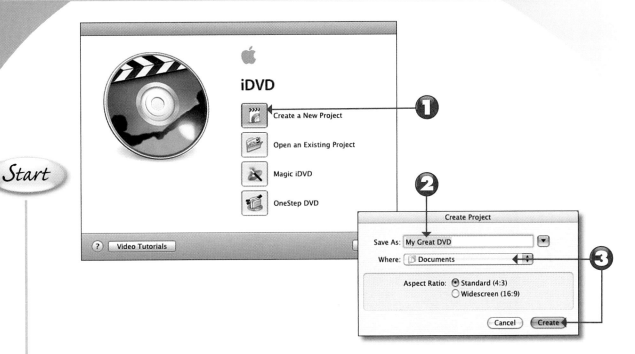

Start

(1) On the iDVD opening screen, click **Create a New Project**.

(2) Enter a name for your DVD project.

(3) Navigate to the location where you want to save the project and click **Create**.

End

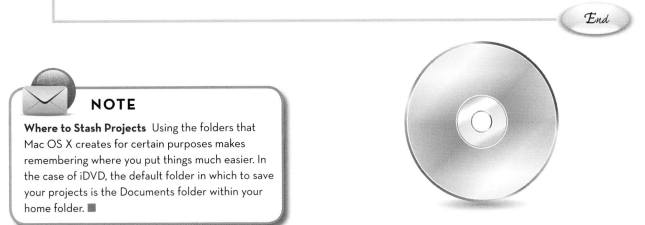

NOTE

Where to Stash Projects Using the folders that Mac OS X creates for certain purposes makes remembering where you put things much easier. In the case of iDVD, the default folder in which to save your projects is the Documents folder within your home folder. ■

PREVIEWING A DVD

It's a well-known fact that creative projects don't always turn out the way they're envisioned. It's far better to catch mistakes and make tweaks before you've burned a DVD than after. That's where iDVD's Preview function comes in handy. Always preview your projects before burning them to disc.

Start

1 Click **Preview** to play the DVD.

2 Click buttons on the remote control to test the way the DVD will work on a TV.

3 Click **Exit** to leave preview mode.

End

TIP

Playing It Safe To be sure the DVD's elements won't extend off the edge of the screen, choose **Advanced, Show TV Safe Area** before you click **Preview**. This command places a rectangle on the screen that defines the boundaries of older TV screens. ■

BURNING A DVD

After your DVD project is set up the way you want it and you've confirmed this by using the Preview feature, it's time to burn an actual DVD disc. You must have a Mac with a built-in SuperDrive to accomplish this with iDVD.

Start

1 In iDVD, click the **Burn** button twice.

2 Insert a blank DVD disc. The process starts automatically and alerts you when it's finished.

End

NOTE

Make Way for DVDs You should quit all other programs while you're burning a DVD. This ensures that no other program will take over the computer while the DVD is being created, which might cause an error in the DVD. ■

NOTE

iDVD Without the Burn Previously, iDVD wouldn't even install if your Mac was SuperDrive-less, but with iDVD 3.0.1 and later versions, you can create iDVD projects on a Mac that doesn't have a Super-Drive. To burn a project, copy it to a SuperDrive-equipped Mac. ■

SHARING YOUR MAC WITH MULTIPLE USERS

Mac OS X is designed to be a multiuser operating system, meaning each user of a single Mac has his or her own account. Each user is either a standard user or an admin user. Admin users can change preferences, install programs, and modify files—in other words, they can make changes that affect all users rather than just the user who implements them. Standard users can only read and modify their own files, and they can only change their own settings.

Your account can be customized with your choice of name, password, and login picture (used both in the login dialog box and for instant messaging with iChat). You also get your very own home folder, named with the short version of your login name. Your home folder is where you can put all your documents, music, pictures, and so on, and you can keep other users from reading, moving, or even seeing what files are in your home folder. When you do want to share files, you can put them in specific places where other users have access to them. Because customizations—such as the desktop picture, screen saver module, monitor resolution, and clock settings—apply only to the user who sets them up, you can also set up user accounts to create different configurations of your Mac for specific purposes, rather than for different people, if you want.

In this chapter, you'll learn how to create user accounts and change their attributes, as well as how to log in and log out. You'll also learn how to add login items—programs and files that open automatically when you log in—and how to manage security with passwords.

ACCOUNT AND SECURITY SETUP

Change your
password, 233

Add login
items, 232

Change your
login picture, 233

Create and
delete users, 227

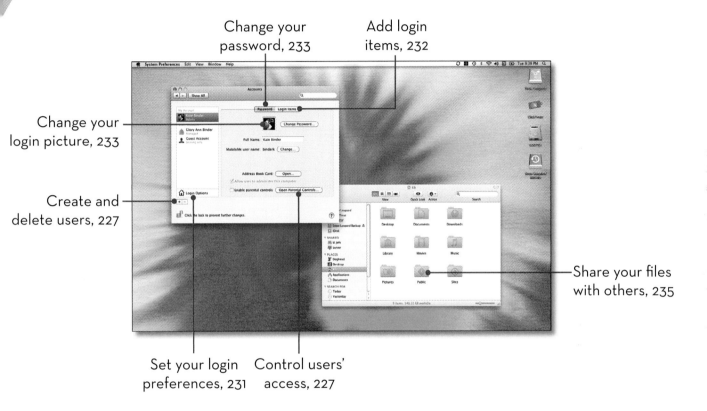

Share your files
with others, 235

Set your login
preferences, 231

Control users'
access, 227

CREATING AND DELETING USERS

Each user of a Mac gets his or her own account, with separate preferences, home folder, and login identity. Each account can have a customized level of access to system functions, and each account is password-protected so that only its user can change its settings.

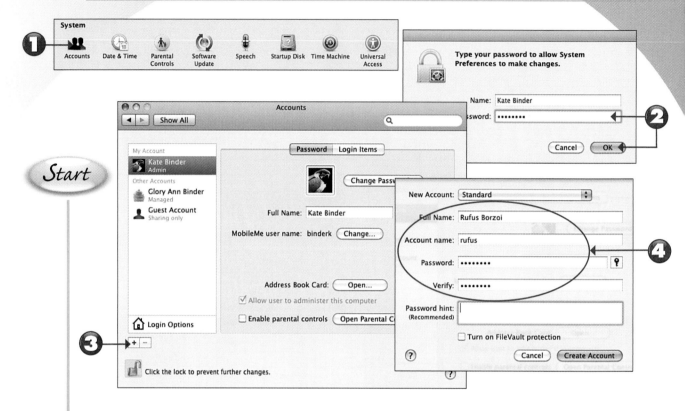

1 Choose **Apple menu**, **System Preferences**, and click **Accounts** to see the accounts preferences.

2 If the preferences are locked, click the **closed padlock** button to unlock them; then enter an admin name and password and click **OK**.

3 To create a new user, click the **Add User** button.

4 Enter the new user's name, a short version of the name (such as initials), and a password.

Continued

TIP

Setting Limits When you create a new user account, you control the user's access to most functions. In the Accounts pane, click Parental Controls. On the System tab, choose the programs and functions you want to make available to the user. On the Content tab, turn on monitoring to limit access to adult content, and on the Mail & iChat tab, set limits on email and instant messaging use. The Time Limits and Logs tabs contain controls for how much time the user can work on the Mac, and for keeping track of what the user does. ■

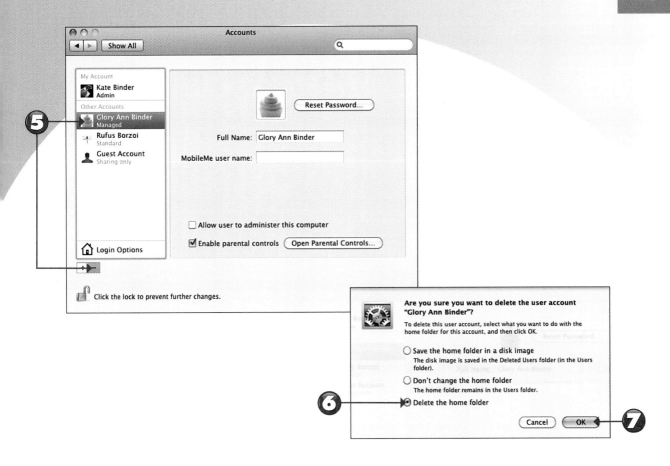

5 To delete a user, click a name in the list and then click the **Delete User** button.

6 Choose what you want to do with the user's files: archive them, level them in place, or delete them.

7 Click **OK** in the confirmation dialog box.

End

TIP

The Stuff They Leave Behind When you delete a user, one of your options is to save the user's files as a disk image that's placed in the Deleted Users folder in the Users folder. Double-click the disk image to see the saved files. If the user was using FileVault, enter the user's password. FileVault or no FileVault, drag the disk image file to the Trash to delete the files. ■

MAKING A USER AN ADMIN

Each Mac has at least one admin user—the first user identity created on your Mac is automatically an admin. You can make any other user an admin as well, which allows that user to control system preferences and make changes to the Mac's setup.

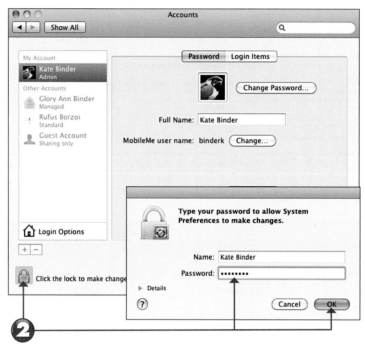

Choose **Apple menu**, **System Preferences**, and click **Accounts** to see the accounts preferences.

If the preferences are locked, click the **closed padlock** button to unlock them; then type an admin name and password and click **OK**.

Continued

NOTE

Admins Beget Admins Only admin users can create other admin users. If you're not an admin user, you'll need to ask someone who is already designated as an admin on your Mac to give you that status. ■

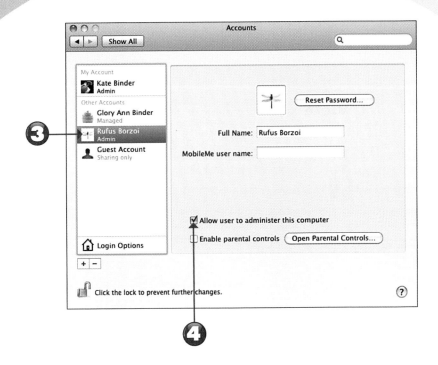

3 Click a name in the account list.

4 Click the **Allow user to administer this computer** check box.

End

NOTE

Wherefore Admin, Anyway? To home users, the term "admin user" can seem strange. It's a result of Mac OS X's emphasis on accommodating multiple users of a single Mac. In most multiuser situations, such as computer labs, only authorized administrators should be able to change the Mac's setup. ■

LOGGING IN AND OUT

Depending on your preferences, you might need to log in to your Mac every day, or you might hardly ever see the login screen. Either way, you do need to remember your login name and password so you can log in when needed—after another user has logged out or after major changes are made to your system.

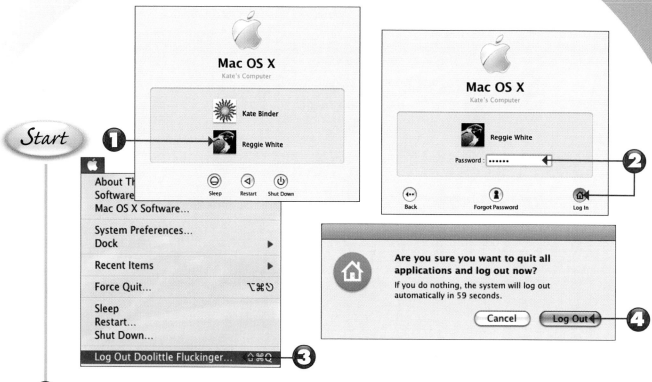

1. In the Login dialog box, click your name in the list of users.

2. Type your password and click **Log In**.

3. To log out, choose **Apple menu, Log Out**.

4. Click **Log Out** in the confirmation dialog box. All the applications quit, along with the Finder, and you're returned to the Login dialog box.

TIP

Skipping the Login Click **Login Options** at the bottom of the Accounts preferences panel in System Preferences; then choose a user from the **Automatically log in** pop-up menu. ■

TIP

Faster Switching Mac OS X's fast user switching feature displays a menu of users; choosing a new user switches instantly to that account. Click **Enable fast user switching** in the **Login Options** tab of the Accounts System Preferences panel. ■

ADDING STARTUP ITEMS

When you log in, your Mac sets itself up the way you like things. One service it can perform for you when you log in is starting up programs you use all the time, such as your email client, your contact manager, and other constant companions. To make this happen, you add these programs to your login items.

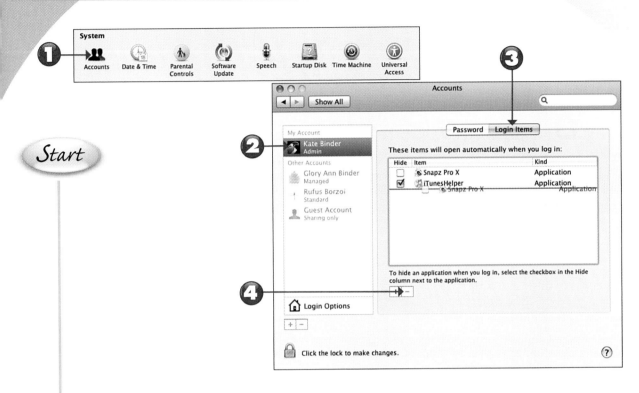

In System Preferences, click **Accounts** to see the accounts preferences.

Click to select the account for which you want to add login items.

Click the **Login Items** tab and then drag programs, documents, bookmark files, or folders into the window from the Finder.

Click an item and click the **Remove** button to remove it from the list.

End

TIP

What a Drag Drag items up and down in the login list to change the order in which they start up. Check the box next to each item to hide it as it starts up—you won't see its windows until you switch to the program. ∎

NOTE

Be Creative Login items don't have to be programs; you can open any file at login. Examples of files you might want to open every time you use your Mac include a sound file of your favorite song, the novel you're working on, or your recipe database. ∎

RESETTING YOUR PASSWORD

Because you need a password to access files on your Mac, be sure to choose a password you can't forget, and take advantage of the Hint feature to provide yourself with a memory-jogging phrase when you need it. If the worst does happen and you just can't figure out your password, here's how to remedy the situation.

1 If you're logged in, choose **Apple menu**, **System Preferences** and click **Accounts** to see the accounts preferences.

2 Click your username in the list and then click the **Password** tab.

3 Click **Change Password**.

4 Type your old password and the new password in the **Password** and **Verify** fields.

Continued

CAUTION

Don't Make It Too Easy This might seem obvious, but if you enter a hint for your password, don't make the hint too obvious. Even if you're tempted to just use the password itself for the hint, don't! ■

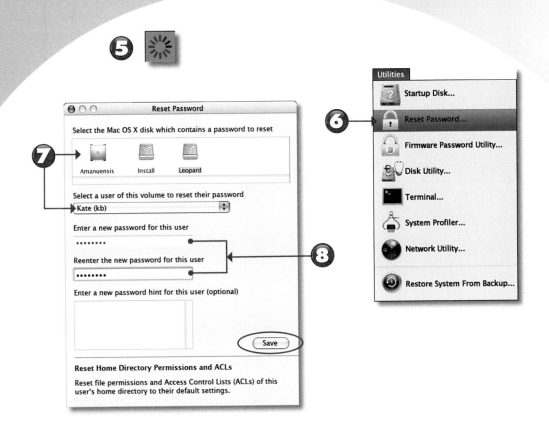

If you have forgotten the Mac's main admin password (the one used by its first admin user), insert the Mac OS X Install Disc and restart. Press **C** on your keyboard until you see the spinning gear symbol.

When the Installer starts up, choose **Utilities**, **Reset Password**.

Choose the hard drive where your system software resides and then select your name.

Enter the new password twice and click **Save**.

End

NOTE

A Little Help from a Friend If you forget your password and can't log in or access your home folder (when you're using FileVault), an admin user can change the password for you. ∎

CAUTION

Safe and Secure Keep your system disc in a safe place so it's not accessible to people who might want to reset the password to gain access to files that aren't theirs. ∎

SHARING FILES WITH OTHER USERS

Some files are meant to be read and even modified by multiple users—a family calendar or a committee report in progress, for example. You can share these files in two designated places, with different results. And you can send copies of your files to other users via their Drop Box folders.

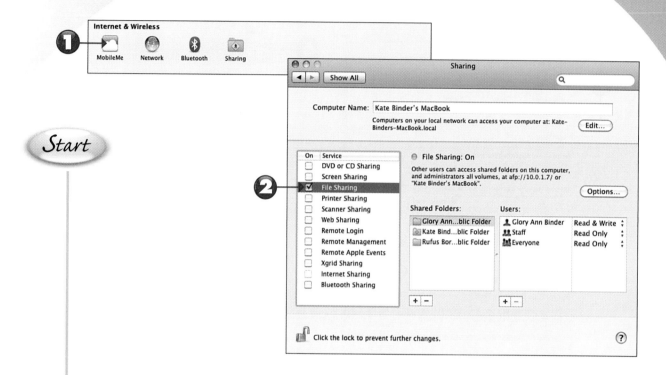

Start

1. To enable network users to access the Public folder in your home folder, open **System Preferences** and click **Sharing**.

2. In the Services list, check the box labeled **File Sharing** to share files with other Mac users on your network.

Continued

NOTE

Skipping It Why all this rigmarole, you ask? The point is to keep your files as safe as you want them to be. If you want to skip the security routine, you can keep your Mac logged in with a single user account and give all users the password. ■

NOTE

It's Good to Share Files you might share in a Public folder or in the Shared folder within the Users folder include databases (of recipes, addresses, or clients, for example), templates for letters or memos that everyone uses, and logo graphics. ■

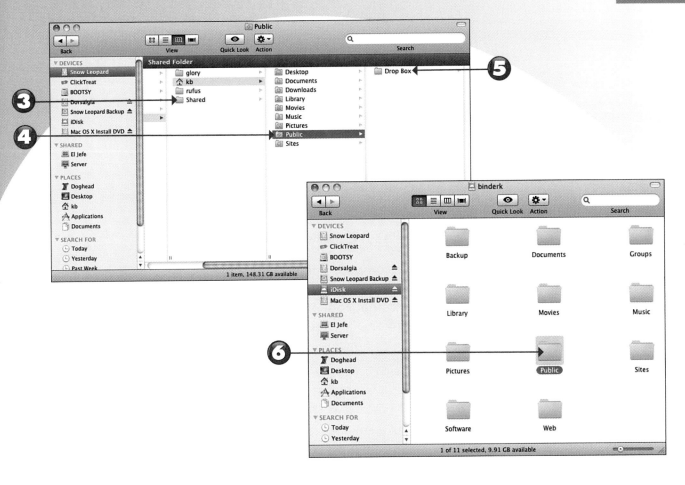

3 Put files you want all your Mac's users to be able to modify in the Shared folder in the Users folder.

4 Put files that you want all your Mac's users to be able to read but not change in the Public folder in your home folder.

5 To give another user of your computer a copy of a file, put the file in that user's Drop Box folder inside his or her Public folder.

6 To share a file with other Mac users on the Internet, copy it to the Public folder on your iDisk.

End

NOTE

Flying Blind When you drag a file into another user's Drop Box, the Mac warns that you won't be able to see the result of the operation. This is its way of saying that you can't open another user's Drop Box folder to see what's in it. ■

NOTE

Large Attachments Many email providers limit the size of file attachments. To send someone a larger file than will fit through your provider's email gateway, put it on your iDisk (step 6) and create a File Sharing web page where she can snag the file. ■

CREATING A HOME NETWORK

A network, whether wireless or composed of physical cables, connects your computer with other computers so you can share files, play network games, and all use the same printers and Internet connection. The Internet, in fact, is simply a huge network comprising many smaller networks. With Mac OS X, setting up your own network in your home or office is easy.

Creating a network has two basic components. First, you need to make the connection by either hooking up your Macs (and Windows PCs, if you like) with Ethernet cables or installing AirPort cards and an AirPort base station so they can talk to each other wirelessly. Then, you need to tell your Mac how your network is set up so the system knows which connector and language to use to communicate with the other computers it's connected to.

In this chapter, you'll learn how to set up your network and turn on file sharing so both Windows users and other Mac users on your network can exchange files with you. You'll also learn how to share printers connected to your Mac with other users on your network. And you'll find out how to share a single Internet connection among all the computers on a network, as well as how to connect to an AirPort network and get online via a wireless AirPort connection.

SETTING UP AND USING A NETWORK

Set up the network
configuration, 239

Get online, 239

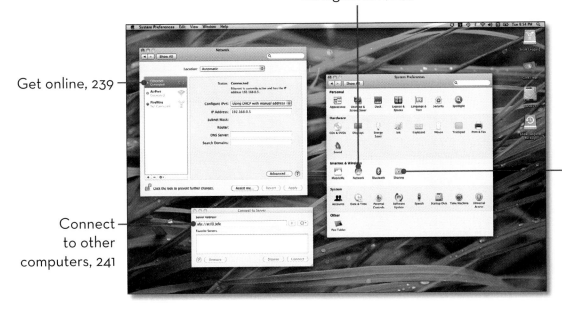

Connect
to other
computers, 241

Share files,
printers, and
Internet con-
nections, 242

GETTING ON THE NETWORK

The first step to setting up a wired home network is this: Connect your computers with Ethernet cables (a regular one for newer Macs and a crossover cable for older Macs). If you have more than two computers, buy a hub and connect each computer to the hub; otherwise, connect your two Macs directly to each other.

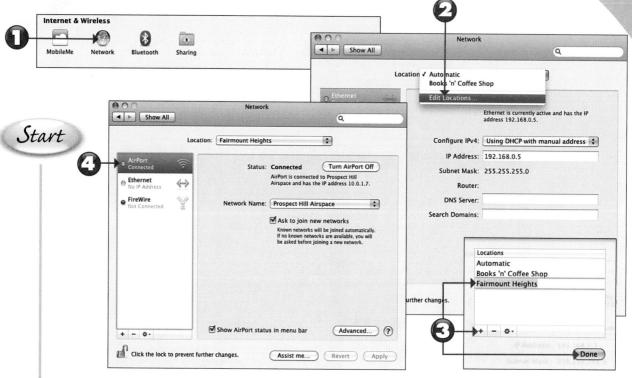

Start

(1) Open **System Preferences** and click the **Network** button.

(2) Choose **Edit Locations** from the **Location** pop-up menu.

(3) Click the **+** button, then enter a name for the network configuration you're about to create and click **Done**.

(4) Click the network port you want to use (usually either **Built-in Ethernet** or **AirPort**).

Continued

TIP

An Even Easier Way If network settings completely befuddle you, try using the Network Setup Assistant to get connected. Start up **System Preferences** and click **Network**; then click **Assist Me** and follow the instructions. ■

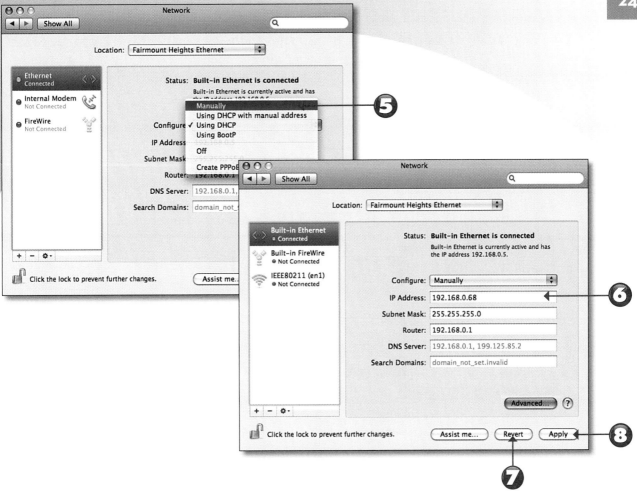

5 Set the **Configure** pop-up menu to either **Using DHCP** or **Manually** (check with your network admin).

6 If you choose **Manually** in step 5, enter settings for the IP Address, Subnet Mask, Router, and DNS Server.

7 Click **Revert** if you want to start over with the original settings.

8 Click **Apply** when you're satisfied with the settings to put them into effect.

End

NOTE

By the Manual When you choose **Manually** in the **Configure IPv4** pop-up menu, you must enter your Mac's IP address, your router's IP address, and the subnet mask. If all this is gibberish to you, go to Threemacs.com (www.threemacs.com) to learn about creating networks. ∎

CONNECTING TO NETWORKED COMPUTERS

Networking has always been easy with Macs, but now the system's networking features are easier to use and more powerful than ever. You can connect to any Mac or Windows computer on your network using either AppleTalk or TCP networking, but all you need to know is the computer's name or IP address.

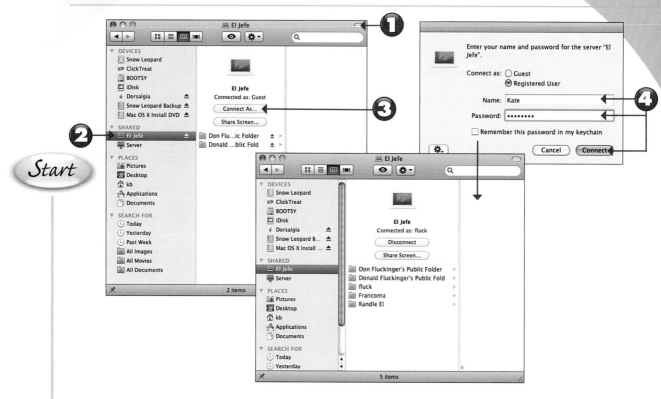

Start

 In the **Finder**, click the transparent button to display the Places sidebar if it's not already visible.

 Click a computer to connect to in the sidebar's **Shared** section.

3 Click **Connect As** to log into a user account on the network computer.

4 Enter your username and password and click **Connect**.

End

TIP
Invisible Friends If the computer to which you want to connect isn't visible, you need to find out its network address (available in the Sharing section of System Preferences). Then choose **Go, Connect to Server** in the Finder and enter the address. ■

TIP
Connecting with the Other Side To connect to a Windows computer, assign it an IP address (refer to Windows documentation). Then choose **Go, Connect to Server** in the Finder, and enter its address in the dialog box in this form: smb://192.168.0.102. ■

SHARING FILES ON A NETWORK

When computers aren't networked, sharing files requires the use of sneakernet: physically walking a removable disk or flash drive to another machine. Fortunately, creating a network is easy enough (see "Getting on the Network," earlier in this chapter) that Mac users rarely have to resort to sneakernet. Here's how to share your files on a real network.

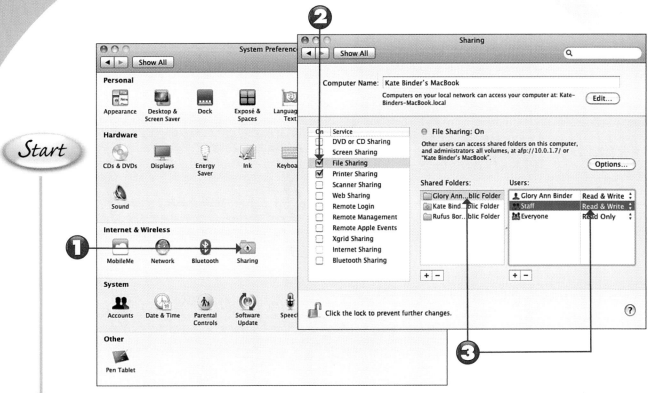

1 Open **System Preferences** and click **Sharing**.

2 Check the box labeled **File Sharing**.

3 To change access privileges for specific users, click a user or group's name and change the privileges status in the column on the right.

End

TIP

When You Get There To connect to another Mac on your network, see the preceding task, "Connecting to Networked Computers." When you connect to another Mac, you'll see the home folders of that Mac's users. If you log in as a registered user of that Mac, you'll be able to access the same folders as if you were sitting in front of the Mac. Otherwise, you must connect as a guest; in this case, you'll be able to see only the contents of the user's Public folder (see "Sharing Files with Other Users," in Chapter 11, "Sharing Your Mac with Multiple Users"). ■

CONTROLLING ANOTHER MAC

If you've ever wanted to reach right through the phone and grab someone else's mouse, screen sharing is for you. Starting with Leopard, this feature has been built right into Mac OS X. It enables you to control the screen of any Mac on your local network, any Mac you can reach through iChat, and any Mac that's logged in to MobileMe using your username.

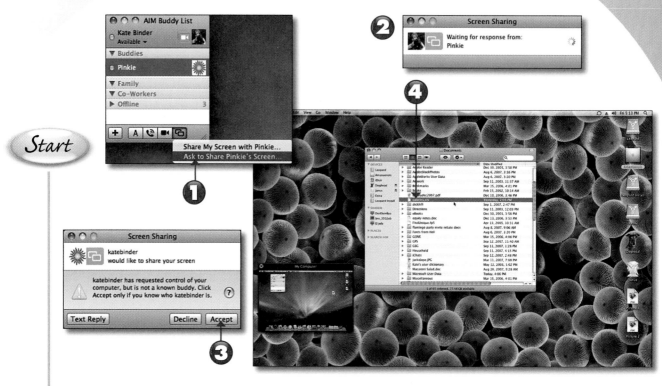

Start

① Click the **Screen Sharing** button at the bottom of the iChat window and choose **Ask to Share [User]'s Screen**.

② A dialog box tells you that your Mac is waiting for a response from the other user.

③ The other user must click **Accept** to begin screen sharing.

④ The other Mac's screen replaces your desktop; you can open folders, files, and programs as if you were sitting in front of the shared Mac.

Continued

TIP

Mother, May I? If you don't see a screen sharing button in iChat or in the Finder, open System Preferences and click Sharing; then click the box labeled **Screen Sharing**. The Mac to which you want to connect must also turn on screen sharing. ■

TIP

Find It in the Finder If you want to share the screen of a Mac on your local network, you don't need to use iChat. In the Shared section of a Finder window's sidebar, click the computer to which you want to connect, then click **Connect As**. ■

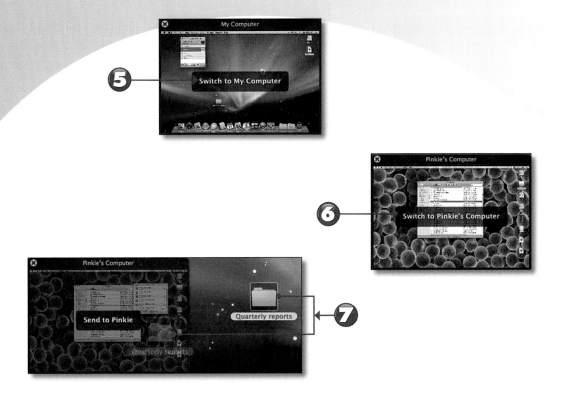

5 Click the thumbnail of your own Mac's desktop to return to your Mac.

6 Click the thumbnail of the shared Mac's desktop to return to using the shared Mac.

7 Drag and drop files or folders onto either thumbnail to copy them to the other Mac.

End

NOTE

Let's Share! You've probably noticed that iChat's Screen Sharing button also gives you the option of sharing your own screen with another user. The process works exactly the same way, except that the other user ends up controlling your Mac. ■

NOTE

If you need access to another of your own Macs, you can use MobileMe to share screens no matter where your two computers are located. Turn to "Accessing Your Mac Remotely," in Chapter 9, to learn more. ■

SEARCHING MULTIPLE MACS

Searching with Spotlight brings the entire contents of your Mac right to your fingertips—and also the contents of other Macs on your local network. That's right; Spotlight can search, almost instantaneously, not only your hard drive but any drive you're connected to on a LAN.

1. In the **Shared** section of the sidebar, click the computer to which you want to connect, then click **Connect As**.

2. Enter your username and password and click **Connect**.

3. Type the terms for your search in the Spotlight field.

4. Click **Shared** to see the search results from network drives.

NOTE

Another Way You'll also see the Shared button at the top of a window showing results from a search done using the Spotlight menu. You can use either method to search—there's no difference in the results. ■

NOTE

The Mac Connection To learn more about connect to other computers on your network, turn to "Connecting to Networked Computers," earlier in this chapter. ■

SHARING A PRINTER ON A NETWORK

You can share printers connected to your computer with other computer users on your network. Starting up printer sharing is simple; you can choose to restrict it to Mac users or enable Windows users to use your printers as well. Network users can add shared printers to their Print dialog boxes just like network printers.

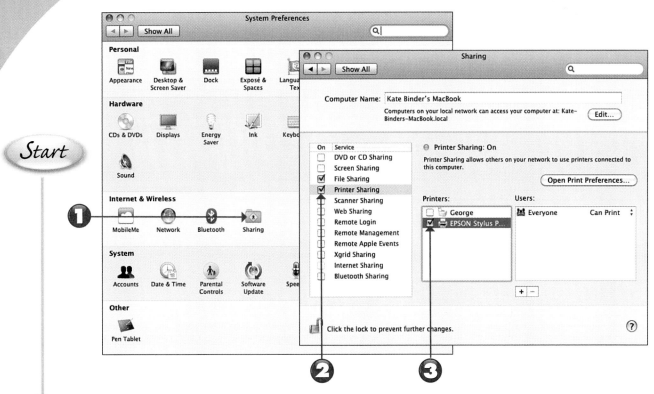

Start

① Open **System Preferences** and click **Sharing**.

② Check the box labeled **Printer Sharing**.

③ Check the boxes next to the printers you want to share.

End

TIP

Where in the Office...? To let other people know where shared printers are physically located, start Printer Setup Utility (in the Utilities folder in Applications). Select the printer and click **Show Info**; then add a description in the **Location** field. ■

NOTE

What It's For Printers on your network are already shared, even if the printers are located in your office. Printer sharing gives network capabilities to devices such as USB inkjets, which don't usually have network connectors. ■

SHARING AN INTERNET CONNECTION

If you've ever suffered through life with two Internet-capable computers and only one network connection, you'll appreciate the ability to share an online connection with all the computers in your house or office. And life gets even better when your connection is broadband, such as a cable modem or a DSL line.

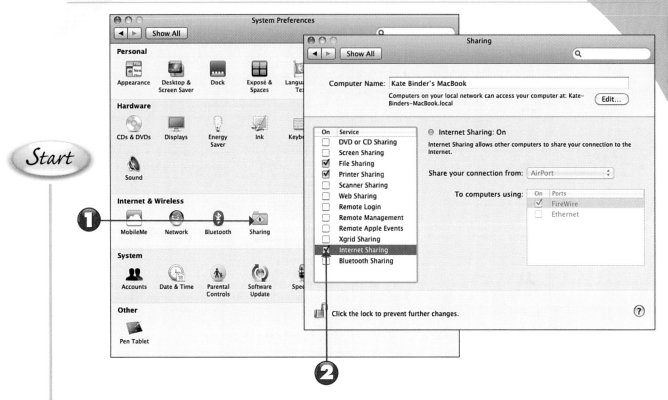

 Open **System Preferences** and click **Sharing**.

 Check the box labeled **Internet Sharing**.

End

NOTE

When Not to Share If you connect to the Internet and your network via the same port, sharing your Internet connection can tell other computers to access the Internet through it when they shouldn't (such as when you take your laptop to the office). ■

NOTE

Another Way to Share If you're sharing an Internet connection through another Mac, you'll be able to get online only when that Mac is up and connected. If that doesn't work for you, consider buying a hardware router that can keep you online all the time. ■

JOINING A WIFI NETWORK

With an AirPort card, you can get rid of those annoying network cables and connect to your network from wherever your computer happens to be, as long as you're close to a WiFi connection point (either an AirpPort base station, or another brand). AirPort is great for laptops—and it comes built into all Apple's current laptops—but you can use it for desktop Macs, too.

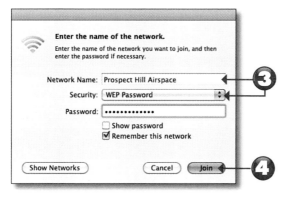

1 Choose a network name from the **AirPort** menu in the menu bar.

2 To join a network that isn't shown, choose **Join Other Network**.

3 Enter the network's name and security method in the login dialog box.

4 Click **Join**.

End

NOTE

AirPort in Your Menu Bar The AirPort menu also enables you to switch networks, turn AirPort on or off, or connect to other AirPort-equipped Macs. ■

TIP

Close to Home Base If AirPort is turned on but you can't get in touch with the network you're looking for, you might be out of range. AirPort base stations have varying ranges; you must be close enough to connect to the base station. ■

MAINTAINING YOUR MAC

Most of the time your Mac just hums right along, cheerfully complying with your requests and sitting quietly in the corner when you're not using it. Every once in a while, however, even the best-behaved Mac needs a little maintenance or a minor repair. This chapter covers the basics of keeping your Mac happy and healthy.

In this chapter, you'll learn how to fix disk errors and reformat disks, both removable disks and hard drives. Also covered are updating your system software, setting the date and time automatically, and calibrating your monitor for accurate color. Some of these techniques are one-time jobs (calibrating your monitor) and others are things you'll do on a regular basis (formatting removable disks).

Along the way, you'll learn a variety of useful tricks, such as how to forcefully quit programs when they're misbehaving. Whether you're a power user or a weekends-only Macster, the tasks in this chapter will teach you things every Mac user should know.

MAC MAINTENANCE AND REPAIR KIT

Repair disks, 252

Force programs
to quit, 261

Calibrate your
display, 257

Update
software, 253

Set the date
and time
automatically, 255

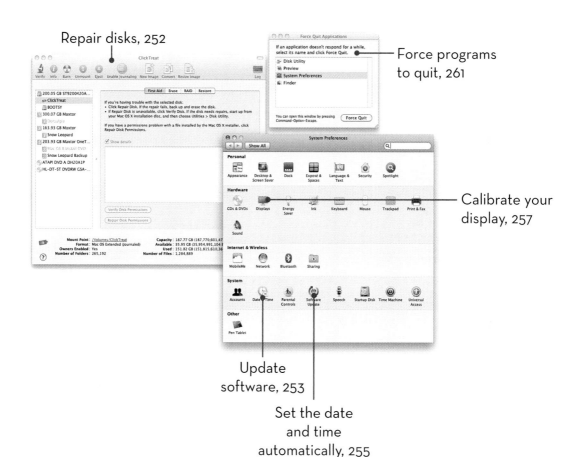

FIXING ERRORS WITH DISK UTILITY

Over time and with use, the formatting structure of a disk can become scrambled, either slightly or seriously. If you have trouble reading files from, or saving files to a disk, or if you experience other mysterious problems, it's time to run the repair program Disk Utility. (To use Disk Utility on your startup disk, see the next task.)

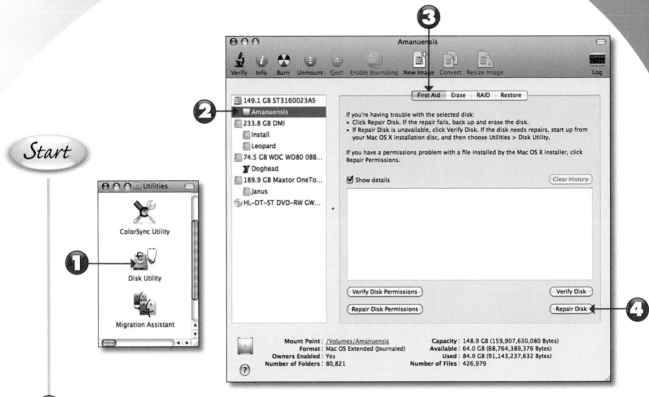

Start

1 Double-click **Disk Utility** to start it (it's in the Utilities folder within Applications).

2 Choose the disk to be repaired in the list.

3 Click the **First Aid** tab.

4 Click **Repair Disk**.

End

TIP

Verify or Repair? If you're concerned about modifying a disk in any way at all, you can check its status without making any repairs by using the Verify commands. And, it's always good to have a current backup before you repair the disk. ■

NOTE

What Are Permissions? Each program, document, and folder in a Mac OS X system has permissions describing who can open and modify it. Incorrect permissions can prevent programs from running or cause them to malfunction. ■

REPAIRING THE STARTUP DISK

Disk Utility can't repair the startup disk because the program can't modify the section of the disk that contains Disk Utility. If you have a second hard drive with a Mac OS X system installed, you can start from that drive to run Disk Utility or use your installation disc, as described here.

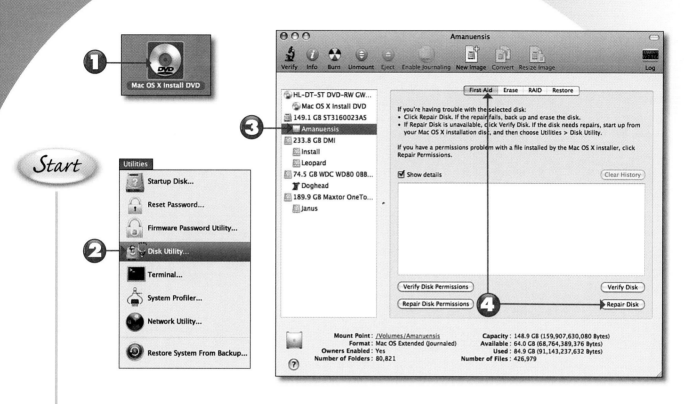

1 Restart from the Mac OS X Installer disk by restarting your Mac with the disc inserted and pressing C as the computer starts up.

2 Choose **Utilities**, **Disk Utility**.

3 Select your hard drive in the list.

4 Click the **First Aid** tab and click **Repair Disk**.

End

NOTE

What's Going On? The Disk Utility command (located in the Utilities menu when you start up from your installation CD) isn't anything special. It simply starts up the Disk Utility program that's installed on the CD, which is the same as the one installed on your hard drive. ■

TIP

Permission Please It's a good idea to repair disk permissions each time you install new software or update existing software, including Mac OS X. ■

UPDATING PROGRAMS WITH SOFTWARE UPDATE

Software Update checks with Apple over the Internet to see whether it finds updated versions of your system software and preinstalled programs. Then it can download and install updates for you. You enter an admin name and password when you update your software. Mac OS X assumes only admin users are authorized to change software. Be aware that many system updates will require you to restart your Mac once they're finished installing.

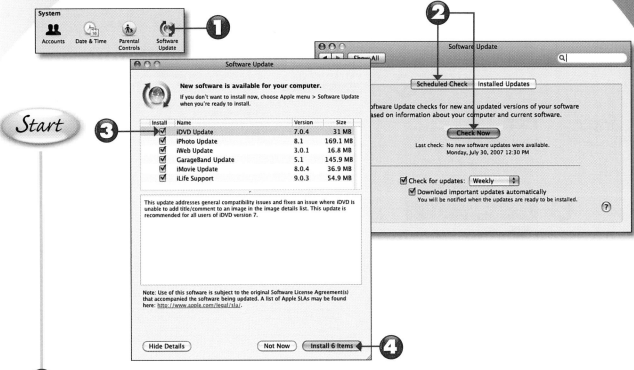

1 Start **System Preferences** and click the **Software Update** button.

2 Click the **Scheduled Check** button and click **Check Now**.

3 If updates are located, click the name of each update to see information about it.

4 Check the boxes next to each update you want to install and click **Install**.

Continued

TIP

Behind the Scenes If you have a broadband Internet connection, check **Check for updates** and choose an interval. Do this when you want the check to occur—Software Update starts counting the time interval from the time you make this setting. ■

TIP

Keeping Track If you want to know which updates have been installed and when, click the **Installed Software** tab to see a list. Click the column headers to sort the list by the date, the update's name, or the version number. ■

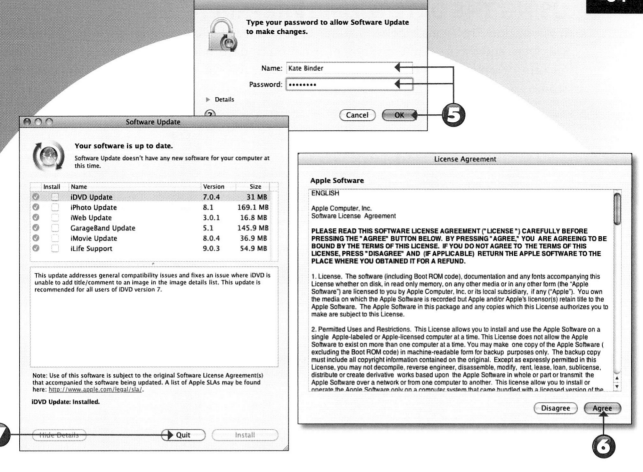

5 Enter an admin name and password and click **OK**.

6 If a license agreement appears, click **Agree**. Software Update downloads and installs the update.

7 Click **Quit**.

End

NOTE

Updating a New System Some updates don't show up until after other updates are installed. After installing system software from your original disk, run Software Update repeatedly until it doesn't show any updates. ∎

TIP

Don't Go First If you're not sure whether to install a system update, take a quick trip to MacFixit (www.macfixit.com) to see whether other users who've already updated their Macs have reported any problems with the update. ∎

USING THE DATE & TIME PREFERENCES

It's important that your Mac know what time it is. Every file on your hard drive is time-stamped, and the system uses that information to determine which files contain the most current data. Using the Date & Time preferences, you can ensure that the date and time stamps on your computer are accurate.

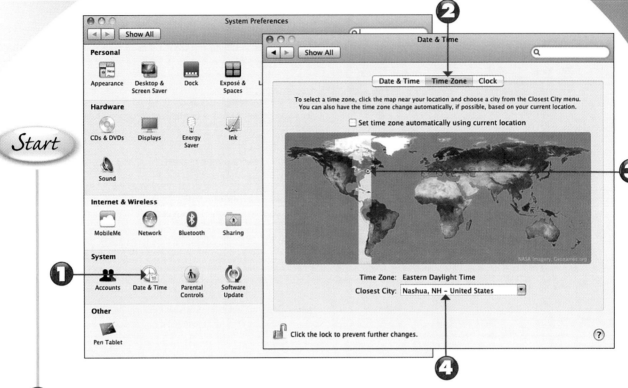

Start

1. Start up **System Preferences** and click the **Date & Time** button.

2. Click the **Time Zone** button.

3. Click the map near where you live.

4. Choose the nearest city from the **Closest City** pop-up menu.

Continued

TIP

Blink Blink Another useful setting in Date & Time preferences is located on the **Clock** tab. Check the box marked **Flash the time separators**. Then, if the colon stops blinking, you'll know your Mac is frozen and you can restart it. ■

NOTE

Today's Date Is... To see the full day and date, click the menu bar clock to reveal its menu. You can also open the Date & Time preferences here, as well as changing the menu bar clock to an analog icon instead of the standard digital display. ■

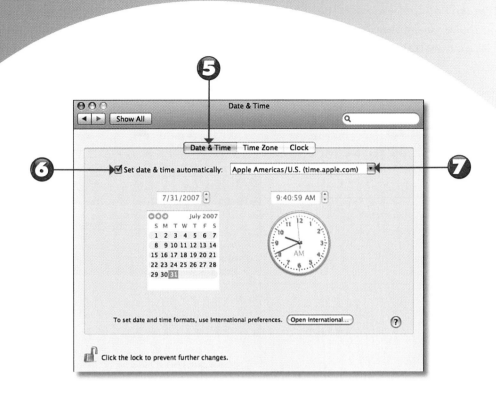

5 Click the **Date & Time** tab.

6 If you have a constant connection to the Internet, check the box marked **Set date & time automatically**.

7 Choose the nearest timeserver from the pop-up menu.

End

NOTE

More About NTP To learn more about how network timeservers work, you can visit the Network Time Protocol website at www.ntp.org. There you'll also find links to lists of alternative timeservers, including servers around the world. ■

CALIBRATING YOUR MONITOR

It wasn't all that long ago that computers had grayscale monitors, but now it's all about color. To make sure color looks right on your screen, however, you need to calibrate your system. Here's how to create a color device profile that tells your Mac how your monitor displays color and makes appropriate adjustments.

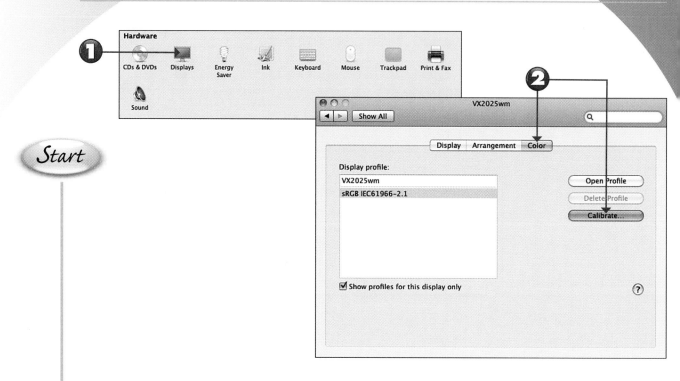

Start

1 Start **System Preferences** and click the **Displays** button.

2 Click the **Color** button and click **Calibrate**. The Display Calibrator Assistant opens.

Continued

NOTE

Managing Color The software components that translate color between your Mac and your monitor comprise a color management system (CMS). In its full-fledged form, a CMS ensures consistent color throughout your system, from scanner to monitor to printer. ■

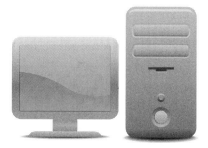

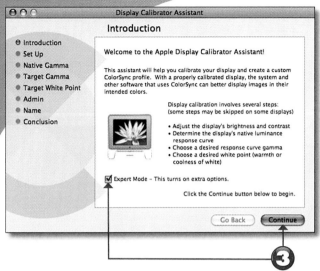

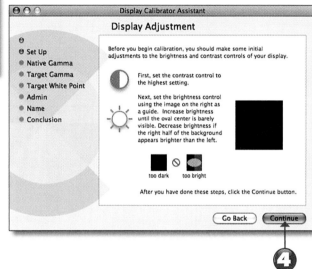

③ Click the **Expert Mode** box to create a more precise profile; then click **Continue**.

④ Make the monitor settings shown in the window and click **Continue**.

Continued

NOTE

Where to Start The **Color** tab of the Displays preference pane includes a list of profiles. If one of those matches, or is close to, the monitor you're using, click to select that profile before you start the calibration process. You'll get a more accurate profile that way. ■

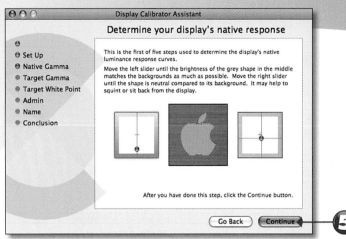

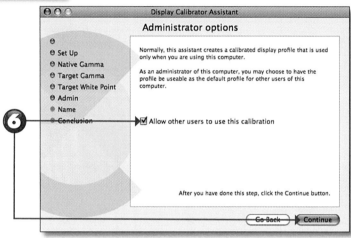

⑤ Follow the instructions on the **Native Response**, **Target Gamma**, and **Target White Point** screens, clicking **Continue** after each screen.

⑥ If you're an admin user, check the box to make the profile available to all users of this Mac; then click **Continue**.

Continued

NOTE

A Step Further If you're in the market for truly accurate color, you'll have to spend a little to get it. Look into a colorimeter such as Eye-One Display 2 (www.gretagmacbeth.com), which sticks to your monitor with suction cups to "see" the color itself as you create a monitor profile. ■

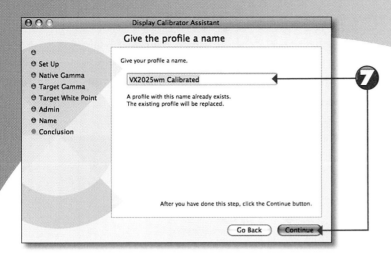

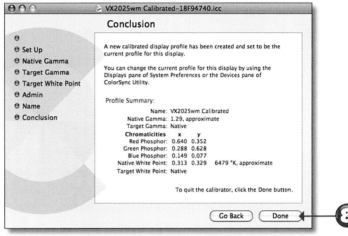

7 Enter a name for the profile and click **Continue**. The Display Calibrator Assistant saves the profile.

8 Click **Done**.

End

NOTE

Greek to Me Native Gamma, Target Gamma, and Target White Point, used in the Display Calibrator Assistant, might sound very technical, but they simply refer to how your eye perceives the lightness, darkness, and overall color cast of your monitor's display. ■

FORCING AN APPLICATION TO QUIT

When a program isn't working right, your first tactic should be to quit and restart it. But sometimes a program is so off-track that the Quit command doesn't work. Then you can force the program to quit. This doesn't affect the other programs that are running, but unsaved changes in documents within the problem application are lost.

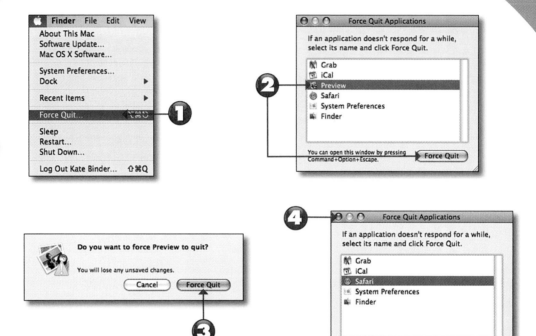

Start

End

1. Choose **Apple menu**, **Force Quit**.

2. Choose the program you want from the list and click **Force Quit**.

3. Click **Force Quit** again.

4. Click the **Close** button to dismiss the Force Quit dialog box.

NOTE

In the Olden Days Apple used to recommend that you restart your Mac after force quitting an application. But in Mac OS X each program runs in its own area of memory so that when it malfunctions, no other program is affected. No need to restart! ■

TIP

The Key to Force Quitting If you're a lover of keyboard shortcuts—they're definitely more efficient than using the mouse—then you'll be thrilled to know that the keyboard shortcut to get to the Force Quit dialog is ⌘+Option+Esc. ■

REFORMATTING A HARD DISK

There are three good reasons to reformat a disk. First, if you want to use the disk on a Windows or Unix computer, it will need a different format. Second, formatting a disk erases all data completely. And finally, reformatting a disk is a last resort if you're having problems opening or saving files on it.

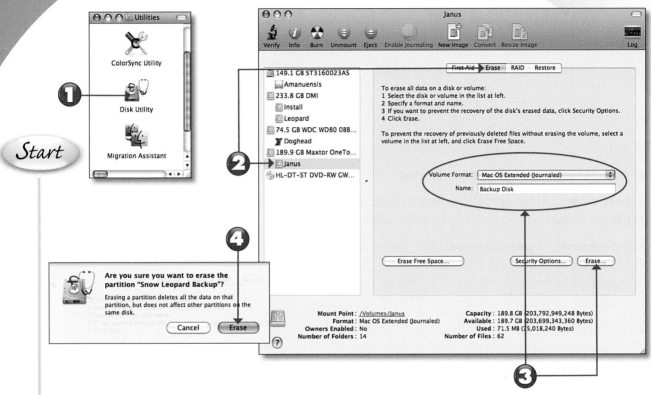

1 Double-click **Disk Utility** to start it (it's in the **Utilities** folder within **Applications**).

2 Choose the disk to be formatted in the list on the left and click the **Erase** button.

3 Choose a **Volume Format** option, type a name for the disk, and click **Erase**.

4 Click **Erase** again.

Start

End

CAUTION

Sensitivity Training Disk Utility's Format menu contains five options, two of which you should definitely avoid. Mac OS Extended is the basic Mac disk format, and Mac OS Extended (Journaled) enables your Mac to keep a list of system operations so that it can restore your disk to its previous state. Mac OS Extended (Case-sensitive, Journaled) and Mac OS Extended (Case-sensitive) should only be used to use the disk with UNIX programs that support case-sensitive file systems. The fifth option, MS-DOS (FAT), is used for Windows partitions that you use with Boot Camp, Apple's utility for running Windows on your Mac. ■

Glossary

A

access permissions   See **permissions**.

accessibility   The degree to which a device or **program** is usable by people with disabilities.

Action menu   A **pop-up menu** that appears in **dialog boxes** and windows in the form of a gear **icon**. It provides access to commonly used commands.

admin user   An administrative user of Mac OS X; a user who can read, write, and move some files that do not belong to her and who can change locked System Preferences settings and install new software.

AIFF   Audio Interchange File Format is a sound file format used by iMovie and other multimedia programs.

AirPort   An Apple-branded combination of hardware (AirPort cards and the AirPort **base station**) and software with which computers can form a **WiFi network** and communicate with each other and the **Internet** without wires.

alias   A small file that, when double-clicked, opens the original file from which it was created.

Apple ID   A **username** for the Apple website and the iTunes Music Store.

Apple menu   The **menu** at the left end of the Mac's **menu bar**, which is accessed by clicking the Apple logo; it contains commands such as Shut Down work no matter which **application** you're using.

application   A program; usually refers to a fully featured program rather than a small accessory program or **widget**.

Application menu   The **menu** that appears to the right of the **Apple menu** in each **program**; it's always labeled with the name of the program.

archive   A compressed version of a file that must be unarchived before it can be opened.

B

back up   To copy important files to a new location in case the originals are damaged or deleted.

base station   A device that creates a **wireless AirPort network** in conjunction with Macs equipped with **AirPort** cards.

Bluetooth   A short-range **wireless** technology that enables computers to communicate with other devices such as PDAs, keyboards, and mice.

bookmark   A record of a **web** page's location, saved for future reference.

boot   To start up a computer.

broadband   A high-speed **Internet** connection such as **DSL** or a **cable modem**.

burn   To write data to a disc; it usually refers to a CD or DVD.

burnable folder   A folder whose contents will be burned to a CD or DVD when the user chooses.

button   Interface equivalent of the real-world object that triggers specified actions when clicked.

C

cable modem A high-speed **Internet** connection that operates over your cable television line.

CD-R Recordable CD, which can be recorded only once.

CD-RW Rewritable CD, which can be erased and recorded again several times.

check box Interface equivalent of the real-world object used to select options in a list or **dialog box**.

clip A short section of video that can be combined with other clips in iMovie to create a movie.

Clip Shelf The area of iMovie's window where individual video clips are stored before they're used in a movie.

Clip Viewer The area of iMovie's interface where clips are combined with transitions, effects, and each other to form a movie.

collection A group of **fonts**.

color management The science of translating and adjusting scanned, displayed, and printed colors to produce consistent color from original art to final printout.

Column view A **Finder** view in which columns of file and folder listings are placed from left to right, with the left columns representing folders closer to the **root** level of a drive.

compressed Refers to a file that's reduced in size by manipulating its underlying data.

contextual menus **Menus** that pop up wherever you click if you use a **modifier key**—specifically, the Control key. Their commands vary according to the context in which you're working.

D

Dashboard An interface for using small, desk accessory programs called **widgets** without switching out of the current program or document.

database A data file in which each type of information is delimited in a field so the data can be sorted or otherwise manipulated based on categories.

desktop The visual workspace in the **Finder**.

device profile A file that describes the color reproduction characteristics of a printer, scanner, or monitor.

DHCP Dynamic Host Configuration Protocol a method of automatically assigning a personal computer an **IP address** so that the computer can connect to the **Internet**.

dialog box A window in which you can click **buttons**, enter text, choose from **pop-up menus**, and drag **sliders** to determine the settings you want to make in a **program** or your **system software**.

dial-up An **Internet** connection over a standard telephone line.

disclosure triangle A **button** to the left of a **folder** or category name in a list; clicking it reveals the folder's or category's contents.

DNS server A computer that translates **URLs** (such as www.apple.com) into the domain name system (DNS) numeric addresses where **web browsers** can find the files that make up websites.

Dock The panel at the bottom of your Mac OS X **desktop** that contains an icon for every running program, as well as **icons** for any other **programs**, **folders**, or documents you want to access quickly.

download To copy files from the **Internet** to the computer you're currently using.

dragging and dropping   Clicking a file's **icon** and dragging it into a **dialog box**, on top of an **application's** icon, into the **Dock**, or elsewhere.

Drop Box   A folder within your **Public folder** that other users can use to give files to you; you are the only person who can see the contents of your Drop Box folder, but each user has his or her own Public folder and Drop Box.

drop-down menu   A menu accessed from the **menu bar**.

DSL   Digital Subscriber Line, a high-speed **Internet** connection that operates over your phone line.

DVD   Digital video disc; a CD-like medium that holds several times as much data as CDs and that is generally used to distribute movies.

E

email   Electronic mail that travels from your computer to another computer, across the **Internet** or over a local network, or **LAN**.

Ethernet   A **networking** technology that enables you to transfer data at high speeds.

export   To store data in a new file, separate from the currently open file.

Exposé   A set of features for moving **Finder** and **application windows** temporarily out of the way.

extension   See **filename extensions**.

F–G

file sharing   A system feature that enables you to transfer files from your Mac to other computers and vice versa; it can also enable other users to access your files if you allow it.

filename extensions   Three-letter (usually) codes placed at the end of filenames to signify the type of file. These may not be visible in the **Finder** or in **application dialog boxes**.

FileVault   A feature that encrypts the contents of a user's **home folder** so they can't be accessed without a password.

Finder   The part of Mac OS X that displays the contents of your **hard drives** and other drives in windows on your **desktop**.

FireWire   A type of connector for digital camcorders, **hard drives**, and other devices.

flash drive   A keychain-sized storage device with no moving parts that plugs into a **USB** port.

folder   A system-level equivalent of a real-world file folder, in which you can store files and other folders to help you organize them.

font   The software that enables your Mac to represent a particular typeface.

format   To prepare a removable disk or **hard drive** to accept data.

function keys   The "F" keys at the top of a keyboard are used for performing special functions that vary depending on the **program** being used.

H

hard drive   A device for data storage, usually found inside a computer.

hardware router   A device that shares an **Internet** connection across a local network, or **LAN**.

home folder   The folder in your Mac OS X system in which you can store all your personal files.

HTML   Hypertext Markup Language, which is the coding language used to create **web** pages.

hub   A device that connects multiple individual computers to form a network.

I–K

icon A picture indicating a file's contents or type.

Icon view A **Finder** view in which files are represented by graphic **icons** rather than just lists of names.

iDisk A storage space on Apple's website that's available to any Mac user who registers for MobileMe.

iLife Apple's bundle of entertainment **programs**, including iMovie, iPhoto, GarageBand, iTunes, and iDVD.

IMAP The Internet Message Access Protocol, which is a less common method of connecting to a mail **server**.

import To retrieve data from a file using a format other than the program's own format.

instant messaging A method of communicating over the **Internet** in which users type short messages and instantly send them to other users.

Internet The global network of computers that encompasses the **World Wide Web**, **instant messaging**, **email**, and many other ways to communicate and share data.

IP address A numerical code that identifies the location of each computer on the **Internet**, including your Mac.

iPod Small, portable Apple device for playing music in **MP3** format.

ISP **Internet** service provider, a company that provides access to the Internet.

JPEG A graphic file format (Joint Photographic Experts Group) commonly used for photos displayed on the **World Wide Web**.

L

label A color applied to a file **icon** in the **Finder**.

LAN Local area **network**, which is a small network enclosed entirely within one building.

List view A **Finder** view in which each **window** displays the contents of a single **folder** or drive in the form of a list of files.

local network address An identifier of a computer on a **LAN**.

log in To identify yourself as a particular user by entering a **username** and password.

login icon A picture representing an individual user that is displayed when that user **logs in** or uses iChat.

M

mail server A computer that directs **email** to and from a local computer on the **Internet**.

memory See **RAM**.

menu A list of commands that appears when the user clicks a keyword or **icon**.

menu bar The wide, narrow strip across the top of the screen that contains **drop-down menus** in the **Finder** and in applications.

menu screens Screens on a DVD containing buttons that lead to other screens or open movies.

minimized A **folder** or document **window** that has been placed in the **Dock**, where you can see a **thumbnail** view of it.

MobileMe An online service available to any Mac user that includes an **email** address and **web** storage space, among other features.

modem A device that enables your computer to connect to the **Internet** over a standard phone, **DSL**, or **cable** line.

modifier keys   Special keys (such as Shift, Option, ⌘, and Control) that enable you to give commands to your Mac by holding them down at the same time as you press letter or number keys or the mouse button.

monitor   A computer's display.

motion menus   DVD menu screens that incorporate moving video in their backgrounds.

mount   To connect to a disk drive (either one connected to your Mac or one connected to a **network** computer) so you can access its files in the **Finder**.

MP3   A compressed music file that's very small but that retains very high quality.

multiwindow mode   **Finder** mode in which double-clicking a **folder** displays its contents in a new **window** rather than in the same window.

N–O

network   A group of computers linked together so that they can exchange information and share functions.

network locations   Groups of **network** settings for specific situations or locations, such as an office **LAN**.

network port   Computer hardware interface used to connect the computer to a **network**.

NTP   Server. *See* **timeserver**.

operating system (OS)   The software that enables a computer to run.

P

pane   A separate page in a **dialog box**, usually accessible by choosing from a **pop-up menu** or (as in the case of System Preferences) clicking a **button**.

pathname   The address of a file on a **hard drive**; it lists the nested **folders** in which the file resides.

PDF   *See* **Portable Document Format**.

peripheral   A device that connects to your Mac, such as a printer, scanner, tape backup drive, or digital camera.

permissions   File attributes that determine which user owns each file and which users are authorized to read it and make changes to it.

pixel   Picture element; a square on the screen made up of a single color.

Places sidebar   A column of disk and **folder icons** that appears on the left side of each **Finder** window in **multiwindow mode**.

playlist   A collection of songs in iTunes.

PNG   Portable Network Graphic format, a graphic file format used on the **World Wide Web**.

POP   Post Office Protocol, the most common method of connecting to a mail **server**.

pop-up menu   A **menu** that appears in a **dialog box** or other interface element rather than dropping down from the **menu bar** at the top of the screen.

Portable Document Format   The file format used by Adobe Reader (formerly Acrobat Reader) and its related software, as well as Apple's Preview. PDF documents look just like the original documents from which they were created.

PPP   Point-to-Point Protocol, a method of connecting to the **Internet** via a phone modem.

PPPoE   PPP over Ethernet, a method of connecting to the **Internet** via a **DSL** modem.

preview   Small or low-res view of a file's contents.

printer driver   A file that describes the characteristics of a printer and enables **programs** to use the printer's features.

processor   The core of a computer; its brain.

profiles   Data files that characterize how a device reproduces color. *See also* **color management**.

program   A file containing thousands or even millions of instructions in such a way that a computer can follow them to perform some useful function for the user.

project   A collection of files used to produce a movie in iMovie or a DVD in iDVD.

protected memory   An **operating system** feature that places barriers around the areas of a computer's memory (or **RAM**) being used by each program, so that if one program crashes, the other programs are unaffected.

proxy preview   A **thumbnail** version of a document, usually in a **dialog box**, that can be manipulated to change the real document in the same way.

Q–R

queue   The list of documents waiting to be printed.

QuickTime   Apple's proprietary video format.

RAM   Random access memory, which is the part of a computer that stores the currently running **programs** and the currently open documents so you can work with them.

reboot   To restart the Mac.

removable disk   Any media that can be ejected from its drive and used in another computer.

resolution   The number of pixels per inch contained in a graphic or displayed on a monitor.

rip   To convert songs on a CD to files on a **hard drive**.

router address   The **IP address** of the computer or device that is providing a shared **Internet** connection.

RSS   Really Simple Syndication, an XML format for distributing **web** content such as news headlines, events listings, and excerpts from discussion forums.

RTF   Rich Text Format, a format for word processor documents that retains information about bold, italic, and other formatting in a form that almost all word processors can understand.

S

screen name   A nickname by which iChat users are identified.

screen saver   A moving display that covers the screen to prevent monitor burn-in.

screen sharing   Feature that enables network users to see another Mac's screen on their own screens and, if authorized, to control the other Mac.

screen shot   A picture of the computer's screen.

script   A simple program that can be created and customized by a user; the Mac OS's built-in scripting language is AppleScript.

search field   Text entry field at the top of a **window** where users enter search parameters.

select   To choose or designate for action; for example, the user must click a file to select it in the **Finder** before he can copy the file.

server   A computer that provides a service to other computers via a **network**, such as forwarding **email** or streaming video.

Services   A set of commands to access programs' features while those programs are not running.

single-window mode   The **Finder** mode in which double-clicking a **folder** displays its contents in the same **window** rather than in a new window.

sleep   A state in which the Mac is still powered on but consumes less energy because it's not being used.

slider   A **dialog box** control for choosing a value along a continuum.

smart folder   A **folder** that collects files from all over the user's **hard drive** based on search criteria set by the user.

smart group   An Address Book group whose contents are updated automatically based on user-determined criteria.

smart mailbox   A mailbox in Mail that displays **email** messages that are actually filed in other mailboxes, based on user-determined criteria.

Space   Custom screen layout that hides extraneous **windows** and **programs**, showing only what's in use at the time.

spam   Junk **email**.

speech recognition   A technology by which the Mac can understand spoken commands.

Stack   An alternate view of a **folder**'s contents accessed by dragging the folder into the **Dock** and then clicking its Dock **icon**.

startup items   **Programs** or documents that open automatically when a user **logs in**.

storage media   A type of computer media used for data storage rather than active information exchange.

submenu   A **menu** that extends to the side from a command in a **drop-down menu**.

SuperDrive   An internal drive for writing CDs and DVDs.

sync   To synchronize data between a computer and a device such as a PDA or cell phone.

system software   See **operating system (OS)**.

T

TCP/IP   Transmission Control Protocol over Internet Protocol, the **networking** method Mac OS X uses; it is an industry standard.

text buttons   **Buttons** in iDVD that don't have video or photo images.

themes   Sets of **menu** and **button** designs that can be applied to iDVD projects.

thumbnail   Miniature image.

TIFF   A graphic file format (Tagged Image File Format) used for images destined to be printed.

timeserver   A computer on the **Internet** that transmits a time signal your Mac can use to set its clock automatically.

title bar   The part of a **window** that displays the **folder**'s or document's title.

toolbar   A row of **buttons** for common functions that appears at the top of a **window** in Preview or another **program**.

track   A component of a song in GarageBand, consisting of the part played by a single instrument.

transition   A special effect inserted between scenes in iMovie.

Trash   The holding location for files or **folders** you want to delete.

U–V

URL   Uniform Resource Locator, an alphanumeric address that points to a specific location on the **Internet**, such as www.apple.com for Apple's website.

USB   Universal serial bus, a type of computer connector.

username   An alphanumeric identifier of a single user.

vCard　A small file containing contact information that can be attached to an **email** message.

video buttons　**Buttons** in iDVD that have video images.

virus　A **program** that damages a computer or the computer's files in some way and then reproduces itself and spreads via **email** or file transfers.

W–Z

Web　*See* **World Wide Web**.

web browser　A **program** used to view websites. Safari is the **web** browser that comes with OS X.

webcam　A small, digital camera used with iChat or to provide a constantly updated image over the **World Wide Web**.

WebDAV　A type of **server** that makes iCal calendars available to subscribers over the **Internet**.

widget　A small program that can be accessed using **Dashboard**.

Wi-Fi　The type of **wireless** networking used by Apple's **AirPort** hardware and software and by other manufacturers' similar devices.

window　A defined rectangular area on the computer screen displaying files or data.

wireless　The capability to communicate without cables; for example, AirPort is Apple's *technology* for creating a wireless network between multiple Macs. *See also* **AirPort** and **Bluetooth**.

word processor　A program used for composing, laying out, and printing text.

World Wide Web　A computerized information source consisting of text, images, and other data displayed on "pages" organized into "sites" that are linked together such that clicking a word or image on one page displays a different page.

Index

D

FREE Online Edition

Your purchase of **Easy Mac OS X Snow Leopard** includes access to a free online edition for 45 days through the Safari Books Online subscription service. Nearly every Que book is available online through Safari Books Online, along with more than 5,000 other technical books and videos from publishers such as Addison-Wesley Professional, Cisco Press, Exam Cram, IBM Press, O'Reilly, Prentice Hall, and Sams.

SAFARI BOOKS ONLINE allows you to search for a specific answer, cut and paste code, download chapters, and stay current with emerging technologies.

Activate your FREE Online Edition at www.informit.com/safarifree

> **STEP 1:** Enter the coupon code: IBVUNCB.

> **STEP 2:** New Safari users, complete the brief registration form. Safari subscribers, just log in.

If you have difficulty registering on Safari or accessing the online edition, please e-mail customer-service@safaribooksonline.com